THE VIOLENCE WITHIN

Cultural
and Political
Opposition
in Divided
Nations

THE
VIOLENCE
WITHIN

Cultural and Political Opposition in Divided Nations

EDITED BY

Kay B. Warren

Westview Press BOULDER
SAN FRANCISCO
OXFORD

Copyright © 1993 by Westview Press, Inc.

Published in 1993 in the United States of America by Westview Press, Inc., 5500 Central Avenue, Boulder, Colorado 80301-2877, and in the United Kingdom by Westview Press, 36 Lonsdale Road, Summertown, Oxford OX2 7EW

A CIP catalog record for this book is available from the Library of Congress.
ISBN 0-8133-1518-2

Printed and bound in the United States of America

 The paper used in this publication meets the requirements
of the American National Standard for Permanence of Paper
for Printed Library Materials Z39.48-1984.

10   9   8   7   6   5   4   3   2   1

For Loy, Camie, and Buddy

Contents

Acknowledgments

Over and above the personal set of colleagues that each of the contributors to this volume acknowledges, we share a collective debt to Henry Bienen, former director of Princeton's Center of International Studies and now the dean of the Woodrow Wilson School, for his intellectual support of the project and his skills in garnering foundation support through CIS for a set of seven interlocking research projects across three disciplines. Bienen along with Libby Schweber, Clarisa Bencomo, Ramesh Venkataraman, Kate Zhou, Cathy Powell, Rosann Fitzpatrick, Joyce Chang, and Aaron Willis were central contributors to our discussions and debates. We are grateful for the ways in which these colleagues from a variety of disciplines compelled us to articulate more precisely our arguments and the differences among approaches. Each of us learned a great deal from intensive exposures to research on other parts of the world and to theoretical literatures from other disciplines. We emerged with new questions to ask of our own materials and with long lists of books to read.

The overall support for these research projects came from the John D. and Catherine T. MacArthur Foundation's Program on Peace and International Cooperation. We are grateful for their support and hope this volume will encourage the foundation to continue funding culturally focused studies of conflict.

Our thanks also to Deborah Poole for a penetrating reading of the volume as a whole and to anonymous reviewers for their critiques and suggestions. At Westview Press, we received generous editorial direction from Dean Birkenkamp as well as Deborah Rich and Cheryl Carnahan. At Princeton, special thanks go to Pauline Caulk for a superb job of taming contributions initially composed in a variety of computer languages and quirky styles, to Carol Zanca, who kept morale up through busy delays, and to Anne Lear for proofreading. Wendy Warren put her creative energies to work in a striking cover design. Loy Carrington employed connective magic to keep people and ideas in touch with each other. And Megan Peterson did an excellent job computerizing our maps and tables.

Kay B. Warren

Introduction:
Revealing Conflicts Across
Cultures & Disciplines

KAY B. WARREN

This book demonstrates the centrality of cultural issues to the study of conflict and violence. The contributors—anthropologists and political scientists who study Guatemala, Brazil, Israel/Palestine, Iran, Egypt, South Africa, the Philippines, and Northern Ireland—argue that one cannot understand current crises without studying longer-term patterns of sociocultural, political, and economic change. At issue is how one conceptualizes the interplay of culture and politics in strikingly volatile situations.

The volume documents the diverse manifestations of contemporary conflicts: ethnic nationalism, religious fundamentalism, political opposition movements, state-guerrilla warfare, resistance to agrarian reforms, and racism in racial democracies. The goal is not to generate universal definitions or totalizing explanations of conflict and violence but rather to capture the complexities of contemporary *intra*national conflicts from the perspective of those caught up in them. Each contributor has written a case study of the cultural and political dimensions of conflict, focusing on specific countries, movements, and communities. These studies are based on larger projects involving intensive fieldwork, participant observation, and interviewing. The chapters look at national culture—at state policies and ideologies of control, containment, and development—in dynamic tension with local populations, pictured as actively formulating their own cultural commitments, modes of control, and politics. From the onset, these analysts challenge the notion that culture is an ancillary or parochial issue. Social cleavages—and the terms of their selective recognition, erasure, or resurgence—are integral to state politics, to movements seeking the transformation of civil society and its authorities, and to local communities attempting to navigate the crosscurrents of change.

First, these chapters expose the distortions of top-down formulations of culture and change that concentrate on the powers of the state, formal institutions, and national leaders, projecting passivity and ignorance onto the wider public. Alternatively, these social scientists examine the political and cultural heterogeneity of national populations and show how groups and individuals create and reformulate their own social critiques and understandings of conflict—that is, how local populations participate in national society by actively promoting and resisting change (Fox 1990b). Struggles for the right to define themselves have compelled many ethnic groups to attempt to redefine national culture (Goldstein 1990). In this light, the chapters analyze states, opposition movements, and local groups with a concern for how conflict produces culture—not just, as some have phrased it, how cultural difference promotes conflict.[1] Notable contrasts emerge, however, among these anthropologists and political scientists as to where one positions analyses of the decentralized production of struggle and culture.

Second, the contributors analyze cultural specificity: the historically and culturally distinctive national settings in which conflict occurs, the diverse and changing identities elaborated by populations within nation-states, and the terms in which competing programs for change are debated. To pursue these issues calls for an awareness of the tendency for analysts across cultural divides to orientalize and essentialize "the other"—that is, to freeze, simplify, and polarize cultural differences through the use of totalizing Western dichotomies, such as traditional/modern, religious/rational, domestic/political, and rural/urban (Said 1978; Clifford 1988). In these chapters, the contributors use a variety of strategies to problematize such contrasts (although assumptions embedded in this language die hard) and to describe the alternative idioms—political, territorial, ethnic, linguistic, religious, gender, class, and work—for social and political commitments.

Third, the contributors are interested in studying the creation of cultural narratives—whether nationalist ideologies, family genealogies, colonial histories, development policies, personal testimonies, or supernatural accounts—as moral and political acts. Each analyst presents narratives through which people communicate their experiences of conflict, express their understandings of shifting realities, and attempt to influence and dispute others' portrayals. Each grapples with the problems of interpreting narratives, as they are appropriated from a variety of sources and reformulated in daily life, and the resulting political implications for movements and communities (Turner and Bruner 1986; Rosaldo 1980, 1989).

Finally, the contributors analyze the jarring ambiguity of violence in national conflicts. State authorities' surveillance and use of coercive force and opposition groups' challenges to the legitimacy of existing political arrangements (as well as the rise of groups exploiting turmoil) collide at distinctive historical and cultural moments in these countries. In examining the nature of these collisions—or, in one significant case, the apparent failure of a historic moment—these chapters argue against conceptions of violence that privilege physical harm and fail to question the ways in which cultural and political practices mediate the experience of violence (Scarry 1985). Domination in various guises, including denials of the existence and expressed needs of subordinate groups, is revealed as a key component of political violence.

Fragmentation, instability, and uncertainty are other components of violence (Taussig 1987, 1992)—particularly as the distinctions among victim, victimizer, and witness are repeatedly called into question (Bourque and Warren 1989; Riches 1986). Such is the case when local communities are caught between armies and armed opposition groups. Part of the terror results from the great uncertainty of when and with what motives particular individuals will be detained, tortured, "disappeared," or freed from captivity. Further at issue is how people mentally and physically endure (and manipulate) the blurring of the statuses of the uninvolved civilian and the possible collaborator, particularly when lines of collaboration are chronically ambiguous and the consequences grave. For analysts of specific cultures and places, the imperative is to dispel the view that violence is inherently chaotic and irrational by tracing the implications of particular forms of domination, resistance, and violence.

CONFLICT THAT COUNTS
IN THE SOCIAL SCIENCES

Until recently, conventional academic divisions of labor and subdisciplinary specializations tended to marginalize the cultural and historical study of intranational conflicts and their implications for longer-term patterns of politics and change. Let me briefly illustrate trends that have influenced research agendas and leave the task of developing a comprehensive literature review across disciplines to others. During the cold war, the conflicts addressed in this volume were dismissed by many political scientists and comparative sociologists who instead focused their research on great power tensions, world wars, and disarmament. National conflicts were relevant to the extent that they could be interpreted as reflections of global tensions.[2] The focus on international relations meant there was relatively little interest in examining localized tensions in their own terms until the late 1980s when escalating ethnic mobilization and the end of the cold war forced scholars to turn their attention to ethnic nationalism.

For their part anthropologists—in concentrating their energies on documenting cultural distinctiveness in religion, economics, and community organization—sometimes dealt with other cultures as if they were equilibrium-maintaining isolates, that is, as distinctive communities somehow set apart from modern history. As Orin Starn (1991) cogently observes, by the way they framed their cultural analyses, such anthropologists risked missing the revolution in front of them—one that involved increasingly regularized rural-urban contacts, growing disaffection with the status quo, and a radicalized potential for political involvements.[3] Although political science and anthropology have widened their scope, and the norms for research are hardly monolithic,[4] these conventions have left their mark in the form of prejudices, blind spots, and evasions in academic research.

An important exception to the marginalization of national conflicts has been the comparative concern with explaining revolutions and rebellions, as in the works of Barrington Moore (1966), Chalmers Johnson (1966), Eric Wolf (1968), Ted Robert Gurr (1970), Joel S. Migdal (1974), James C. Scott (1976), Charles Tilly (1978), and Theda Skocpol (1979). Perhaps as a legacy of the 1960s, many of these studies define *change that counts* as political mobilization and revolutionary structural transformation—commonly focusing on Mexico, Russia, China, Vietnam, Cuba, and Nicaragua for twentieth-century examples—at the expense of the many striking transformations, conflicts, and national situations that stand outside this grammar of change. In such conceptualizations mass revolutionary mobilization must transcend (or its leaders strategically manipulate and eventually neutralize) cultural difference if violent challenges to the status quo are to be successful. Although cultural diversity within states (particularly ethniclike cleavages) may boil over into riot, rebellion, or civil war, by definition pluralism does not foster the systemic transformations that serve as the frame of reference for these scholars (Enloe 1973). Revolution-centered views of conflict and change see cultural difference as a barrier, a selective conduit for mobilization, a special interest that can contribute to or impede the wider movement, not as a source of alternative agendas and analyses to be understood in its own terms. Thus, cultural issues suffer an uneven fate in these analyses of conflict that look to structural explanations and that concentrate on class as the central, proactive cleavage and identity in social life. As James C. Scott (1976, 1985, 1990) has detailed in his ground-breaking studies of rebellion and local resistance, large areas of daily conflict and resistance to domination—not to speak of other identities and sources of ideology—remained to be conceptualized and explored because of the emphasis on the relatively infrequent instances of revolutionary transformation.

A second exception to the marginalization of national conflicts has been the literature on decolonization and the formation of new states, especially since the 1940s. The backdrop for this research has been studies of nineteenth- and twentieth-century capitalist expansion and transformation, which generated broad, comparative generalizations about agrarian class relations and global divisions of labor as conceptualized by Marxist, dependency, and liberal forms of economic determinism (Chilcote 1982; Migdal 1974). Current literature reveals a range of intellectual projects rather than a consensus about methods, questions, and goals of research. Increasingly, political scientists have replaced unilinear formulations with nuanced and multi-centered views of the politics of change (Grindle 1986; Migdal 1988). In the process, they have pursued more comprehensive analyses of the social and political implications of national development policy. Some continue to see social movements and political resistance as the dangerous consequences of states' modernizing so quickly or chaotically that political authority is unable preemptively to channel and institutionalize political activism (Huntington 1968; Horowitz 1985).

Among interpretive anthropologists and historians (Geertz 1973; Guidieri et al. 1988; Thompson 1963; Hobsbawm and Ranger 1983) as well as scholars of subaltern studies and deconstructionism (Bhabha 1990; Chatterjee 1986; Guha and Spivak 1988; Klor de Alva 1992), there has been a growing concern with the dialogic invention of culture in metropolitan and colonial societies, the cultural and political struggles for independence from colonial rule,[5] and the unfinished business of national domination and cultural pluralism in contemporary states. The cultural critics among these scholars have directly challenged Western epistemologies and the political interests served by anthropology and political science on postcolonial societies.

Postcolonial governments (and their oppositions) have had to author convincing nationalisms to compete—at least situationally—with powerful and divergent loyalties to language, religion, ethnicity, and region. Such loyalties, be they localized or transnational, are portrayed as primordial by movements seeking to legitimize their claims historically as well as by social scientists using static notions of traditionalism. But it would be a mistake not to see these identities and cultural practices as dynamic and subject to strategic manipulation because they have also been shaped by colonial and postcolonial histories (Clifford 1988; Fox 1990a; Warren 1992).

New states have found, as had colonial powers, that the assimilation and appropriation of dominant culture and the dislocations that followed integration into volatile international markets spurred various forms of militancy and resistance. Historical materialists concerned with culture have interpreted resistance as a manifestation of class conflict and alienation imposed by capitalist forms of production and exploitation (Nash 1979; Taussig 1980; Ong 1987). The question has been how to read particular cultural acts—such as ritual offerings to heterodox gods, beliefs about the magical properties of money, and spirit possession on the global assembly line—as appropriations of older cultural symbols and codes to address the dehumanizing nature of work in exploitative situations. Or, from a liberal perspective, resistance has been seen as the channeling of the competition for resources through ethnic blocks (Horowitz 1985; Newman 1991). Stanley J. Tambiah (1990), for example, has shown how minor disputes are manipulated by the politics of the moment into escalating communal conflicts as part of the process through which groups compete for resources and status.

The 1980s and 1990s have witnessed the direction of research to a wider range of conflicts and ways in which civil society is transformed. One sees in this reorientation heightened interest in social movements from feminism to human rights and ethnic nationalism (Eckstein 1989), reconsiderations of the role of local culture in resistance and opposition movements (Colburn 1989; Lan 1985; Warren 1989), reappraisals of colonial culture and domination (Stoler 1985; Taussig 1987; Comaroff and Comaroff 1991), questions about the interplay of cultural diversity and nationalism (Fox 1990b; Gellner 1983; Kapferer 1988; Tambiah 1986), and the recognition of the cultural paradoxes occupied populations make their own through allegory (Lavie 1990). In anthropology there is growing interest in discussing agendas for a culturally sensitive field of conflict studies. As the Carolyn Nordstrom and JoAnn Martin collection (1992) demonstrates so admirably, this project calls for rethinking social theory and the role of the social scientist.

DIALOGUES ON CULTURE AND POLITICS

This volume explores the approaches and concepts anthropologists and political scientists bring to their studies of conflict and cultural meaning. Interestingly, the process through which we developed the collection both reproduced and eroded entrenched theoretical differences and tacit divisions of labor between the fields. Unlike many collections whose contributors are in tenuous contact with each other, after completing their fieldwork these researchers met in an advanced research seminar to share their emerging analyses and read theoretical works across disciplines. As we listened to detailed descriptions of culture and politics in Israel, Northern Ireland, South Africa, and the rest, seminar participants debated the significance of Antonio

Gramsci's *hegemony* (Gramsci 1971; Williams 1977), James Scott's *weapons of the weak* (1985), Benedict Anderson's (1983) nation-state as the preeminent *imagined community,* Joseph Gusfield's (1981) resource versus identity-based social movements, Joan Scott's (1988) gender representations as discourses of power, and Michael Taussig's (1987) *culture of terror.* The early gestation of this volume occurred during seminar discussions and presentations of field-work findings.

The seminar did not lack fireworks and diverse, sometimes discordant languages of analysis. Comparative politics and policy studies are most commonly informed by images of social research as science: a comparative search for abstract and predictive explanations that identify key *variables* accounting for patterns of conflict and change. For example, in our seminar sessions Tony Marx explained cleavages and changes in ideologies and forms of political action for the black opposition to apartheid in South Africa. In addition to studying the dynamics and ideologies of this movement, Marx explored the interaction of periods of political organizing or unrest with variables such as cycles of national economic growth and recession on the one hand and government repression on the other. As background to his considerations of agrarian reform, Jeff Riedinger was concerned with models of rebellion and resistance, developed by a range of theorists, as they predict peasant responses to the commercialization of agriculture in the Philippines. His analysis reconstructed the cost-benefit calculations believed to be implicit in peasant behavior as individuals decided between siding with the insurgent New People's Army or rural landlords and their own private armies. Guilain Denoeux structured his discussions of the political mobilization of urban populations by examining coalitions of informal networks in the Middle East. His goal was to specify the social and political variables that account for what he identified as the shift of nonelite networks from regime-supporting and politically stabilizing to oppositional and destabilizing, as happened in the case of the Iranian Revolution against the shah but failed to materialize to the same extent in Egypt.

The quest for causal statements—in a systems rather than a mechanically deterministic sense—and for theoretical frameworks that generate comparative generalizations remains the signature of political science, although, as we will see, it is not the only form of political analysis for this or other disciplines. In these explanations of conflict and change, the most significant context of people's lives is abstracted to their structural position in the wider political economy. The comparative approach identifies salient variables in order to capture key commonalities and contrasts across societies with the

goal of demonstrating a wider truth. Anything not amenable to this comparative language tends to disappear as analyses proceed from case studies to comparisons. Thus, as the explanations gain scope and power, the substance and
complexity of cultural difference, historical distinctiveness, and individual
agency are often diminished, except where they relate directly to the key variables. Individuals in all their variety become rational actors or role-players.
Their diverse and contingent subjectivities are shunned for what is judged to
be the more stable objectivity of groups and systems. The measure of change
is its contribution to nation building (Young 1976).[6] In the seminar, the challenge to the political scientists was to work toward a fuller cultural analysis
that for their purposes would still be comparatively significant.[7]

Not all of the political scientists pursued classical comparative strategies.
In particular, Mike Hanchard discussed the variousness, ambiguities, and
paradoxes of racial identification in Brazil. Rather than focusing on collective
identities or individualized cost-benefit calculations for action, he explored
the difficult connection between the moments of racial recognition and identification among Afro-Brazilians and the emerging political movements that
critique existing social arrangements and violence against blacks. Hanchard
provided a cross-national twist to comparative analysis in his examination of
the political significance of the ways Brazilian activists have appropriated (and
transformed) ideas of Negritude from Africa and civil rights and Black Power
from the United States.

Cultural anthropology is explicitly concerned with problems of experience, representation, interpretation, and the arrays of meaning elaborated in
the practice of culture by people with a multiplicity of identities and social
connections—in particular historically created communities. Violence,
whether surgical or diffuse, is not a social fact or a cultural experience until it
is given significance by analyzing subjects. The issue for anthropologists is to
unlock the meanings of conflict and change in cultures and political systems
in which symbolic languages, social realities, and conflicts are not easily translatable into conventional Western categories of social analysis, however Westernized the population appears to be. As this volume shows, cultures of terror
and resistance take many forms. Although cultural analysis can be conducted
from national or local vantage points, the anthropologists in this collection
worked on the interface between social movements and people's daily lives.

In the seminar, Davida Wood argued that one cannot understand the
meaning of political activism for the Palestinians living in Israel's Galilee region by listening to the rhetoric and ideologies of the political parties alone.
Rather, one must understand more about Palestinian culture—specifically

the intersections of how and when particular individuals evoke understandings of authority and honor, the ways clanship as well as party membership continues to define key social relationships, and the embeddedness of Palestinian society in Israeli politics. Begoña Aretxaga sought a deeper understanding of the troubles in Northern Ireland by examining the impact of British militarization and Irish Republican Army (IRA) responses on Belfast's Catholic population. She described distinctive political memories that for the British justify the continued domination and use of force to subdue the Irish "barbarians" and for the Catholics yield images of injustice and resistance that resonate with the present. Aretxaga showed how political commitments cannot merely be understood in terms of the classical political ideologies of liberation movements but must also be seen in the context of individuals struggling to make meaning of the politics of everyday life. My presentation described how rural Mayan communities in Guatemala were caught between military and guerrilla forces in the 1970s and 1980s. I focused on the ways the Mayas of San Andrés survived the horror of random killings and disappearances, discovered the realities of political betrayal yet resisted the internalization of violence in community affairs, and found ways to express in veiled languages the conflicts and dilemmas unleashed in the clash between insurgents and counterinsurgency forces.

These anthropologists are interested in the agencies and agents behind particular constructions rather than attributing cultural production to generalized political interests or abstract economic forces. The interpretive quest involves making central what is often muted: people's varying experiences of dislocation, repression, and dissent and their struggles to make sense of their own violence as well as the violence of those in power. How are these experiences lived in different cultural worlds? How do individuals refashion their cultures to deal with the uncertainty and paradoxes of their situations? How do people find ways to represent the inarticulable, fragmenting, disorienting, and dominating nature of terror and simultaneously find routes to resist or perhaps succumb to its pressures?

In contrast to political science, the anthropological context of people's lives includes the variety of social worlds in which they live—their families, kinship networks, work groups, cooperatives, religious organizations, communities, and political action groups—which mediate personal agency and wider politics and economics. Additionally, anthropologists raise epistemological questions about how we know what we know across cultural cleavages, given that researchers are also cultural beings with their own identities, cultural categories, social and political positions, and changing contexts. This reflexivity

questions the cultural assumptions of the investigator and the appropriate-
ness of the narrative forms used in conveying research findings (Clifford
1988; Clifford and Marcus 1986) as it works to reveal the inner dynamics of
other societies. In the seminar, the challenge to the anthropologists was to
demonstrate the ways meanings are in fact linked to political practice, how
local culture is relevant to the understanding of national society, and how
state politics can be brought into a cultural analysis.

Distinctive formulations of explanation, interpretation, and comparison;
transnational, national, and local levels of analysis (or the suspicion that *level*
is not the best analytic metaphor); and different definitions of the context of
social life all produce striking differences between political science and anthropology. These distinctions tie into a wider set of hierarchies in Western
social science that contrast scientific ways of knowing as objective and hu-
manistic ways of knowing as subjective.[8] Even though anthropologists and
historians of science have explored the ironies of this language, the construction continues to guide political research and limit the development of the
subfield of political culture. The tenacity of this paradigmatic contrast—coupled with political science's emphasis on predictive explanations, lawlike generalizations, changes that count, and regime stability and instability—may be
due in part to political science's important constituencies in foreign policy
and development economics.[9] Cultural specificity, which calls for a meaning-
centered rather than a nation-centered standardized analysis, is often deemed
irrelevant or at worst threatening to policymakers' goals. Culture is reduced
to the status of a variable, which if necessary can be controlled for, evoked
when other explanations are insufficient, or treated as a form of universal psychology.[10] Fortunately for our seminar and these chapters, disciplinary conventions do not preclude experiments, although reward structures in and
among fields make interdisciplinary projects less common than they should
be.

As the research seminar continued, participants noticed areas of convergence in their projects. The contributors built upon and extended these areas
of common interest in their chapters for this volume, further shifting disciplinary boundaries by foregrounding cultural politics in their research. They
would second Geertz's (1983: 143) observation that "political authority still
requires a cultural frame in which to define itself and advance its claims, and
so does opposition to it." For this volume, the political scientists Riedinger,
Denoeux, and Marx wrote what they consider special cross-disciplinary experiments in cultural analysis; Hanchard offers his approach as an explicit
challenge to the conventional distinction between cultural and political stud-

ies. In their case studies, the political scientists make particularly insightful contributions to our understanding of the processes through which groups formulate ideologies to appeal to wider populations and challenge constructions dominant in national politics.

The anthropologists Aretxaga, Wood, and Warren write against apolitical cultural studies, whether in the guise of arguments that essentialize cultural difference or reinvent functionalism. Some cultural studies simply ignore issues of domination and politics, treating culturally distinctive communities as if they practice autonomous systems of belief despite sustained periods of colonial domination. Other cultural studies examine conventionalized activities and roles as mechanisms that channel internal conflict, promote solidarity, reaffirm collective commitments to the system, and regulate human ecology.[11]

By contrast, the anthropologists in this volume are concerned with multiple and contested political cleavages, the lack of consensus and clearly bounded groups, structures of domination, and cultural meaning in societies inevitably enmeshed in wider historically forged political relations. In particular, their analyses contribute to knowledge of the ways in which cultures of resistance to domination are elaborated by concrete individuals in situations where repression and violence have become central facts of everyday life. These anthropologists pursue an interpretive approach that stresses the production of cultural meaning in ongoing social practice (Bourdieu 1977). Individuals and groups become agents—despite structural subordination— through the reworking of local culture and received ideologies, which may be designed to control but are reconfigured to buffer and critique structures of domination. The question, of course, is the substance (or lack of explicitness) of social critiques, the actions they make meaningful, and the character and goals of actions analysts read as resistance.[12]

Together, these chapters reflect the direct and diffuse influence of a variety of culture theorists (who as I have indicated are read and appropriated by the researchers in varying ways given the disciplines' different positioning of ideological struggle) including Clifford Geertz (1973, 1983), Raymond Williams (1977), Antonio Gramsci (1971), Pierre Bourdieu (1977), James Clifford (1988), Michel Foucault (1979, 1983), James Scott (1985), Michael Taussig (1987, 1992), Joan Scott (1988), Renato Rosaldo (1989), and others. Culture is no longer an anonymous given in a particular society, unproblematically passed from one generation to the next as an established consensus about what is socially, politically, and religiously authoritative. Rather, as Renato Rosaldo (1989: 26) observed, "Culture can arguably be conceived as a

more porous array of intersections where distinct processes crisscross from
within and beyond its borders." These intersections occur when the confluence of meaning and politics becomes significant for those caught in its wakes
and eddies. The researchers in this volume identify and analyze key intersections in societies in which political realities are volatile and changing.

CONTOURS OF RESISTANCE, REPRESSION, AND OPPOSITION

Kay B. Warren explores the political ironies and the culture of terror that
engulfed Mayan Indian populations following military-guerrilla clashes and
the militarization of civilian life in Guatemala from the late 1970s through
the 1980s. During *la violencia* (the violence) threats of guerrilla attacks and
rural radicalization drove many large landowners out of the highlands, potentially increasing agriculturalists' access to land and their authority in local
government. Killings, disappearances, tortures, and armed sweeps, however,
created a climate of overwhelming anxiety and uncertainty because no one
knew who might be detained or killed next. Warren's study shows how Mayans struggled to interpret an increasingly chaotic world and attempted to resist the internalization of national violence in community affairs. Mayans
from San Andrés communicated their fears and the inchoate consequences of
their experiences through strategic silences and evasions as well as through social realist narratives that described the arbitrariness of often ambiguous political powers that threatened without warning or necessary reason to con-
demn Mayans as subversives or collaborators. Perhaps because their
universalistic religious languages, built on the moral agency of individuals,
appeared to falter in the face of disruptions of meaning and experience, Mayan Catholics in contemporary religious groups such as Acción Católica began to revitalize older forms of traditionalist religion—particularly Mayan beliefs that portray certain "selves" as potentially unstable and capable of
transformation into supernatural beings (*rajav a'a'*), betraying others in the
process. Warren argues that these cultural constructions have been appropriated as a veiled language through which to express the existential dilemma
raised by violence: Who can I trust in a world in which I may be betrayed by
my neighbors, the very people I am dependent on for information crucial to
my personal survival? An analysis of the range of Mayan narrative and
nonnarrative strategies for resisting terror allows for a fuller accounting of the
effects of genocidal violence on Guatemala's four million Mayan Indians.

Michael Hanchard analyzes the coercive, depoliticizing nature of Brazilian national culture by asking who creates and who neutralizes the cultural forms for articulating dissent. He examines the ideology of racial democracy, developed by major figures such as Gilberto Freyre, as a persuasive nationalist claim that Brazil had uniquely resolved the problem of racism unlike countries such as the United States or South Africa. Hanchard is interested in the fact that despite continuing racial stratification in economics and politics and the violence Afro-Brazilians face in their daily lives, there has been no crystallization of opposition, no "historical moment"—as occurred in the United States or South Africa—when blacks could create a sustained political challenge to racism. His analysis of the Brazilian *movimento negro* in the 1970s and 1980s documents a variety of attempts by black activists to create social movements building on the symbols of Negritude, diaspora, and Black Power. According to Hanchard, these movements fail to attract wider followings because of their limited financial resources and the particularly hostile reactions of those in the wider society who deny the legitimacy of any claims of racism. Just as important has been the process through which the *movimento negro* has internalized the tensions between the myth of racial democracy and race-focused political consciousness as well as the contrast between Brazilian culturalism (the national celebration of Afro-Brazilian heritage) and cultural politics (the critique of the political stakes inherent in any cultural revitalization).

Davida Wood identifies and analyzes Palestinian idioms for politics in Israel: how they shape what becomes political and how politics is contested through events such as nationalist protests, arrests, elections, marriages, and blood feuds. At issue is the significance for Palestinian Israelis of simultaneously being an ethnic minority with citizenship in a parliamentary democracy and a terrorist enemy existing in an ungovernable space the state attempts to dominate. As part of its policy to contain minority political demands, Israel localized Palestinian political representation to what it defined as the "traditional" level, using the patrilineal kinship system—the *ḥamūlas*—as the framework for integrating Palestinians into Israel's administrative structure. In practice, however, the *ḥamūla* is not a rigid or autonomous structuring of authority but is a complex field of social relations and ideas about binding but vulnerable collective honor and power. Kinship-based politics exists in dynamic tension with Palestinian nationalism and opposition groups such as the Communist party, the Marxist-Leninist Sons of the Village, the Progressive List for Peace (each of which is identified with factions of the Palestine Liberation Organization [PLO]), and the fundamentalist Islamic Association.

Wood shows how individuals appropriate *ḥamūla* honor and nationalist ideology as they intensify or diffuse violent conflicts in their families, community, and nation. The dilemma for Palestinians in Israel is to devise frameworks with which to interpret political developments in an environment in which the state actively supports collaborators and the resulting possibility of betrayal generates unresolvable uncertainty about the motives and meanings behind individual actions.

Guilain Denoeux examines the social forms and cultural processes through which Islamic fundamentalism coalesced in certain Middle Eastern countries, but not in others, to become a major political movement opposing Westernization. Central to his argument are the informal urban networks the poor and working classes create as they search urban environments for economic resources, information, patrons, social ties, resolutions of disputes, and reaffirmations of their cultural and religious identities. Networks have often been interpreted as stabilizing and integrative, linking populations that have been marginalized by social change into cross-class, patron-client reciprocities that can be used by power brokers to deliver support for existing authorities in exchange for access to goods and services. Denoeux argues that under certain political, economic, and cultural circumstances, however, networks can become powerful organizational and ideological avenues for channeling political dissent. He examines informal religious groups—such as the *jama'at islamiyya* on Egyptian university campuses and the *hay'at-e senfis* of the bazaar and the *hay'ats* of the urban poor in Iran—and finds that such associations offered members systematic critiques of the dislocating aspects of change as "moral corruption." In appealing to millions of apolitical Iranians after the fall of the shah, Khomeini appropriated these themes, linking the "cultural decadence" fostered by the shah's modernization programs with the growing influence of Westerners in the country and the regime's perceived subservience to the United States and Israel. In the process, religious nationalism was used to forge the close identification of personal dilemmas with national problems, thus supporting the increasing authority of clerics in the emergent political order. Denoeux also examines the culture of radical-utopian Islamic networks and the ways they legitimize present actions through the memory of Muhammed's withdrawal (*hijra*) from a world denounced as corrupt.

Anthony W. Marx examines the ways black opposition groups in South Africa have challenged, with their own alternative formulations, the state's claim to the authoritative version of nationhood. Following Benedict Anderson, he argues that nation-states are not static units of comparison but are variable historical and political constructions. South Africa as a nation has been formed by a history of recurrent and still unresolved tensions between oppression and self-determination. Marx is struck by the progressive and conservative goals of oppositional nationalism, the use of unrest to challenge authorities, and the attempted suppression of certain cleavages in order to create a widely appealing imagined community. The history of competing formulations in South Africa includes the apartheid policy of Afrikaner nationalism, the inclusive nationalism of the African National Congress (ANC), the racially separatist formulation of the Pan Africanist Congress (PAC), the race-affirming psychology of the Black Consciousness Movement (BC), the Zulu ethnic nationalism of Inkatha, and the umbrella opposition to apartheid of the United Democratic Front (UDF). Marx seeks to explain the interplay of ideologies, groups, experiences with state policies and repression, and the economic conditions that have shaped the activism of successive generations of the black opposition, leading in the 1980s to a reappropriation of the earlier ANC Charterist formulation that is shaping current political transitions. Critical to this process in the climate of increasing violence and repression during the mid-1980s was the escalation of opposition demands for the release of Nelson Mandela and the end to apartheid.

Jeffrey M. Riedinger asks whether significant agrarian reform is feasible as an attack on growing rural poverty and landlessness in countries such as the Philippines that are involved in conflictual "transitions" from authoritarian to democratic governments. As his analysis demonstrates, the answer is not a narrow technical one about productivity gains or losses with the redistribution of land resources precisely because the terms of national debate are culturally and politically constructed. The conflicting realities and representations of agrarian reform in the Philippines are shaped by histories of agrarian relations and democratic reforms that allowed rural elites to consolidate national powers during the 1898–1946 U. S. administration; by the ambivalence of the Aquino government, which designed and then emasculated a redistributive reform; by landowning elites who maintain private armies and seek to bolster resistance to reform by defining peasants as well maintained within existing paternalistic arrangements; and by continued pressures for change from the New People's Army, the union movement, and the Catholic church's Basic Christian Community movement. In recent efforts to shape policy, both elites and peasants debated images of landowners and laborers, connections to the land, economies of scale in agricultural productivity, peasant capacities and aspirations, and the implications of paternalism. Riedinger concludes that planters, congressional representatives, and President Corazon Aquino used similar rhetorical strategies to limit the scope and direction of the reform that at this juncture makes available only 13–16 percent of the farm land for redistribution. Although the new reform law reflects the continuing dominance of the planters' formulation of agrarian relations, challenges to that formulation have mounted in an increasingly militarized countryside.

Begoña Aretxaga illustrates the ways in which history has been used in Northern Ireland to justify interpenetrating and antagonistic political realities for Irish Republicans and the British. British domination and the militarization of daily life have produced a culture of terror for Irish Catholic civilians, exemplified by the arbitrariness of the meanings imposed by patrolling police and soldiers as they decide at each encounter who is a terrorist or a civilian, and by jailers at the Long Kesh prison who in the late 1970s transformed political prisoners into common criminals by stripping them of the markers of their political and moral reasons for incarceration. In personal accounts of police and ethnic persecution that began in their childhoods, Irish nationalists describe their experience of the arbitrariness of oppression and the anxious feelings the fragmentation of reality has produced for its survivors. Aretxaga centers her chapter on the existential dilemmas faced by Bobby Sands, the other hunger strikers of 1981, and their families who resisted their definition as common criminals by elaborating counternarratives of protest and resistance, reclaiming the agency to create meaning and contest power even as they were imprisoned. Their decision to protest their treatment through a hunger strike intensified the cultural paradoxes: For the prisoners, there was no choice between dignity or death; for their mothers, there was the unbearable dilemma of supporting sons they had struggled to nurture in the midst of grinding poverty in their decision to fast to death. The decision to live out the tragedy became personally compelling. It was made more powerful as Sands explored the echoes of Christ's suffering and political martyrdom in his poetry and as nationalists linked the hunger strikes to other instances of fasting protests by people of ancient Gaelic times and by Nationalist heroes of the early twentieth century, thereby asserting the continuity of moral resistance and ethnic nationalism.

Although the chapters in this volume can be approached as distinctive contributions to their fields and regions of study, clearly, much is to be gained through a comparative, interactive reading. The chapters speak to each other on such issues as the emotional force of violence and the ruptures of meaning involved in surviving and resisting violent repression (see Aretxaga, Warren, and Wood);[13] the interplay of dissent and coalitional politics in the emergence or breakup of opposition movements (see Hanchard, Marx, Denoeux, Aretxaga, Riedinger, Wood, and Warren); the significance of cultural memory—the historical and the mythic—to current directions of resistance and ethnic nationalism (see Wood, Hanchard, Denoeux, Warren, Marx, Aretxaga); distinctive national experiences and constructions of modernity (see Denoeux, Riedinger, Aretxaga, Marx); the resistance of democratic and democratizing states to reforms redistributing power and resources (see Riedinger, Aretxaga, Hanchard, Wood, Warren); and the choices faced by formerly marginalized groups as they achieve increasing powers in their political systems (see Marx, Denoeux, Riedinger).

This volume makes the case for an *anthropology of politics* in which culture—in its contested, contingent, and historically grounded sense—is a constituting element of political action and identity. Our goal is to examine contemporary conflicts in divided nations, the struggles involved in their intensification (or denial), and the long-term cultural clashes that define and complicate their terms. In the process, these chapters attempt to refocus studies of conflict on cross-cutting internal divisions, dislocations, and voices of dissent; on the consequences of political violence for the ongoing social life of political groups, communities, and families; and on the genesis of movements to contest and support existing political arrangements. The search is not for prisoners' dilemmas or hidden transcripts to unify this diversity but for meaning-centered accounts that will more fully communicate the dilemmas and lessons of change.

NOTES

My thanks to Mike Hanchard, Peter Smith, Davida Wood, Begoña Aretxaga, Judith Barish, Jim Boon, Deborah Poole, Rosann Fitzpatrick, Jeff Riedinger, Tom Johnston-O'Neill, and Aaron Willis as well as participants in the Princeton, MacArthur Foundation, and Alfred Stepan's Arden Homestead seminars for discussions of the issues raised in this introduction.

1. Horowitz's argument (1985) that too much ethnicity creates conflict yet that one can "control" for culture as a variable in the study of pluralism is a good example of the formulation I am attempting to problematize.

2. See, for instance, Hammond (1969), Kissinger (1974), Giddens (1987), Papp (1988), Spanier (1990). Anthropologists have dealt occasionally with cultural issues inherent in great power tensions and formulations of conflict, but often from afar and without their most powerful ethnographic tools. See Rubinstein and Foster (1988) and Turner and Pitt (1989).

3. This is not a linear process but an interplay of local culture, wider political movements, and the state, as Isbell (n.d.) demonstrates for Peru and the Shining Path.

4. Important examples of political science research that foreshadowed these current trends include the works of Bienen (1968) and Enloe (1973); for anthropology, historically sensitive ethnographies such as Geertz (1965), Friedrich (1970), and Wallace (1972), as well as Hobsbawm's (1959) classic historical analysis, demonstrated the importance of a wider framing of cultural research on conflict and change.

5. Klor de Alva (1992) has challenged the applicability of the new-states formulation for Latin America, reminding us of the danger of overgeneralizing colonial experiences from any one model of domination or cultural identity.

6. Thus the focus on regime transitions, stabilizing or destabilizing movements for national governments, system maintenance (when for anthropologists and historians "the system" is not the same over time), and the nation-state as the consummate modern imagined community. That nation-states are seen as naturally appropriate and comparable units is a historically grounded idea of recent vintage, as Anderson (1983) and Gellner (1983) have shown. That this natural unit—could we have political order without it?—is currently being eroded through the European Community and other regional associations, the breakup of the Soviet Union, and the rise of ethnic nationalism may call for a reconsideration of this language and the goals of the comparative project.

7. Geertz (1973, 1983), Kapferer (1988), and Tambiah (1986) provide alternative strategies for comparative analysis that attempt to devise historically grounded holistic contrasts and that deal with different cultural centers of gravity rather than with standardized variables. Wolf (1982) offers an important historical critique of bounded comparisons.

8. Rubinstein (1988) argues that this contrast has inhibited policymakers from taking cultural studies seriously in international security studies. Poole and Renique (1991) denounce comparative methods that fail to deal with historical specifics, arguing that the resulting distortions of cultural realities may have implicit political motivations.

9. Of course anthropological fieldwork was undertaken in colonial situations, assisting European administrators by producing useful structural-functionalist descriptions of local cultures while ignoring culture contact and domination. Then as well as in postcolonial research, field-workers' subject positions have been influenced by the multiple political contexts they engage at home and abroad (cf. Asad 1973). To extend Stocking's observations (1991: 5) to both disciplines, a more comprehensive consideration of these issues would empirically examine the actual research situations, relationships created in the process of fieldwork, and the ways in which concrete practices influence the production of knowledge. Anthropologists now attempt greater reflexivity in their writings to deal with these issues.

10. That ethnic pluralism and religious fundamentalism, for instance, can be seen as both products and mediations of economic and political change demonstrates the difficulties in thinking of culture as a singular variable.

11. Functionalist arguments range from Harris's (1974) vulgar materialism to the much more subtle forms of functionalism found in Rappaport's (1967) cultural ecol-

ogy, Sahlins's (1961) strategic political functionalism, Turner's (1969) ritual communitas, and Geertz's (1973: 142–169) concern with meaning systems rendering the world comprehensible. The contributors in this volume would also challenge decontextualized examinations of behavior in fields such as sociobiology or psychology (cf. Haas 1990; Chagnon and Irons 1979; Groebel and Hinde 1989), which do not address individual agency, meaning, history, and multiple sources of power (cf. Boon 1986).

12. This approach contrasts in its framing of the issues with other variants of interpretive anthropology that focus on discourse, text, internalized discipline, hegemony, structures of conjuncture, and transformations of deep structures. See Comaroff and Comaroff (1991), Foucault (1979, 1983), Nash (1989), Sahlins (1981), and Lévi-Strauss (1963) for contrasting approaches.

13. See Rosaldo (1989: 2) on the issue of emotional force and Taussig (1987, 1992) on terror and fragmentation.

BIBLIOGRAPHY

Anderson, Benedict. *Imagined Communities: Reflections on the Origin and Spread of Nationalism.* London: Verso, 1983.

Asad, Talal. *Anthropology and the Colonial Encounter.* Atlantic Highlands, N.J.: Humanities Press, 1973.

Bhahba, Homi. "DissemiNation: Time, Narrative, and the Margins of Modern Nation." In Homi Bhahba, ed., *Nation and Narration.* London: Routledge, 1990, 291–322.

Bienen, Henry. *Violence and Social Change.* Chicago: University of Chicago Press, 1968.

Boon, James. "Symbols, Sylphs, and Siwa: Allegorical Machineries in the Text of Balinese Culture." In Victor Turner and Edward Bruner, eds., *The Anthropology of Experience.* Urbana: University of Illinois Press, 1986, 239–260.

Bourdieu, Pierre. *Outline of a Theory of Practice.* Cambridge: Cambridge University Press, 1977.

Bourque, Susan C., and Kay B. Warren. "Democracy Without Peace: The Cultural Politics of Terror in Peru." *Latin American Research Review* 24, no. 1 (1989): 7–34.

Chagnon, Napoleon, and W. Irons, eds. *Evolutionary Biology and Human Social Behavior: An Anthropological Perspective.* North Scituate, Mass.: Duxbury Press, 1979.

Chatterjee, Partha. *Nationalist Thought and the Colonial World—A Derivative Discourse?* London: Zed Press, 1986.

Chilcote, Ronald H. *Dependency and Marxism: Toward a Resolution of the Debate.* Latin American Perspectives Series, no. 1. Boulder: Westview Press, 1982.

Clifford, James. *The Predicament of Culture.* Cambridge: Harvard, 1988.

Clifford, James, and George Marcus, eds. *Writing Culture*. Berkeley: University of California Press, 1986.

Colburn, Forest, ed. *Everyday Forms of Peasant Resistance*. Armonk, N.Y.: M. E. Sharp, 1989.

Comaroff, Jean, and John Comaroff. *Of Revelation and Revolution: Christianity, Colonialism and Consciousness in South Africa*. Chicago: University of Chicago Press, 1991.

Eckstein, Susan, ed. *Power and Popular Protest: Latin American Social Movements*. Berkeley: University of California Press, 1989.

Enloe, Cynthia H. *Ethnic Conflict and Political Development*. New York: Little, Brown and Company, 1973.

Foucault, Michel. *Discipline and Punish: The Birth of the Prison*. Alan Sheridan, trans. New York: Vintage, 1979.

_____ . *Power/Knowledge: Selected Interviews and Other Writings, 1972–1977*. Colin Gordon, ed. New York: Pantheon, 1983.

Fox, Richard G. "Hindu Nationalism in the Making, or the Rise of the Hindian." In Richard G. Fox, *Nationalist Ideologies and the Production of National Cultures*. American Ethnological Monograph Series, no. 2. Washington, D.C.: American Anthropological Association, 1990a, 63–80.

_____ . *Nationalist Ideologies and the Production of National Cultures*. American Ethnological Monograph Series, no. 2. Washington, D.C.: American Anthropological Association, 1990b.

Friedrich, Paul. *Agrarian Revolt in a Mexican Village*. Chicago: University of Chicago Press, 1970.

Geertz, Clifford. *The Social History of an Indonesian Town*. Cambridge, Mass.: MIT Press, 1965.

_____ . *The Interpretation of Cultures*. New York: Basic Books, 1973.

_____ . *Local Knowledge: Further Essays in Interpretive Anthropology*. New York: Basic Books, 1983.

Gellner, Ernest. *Nations and Nationalism*. Ithaca: Cornell University Press, 1983.

Giddens, Anthony. *The Nation-State and Violence*. Berkeley: University of California Press, 1987.

Goldstein, Judith C. "An Innocent Abroad: How Mulla Daoud Was Lost and Found in Lebanon, or the Politics of Ethnic Theater in a Nation at War." In Richard G. Fox, *Nationalist Ideologies and the Production of National Cultures*. American Ethnological Society Monograph Series, no. 2. Washington, D.C.: American Anthropological Association, 1990, 15–31.

Gramsci, Antonio. *Selections from the Prison Notebooks of Antonio Gramsci*. Quintin Hoare and Geoffrey Nowell Smith, eds. New York: International Publishers, 1971.

Grindle, Merilee S. *State and Countryside: Development Policy and Agrarian Politics in Latin America*. Baltimore: Johns Hopkins University Press, 1986.

Groebel, Jo, and Robert A. Hinde. *Aggression and War: Their Biological and Social Bases.* Cambridge: Cambridge University Press, 1989.

Guha, Ranajit, and Gayatri Chakravorty Spivak, eds. *Selected Subaltern Studies.* New York: Oxford University Press, 1988.

Guidieri, Remo, Francesco Pellizzi, and Stanley Tambiah, eds. *Ethnicities and Nations: Processes of Interethnic Relations in Latin America, Southeast Asia, and the Pacific.* Austin: University of Texas Press, 1988.

Gurr, Ted Robert. *Why Men Rebel.* Princeton: Princeton University Press, 1970.

Gusfield, Joseph. "Social Movements and Social Change." *Research in Social Movements, Conflict, and Change* 4 (1981): 317–336.

Haas, Jonathan. *The Anthropology of War.* A School of American Research book. Cambridge: Cambridge University Press, 1990.

Hammond, Paul Y. *The Cold War Years: American Foreign Policy Since 1945.* New York: Harcourt, Brace, Jovanovich, 1969.

Harris, Marvin. *Cows, Pigs, Wars, and Witches: The Riddles of Culture.* New York: Vintage Books, 1974.

Hobsbawm, Eric. *Primitive Rebels: Studies of Archaic Forms of Social Movements in the 19th and 20th Centuries.* New York: Norton, 1959.

Hobsbawm, Eric, and Terrance Ranger, eds. *The Invention of Culture.* Cambridge: Cambridge University Press, 1983.

Horowitz, Ronald. *Ethnic Groups in Conflict.* Berkeley: University of California Press, 1985.

Huntington, Samuel P. *Political Order in Changing Societies.* New Haven: Yale University Press, 1968.

Isbell, Billie Jean. "Responses to Shining Path in Provincial Ayacucho in the 1980s." In David Scott Palmer, ed. *The Shining Path of Peru.* New York: St. Martin's Press, in press.

Johnson, Chalmers. *Revolutionary Change.* Boston: Little, Brown, 1966.

Kapferer, Bruce. *Legends of People, Myths of State: Violence, Intolerance, and Political Culture in Sri Lanka and Australia.* Washington, D.C.: Smithsonian Institution Press, 1988.

Kissinger, Henry. *American Foreign Policy.* New York: W. W. Norton, 1974.

Klor de Alva, J. Jorge. "Colonialism and Postcolonialism as (Latin) American Mirages." *Colonial Latin American Review* 1, no. 2 (1992).

Lan, David. *Guns and Rain: Guerrillas and Spirit Mediums in Zimbabwe.* Berkeley: University of California Press, 1985.

Lavie, Smadar. *The Poetics of Military Occupation: Mzeina Allegories of Bedouin Identity Under Israeli and Egyptian Rule.* Berkeley: University of California Press, 1990.

Lévi-Strauss, Claude. *Structural Anthropology.* New York: Anchor Books, 1963.

Migdal, Joel S. *Peasants, Politics, and Revolution.* Princeton: Princeton University Press, 1974.

_____ . *Strong Societies and Weak States: State-Society Relations and State Capabilities in the Third World.* Princeton: Princeton University Press, 1988.

Moore, Barrington. *The Social Origins of Dictatorship and Democracy.* Boston: Beacon Press, 1966.

Nash, June C. *We Eat the Mines and the Mines Eat Us: Dependency and Exploitation in Bolivian Tin Mines.* New York: Columbia University Press, 1979.

_____ . *From Tank Town to High Tech: The Clash of Community and Industrial Cycles.* Albany: SUNY Press, 1989.

Newman, Saul. "Does Modernization Breed Ethnic Political Conflict?" *World Politics* 43 (1991): 451–478.

Nordstrom, Carolyn, and JoAnn Martin, eds. *Paths to Domination, Resistance, and Terror.* Berkeley: University of California Press, 1992.

Ong, Aiwah. *Spirits of Resistance and Capitalist Discipline: Factory Women in Malaysia.* Albany: SUNY Press, 1987.

Papp, Daniel S. *Contemporary International Relations,* 2d ed. New York: Macmillan, 1988.

Poole, Deborah, and Gerardo Renique. "The New Chroniclers of Peru: U.S. Scholars and Their 'Shining Path' of Peasant Rebellion." *Bulletin of Latin American Research* 10, no. 2 (1991): 133–191.

Rappaport, Roy. *Pigs for the Ancestors.* New Haven: Yale University Press, 1967.

Riches, David, ed. *The Anthropology of Violence.* Oxford: Basil Blackwell, 1986.

Rosaldo, Renato. *Ilongot Headhunting 1883–1974: A Study in Society and History.* Stanford: Stanford University Press, 1980.

_____ . *Culture and Truth: The Remaking of Social Analysis.* Boston: Beacon, 1989.

Rubinstein, Robert A. "Anthropology and International Security." In Robert A. Rubinstein and Mary LeCron Foster, eds. *The Social Dynamics of Peace and Conflict: Culture in International Security.* Boulder: Westview Press, 1988, 17–34.

Rubinstein, Robert A., and Mary LeCron Foster, eds. *The Social Dynamics of Peace and Conflict: Culture in International Security.* Boulder: Westview Press, 1988.

Sahlins, Marshall. "The Segmentary Lineage: An Organization of Predatory Expansion." *American Anthropologist* 63 (1961): 322–345.

_____ . *Historical Metaphors and Mythical Realities: Structure in the Early History of the Sandwich Islands Kingdom.* Ann Arbor: University of Michigan Press, 1981.

Said, Edward. *Orientalism.* New York: Random House, 1978.

Scarry, Elaine. *The Body in Pain: The Making and Unmaking of the World.* Oxford: Oxford University Press, 1985.

Scott, James C. *The Moral Economy of the Peasant: Rebellion and Subsistence in Southeast Asia.* New Haven: Yale University Press, 1976.

_____ . *Weapons of the Weak: Everyday Forms of Resistance.* New Haven: Yale University Press, 1985.

_____ . *Domination and the Arts of Resistance: Hidden Transcripts.* New Haven: Yale University Press, 1990.

Scott, Joan. *Gender and the Politics of History.* New York: Columbia University Press, 1988.

Skocpol, Theda. *States and Social Revolutions: A Comparative Analysis of France, Russia and China.* Cambridge: Cambridge University Press, 1979.

Spanier, John. *Games Nations Play,* 7th ed. Washington, D.C.: Congressional Quarterly Press, 1990.

Starn, Orin. "Missing the Revolution: Anthropologists and the War in Peru." *Cultural Anthropology* 6, no. 1 (1991) : 63–91.

Stocking, George W. *Colonial Situations: Essays on the Contextualization of Ethnographic Knowledge.* Madison: University of Wisconsin Press, 1991.

Stoler, Ann. *Capitalism and Confrontation in Sumatra's Plantation Belt, 1870–1979.* New Haven: Yale University Press, 1985.

Tambiah, Stanley J. *Sri Lanka: Ethnic Fratricide and the Dismantling of Democracy.* Chicago: University of Chicago Press, 1986.

_____ . "Reflections on Communal Violence in South Asia." *Journal of Asian Studies* 49, no. 4 (1990): 741–760.

Taussig, Michael. *The Devil and Commodity Fetishism in South America.* Chapel Hill: University of North Carolina Press, 1980.

_____ . *Shamanism, Colonialism, and the Wild Man: A Study in Terror and Healing.* Chicago: University of Chicago Press, 1987.

_____ . *The Nervous System.* New York: Routledge, 1992.

Thompson, E. P. *The Making of the English Working Class.* London: Penguin, 1963.

Tilly, Charles. *From Mobilization to Revolution.* Reading, Mass.: Addison-Wesley, 1978.

Turner, Paul R., and David Pitt, eds. *The Anthropology of War and Peace: Perspectives on the Nuclear Age.* South Hadley, Mass.: Bergin and Garvey, 1989.

Turner, Victor. *The Ritual Process.* Chicago: Aldine, 1969.

Turner, Victor, and Edward Bruner, eds. *The Anthropology of Experience.* Urbana: University of Illinois Press, 1986.

Wallace, Anthony F. C. *The Death and the Rebirth of the Seneca.* New York: Vintage, 1972.

Warren, Kay B. *The Symbolism of Subordination: Indian Identity in a Guatemalan Town,* 2d ed. Austin: University of Texas Press, 1989.

_____ . "Transforming Memories and Histories: The Meanings of Ethnic Resurgence for Mayan Indians." In Alfred Stepan, ed., *Americas: New Interpretive Essays.* Oxford: Oxford University Press, 1992, 189–219.

Williams, Raymond. *Marxism and Literature.* Oxford: Oxford University Press, 1977.

Wolf, Eric. *Peasant Wars of the Twentieth Century.* New York: Harper and Row, 1968.

_____ . *Europe and the People Without History.* Berkeley: University of California Press, 1982.

Young, Crawford. *The Politics of Cultural Pluralism.* Madison: University of Wisconsin Press, 1976.

1 Interpreting *La Violencia* in Guatemala: Shapes of Mayan Silence & Resistance

KAY B. WARREN

During the 1970s and 1980s Guatemala was engulfed in intense internal warfare, *la violencia* (the violence)[1] as it is called in that country. Between 1978 and 1985, an estimated 50,000 to 70,000 people were killed; half a million people out of a national population of 8 million became internal refugees; 150,000 fled to Mexico as political and economic refugees; and 200,000 found their way to other countries such as the United States (Manz 1988: 30, 209).

Explicitly, *la violencia* was a confrontation between military and guerrilla forces. From the military's point of view, it was a battle against communism, against an armed and dangerous menace within.[2] Guerrilla terror needed to be met with counterterror. The counterinsurgency war began with the successful routing of guerrilla forces in eastern Guatemala in the 1960s. In the late 1970s and early 1980s, during the regimes of General Lucas García (1978–1982) and General Ríos Montt (1982–1983), the situation intensified as guerrilla groups mounted attacks on military installations, took over towns, and threatened major landowners in the western highlands.[3]

Whereas the guerrillas extended and unified their operations through an umbrella movement known as the *Unidad Revolucionaria Nacional Guatemalteca* (URNG), many Mayan communities expressed their frustration with party politics and the lack of government support for rural needs by joining activist grass-roots networks such as the *Comité de Unidad Campesina* (CUC) (Davis 1988b). From the guerrillas' point of view, this was an armed struggle to challenge the legitimacy of the state and the exploitation of Guatemalan peasants by wealthy landowners and export-oriented commercial elites. They recruited combatants from the countryside and sought support from peasant populations. In their terms, this was a war of liberation to resolve brutally conflicting class interests in a country with the lowest physical quality of life index in Central America and the third lowest, after Haiti and Bolivia, in all of Latin America (Painter 1987: 3).

In Guatemala, however, the relation of landowner to peasant, or officer to foot soldier, is lived out in a world of ethnic difference. The first-order contrast distinguishes *ladinos* (or whites[4])—the New World descendents of the Spaniards who conquered and colonized Guatemala in the sixteenth century and rebelled in the nineteenth century to formulate their vision of Latin American nationhood—and *indígenas* (or Indians)—the descendents of a variety of Mayan ethnic groups that jockeyed for territory after the collapse of the Mayan empire many centuries before the European conquest and served as laborers for colonial plantation economies (Carmack 1981; Handy 1984). As I argue here and elsewhere, the *ladino-indígena* contrast is hardly static; rather, these terms represent identities that are continually redefined in practice and in representation (Warren 1989; 1992). For their part Mayan populations are not homogeneous in language or identification. Twenty-three Mayan languages and approximately one hundred community-specific dialects are spoken in Guatemala. Most Mayans identify closely with their home communities, where membership is visually marked by similarities in dress, and recognize weaker affinities with members of their regional language group. Pan-Mayan groups have grown in importance since the mid-1980s, although in the face of language diversity they have appropriated Spanish as their lingua franca.[5]

What were the implications for ethnicity of this war of liberation and counterinsurgency? First, *la violencia* was a manifestation of unresolved tensions in Guatemalan racism. Although it would be a mistake to reduce ethnic difference to agrarian class relations in Guatemala, colonial and modern plantation economies were built on social ideologies and state development strategies that harnessed the labor of impoverished Mayans and kept them poor (Handy 1984; Painter 1987; Sherman 1979; Stavenhagen 1970). Racism, which justified an ethnic division of labor delegating manual labor to Mayans and nonmanual labor to Spaniards (and later to their cultural offspring, the *ladinos*), lies at the heart of the 470-year history of plantation economics. The guerrillas sought to radicalize the poor, and the army sought to punish them so they would not collaborate with or join the opposition.

Second, *la violencia* was understood by all sides as a conflict with strong ethnic overtones. Many Mayans felt the government used the counterinsurgency war as an excuse to destroy Mayan populations (Menchú 1984). Both their desire for wider political participation and their distinctiveness in language and community were seen as political threats by rightist political groups and the military. The ironic fact that the foot soldiers for this counterinsurgency effort were overwhelmingly Mayan was not lost on rural populations.

Third, *la violencia* was to have a great impact on interethnic relations in many communities. The war served as a vehicle for the expression and intensification of ethnic distrust along two axes. *Ladino* hacienda owners were targets for assassination by guerrilla groups. Mayans, on the other hand, feared the special connections local *ladinos* had with military authorities through the system of civilian-military cooperation set up in 1938 (McClintock 1985: 65–69). Most populations assumed that military officers would automatically side with those who were identified as members of national culture—that is, with the *ladinos*. In addition, Mayan strangers from other language groups were feared as collaborators.

Fourth, rather than leading to an abandonment of ethnicity as happened in the 1930s in El Salvador (Anderson 1992), *la violencia* has been accompanied by a resurgence of Mayan identity on a local level and by the growing importance of experiments in ethnic nationalism as a pan-community elite movement. Recently, international development groups and the Catholic church, after decades of promoting the assimilation of Mayans into national society, have begun to support ethnic revitalization.

Studies of *la violencia* by North American, European, and Latin American scholars have been influenced by international human rights discourse, with its goal of documenting the abuses of power by states and the systematic ways basic rights are violated. The human rights movement seeks a factual account of incidences of violence and the creation of domestic human rights monitoring organizations so pressure can be put on governments to release detainees and to curb the politically motivated excesses of the armed forces and the police. The movement's understandings are conveyed in realist narratives that, as this chapter argues, are not the only way to represent the impact of *la violencia* on local populations (Americas Watch 1984; Americas Watch and the British Parliamentary Human Rights Group 1987; Simon 1986).

For anthropologists, now that it is "safe" to return to Guatemala, the goal of research has been to show the impact of *la violencia* on Mayan communities and to explore the internalization of violence, which in some cases has led to chronic killings and death squads within communities. These studies have sought to understand conflict by revealing patterns in the killings; documenting the escalating, personal character of intracommunity violence; and revealing the social characteristics of the perpetrators and the victims of violence (Carmack 1988b).

What have these two streams of scholarship discovered in their examinations of Guatemalan violence? Michael McClintock has documented the nature of state violence and human rights violations and found that many of the counterinsurgency techniques employed in Guatemala in the early 1960s were later used in Vietnam in the late 1960s and then reincorporated into Guatemala in the 1970s and 1980s. He presents convincing evidence that rightist death squads operating out of the capital with the goal of eliminating the opposition—whether political candidates, union leaders, or students— were not independent vigilante groups but were tied closely to the police, the military, and at times directly to the office of the presidency (McClintock 1985).

In rural areas, the militarization of civilian life in Guatemala took the form of setting up military bases (*destacamentos*) and mobile outposts as well as creating civilian patrols (*patrullas de autodefensa civil*), which were organized to "protect" towns from outsiders and, much more important, to help monitor local populations. The presidency of General Ríos Montt organized the patrols in 1982 as a counterinsurgency measure; by 1985, under General Mejía Víctores, the military estimated that one million rural Guatemalans were involved in patrolling their own communities (Simon 1986: 26).

Finally, current studies analyze the political and economic impacts of *la violencia* on rural communities in the western highlands where most of the warfare has occurred. Conflict did not have the same intensity in all parts of the highlands. Zones of major guerrilla activity, such as the Ixil Trixangle in the Department of El Quiché, were the most heavily militarized, although military bases and civilian patrols were set up throughout the highlands. To resettle populations dispersed by the violence, the government created thirty-three model villages (*polos de desarrollo*), which have left civilian populations directly under military control (Manz 1988). The effects of *la violencia* ranged from the massacre and physical destruction of an estimated four hundred hamlets (*aldeas*) and municipal centers (*cabeceras*) to periodic sweeps, repression, and killings in other settlements; to strategic involvements in civil patrols and mass evangelical conversions; to economic devastation with only scattered casualties in other areas; to situations in which some populations were relatively unaffected and people are said to have discovered their own country's experience by watching the movie *El Norte* (Falla 1992; Davis 1988a; Carmack 1988b; Stoll 1992; Ehlers 1990).

We need more research, however, on how Mayan populations express and communicate their anguish in the face of military and guerrilla violence. Mayan anthropologists and political commentators have written powerful personal testimonies (Menchú 1984; Montejo 1987; Montejo and Akab' 1992) and wide-ranging historical analyses of patterns of domination and cultural resistance (Cojtí Cuxil 1991; Sam Colop 1991). Foreign anthropologists are now beginning to address Mayan constructions and representations of violence (Wilson 1991; B. Tedlock n.d.; D. Tedlock n.d.). In this analysis, I discuss the cultural construction of terror—that is, how Mayans shape their understandings of the militarization of civilian life and the tortures, disappearances, and killings that became a daily occurrence in the late 1970s and early 1980s. I gathered the ethnographic materials for this analysis during five months of fieldwork in the *municipio,* the nucleated center and surrounding hamlets, of San Andrés Semetabaj in the western highland Department of Sololá in the spring and winter of 1989.[6]

This analysis is divided into three sections. I begin with a discussion of the issues that emerge in people's accounts of their experiences of *la violencia* in San Andrés. Then I describe the recent revitalization of certain elements of traditionalist Mayan culture—specifically, narratives about the capacity of certain people to transform themselves into supernatural beings—by Mayan leaders who, ironically, had struggled to destroy the institutional bases of these same Mayan *costumbres* in the 1960s and 1970s (Warren 1989).[7] I argue that current interest in these narratives stems from the way they resonate with painful dilemmas Mayan populations faced during *la violencia.* In closing, I consider the shapes of silence and resistance and the role of the anthropologist in the study of cultures of terror.

San Andrés Semetabaj is a *municipio* of about 1,500 people with another 3,000 living in outlying hamlets. It is an agricultural community that grows corn—the staple for tortillas—and beans for subsistence. Earlier in this century San Andrés produced wheat, milk, and cheese for regional markets; agricultural laborers for coastal plantations that grew coffee, cotton, and corn; and builders and back-strap loom weavers for the neighboring tourist center of Panajachel. Before the establishment of the regional cooperative, most Mayans worked seasonally on coastal plantations in exchange for access to agricultural land on which to grow corn and for minimal wages. In the off-season, families returned to San Andrés to cultivate whatever land they had in the *municipio.* Others worked for local landowners during labor-intensive parts of the agricultural cycle. Local plantations supported few permanent workers. In the early 1960s, an agricultural cooperative began offering extension services and credits for seed and fertilizer, which significantly increased local yields. As a result, people were able to work on local microplots instead of facing the difficult and risky prospect of contracting as migratory laborers on the south coast. The town gained fame for this successful regional agricultural cooperative.

In the 1950s and 1960s, the *municipio* also became known for its successful establishment of *Acción Católica,* or Catholic Action, the revitalization movement that sought to win converts to sacramental orthodoxy from the traditionalist Mayan-Catholic religious brotherhoods, the *cofradías,* which as locally administered Mayan organizations had been central to religiosity and community life since the Spanish missionization of the colonial period. Initially the young catechists of Catholic Action worshiped with members of the traditionalist civil-religious hierarchy as fellow Catholics. But their different notions of religious authority, moral action, personhood, and ritual celebration led to a struggle and a climactic separation as catechists founded their own congregation.

By 1975 the worst fears of the traditionalist elders and *principales* of the town had been realized: The civil-religious hierarchy collapsed because of the reluctance of the younger generations to serve in the religious brotherhoods.[8] Only two of the eight brotherhoods were able to function, and even these had lost the hierarchical ordering of the *cargos* (positions, or "burdens") so central to earlier rituals. The ritual guides, called *k'amol b'ey,* who earlier spoke the religious discourses in the brotherhoods, had died or retired, and there was no next generation to take their place. The Mayan divining priests, the *aj q'ij,* had also been marginalized in the process of the catechists' consolidation of religious power. Catholic constructions of orthodoxy, which stressed the polarity of good and evil and the heterodoxy of traditionalist religion, in contrast to the traditionalist Mayan-Catholic religion, which did not use the same dichotomous formulations and was highly syncretic, were used to portray the diviners—the *aj q'ij*—and sorcerers—the *aj itz*—as heretically serving evil. Catholic Action along with two Protestant denominations, the Assembly of God and the Central American Mission, which had established small congregations over the same period, gradually eroded the diffuse powers of the aging traditionalist leadership. The *costumbre* of the ancestors appeared to be all but dead in the town. But as we will see, appearances can be deceiving.

REPRESENTATIONS OF *LA VIOLENCIA* IN SAN ANDRÉS SEMETABAJ

Trixanos, as Mayans in San Andrés call themselves, had their initial experiences of *la violencia* in the late 1970s. They had heard of troubles in other areas; then bodies began to appear in the Department of Sololá. During our discussions, Trixanos recalled their encounters with death in these words:

> There was great fear. People frequently appeared along the highways dead, dumped. You didn't know what town they were from.

> During *la violencia,* bodies were left dumped on the roadsides—those from another town here, those from here in another town. Now they bury them.

The immediacy of the horror is evoked by tortured and abandoned bodies, corpses out of place in a country in which one's home community is the crucial part of one's ethnic identity. For the public, violence was inscribed on the bodies of strangers, foretelling what might happen to one's own people. For each body out of place, a family somewhere was worrying about a brother, son, or daughter who had vanished. They are called *desaparecidos,* "those who have [been] disappeared." Styles of violence changed from making the public a witness to death, when bodies were purposely dumped beside major roads in the late 1970s during the Lucas García regime, to the hidden burials and clandestine cemeteries of the early 1980s during Ríos Montt's presidency. But the fact of torture and *desaparecidos* continued.

Por miedo, "out of fear," people stayed in their homes. Kidnappings occurred most often in outlying hamlets, said to be closer to the routes taken by guerrillas as they moved from the coastal regions south of Lake Atitlán to the more active areas north of the lake. Some victims vanished and were never seen again; others wandered back, frightened and mistreated, after being held for several days. Some surprised mourning relatives, writing months later to explain that they had been kidnapped only to be forced to join the army. After losing adult males, some families fled from the outlying hamlets to the county seat to find shelter from army sweeps designed to punish any who had been reported as sympathetic to the guerrillas. But San Andrés was fortunate; it did not suffer the displacements or massacres of local populations that occurred to the north and west (Carmack 1988b; Manz 1988; Montejo 1987; Falla 1992).

The economic effects on San Andrés, however, were substantial. European and North American tourism to Lake Atitlán evaporated (Hinshaw 1988); "even the long-haired *jipis* ('hippies') left," as one Trixano dryly observed, so there was no demand for handwoven fabric, agricultural surpluses for restaurants, and construction workers for new hotels. Trixanos were very aware of the town's dependence on the neighboring tourist center of Panajachel, which

absorbs excess labor and generates additional income for agriculturalists and
weavers, even though tourists are rarely seen in San Andrés itself.

Most important, agriculturalists were afraid to go to the outlying fields because their movements were closely monitored and army sweeps were common. Herbs, mushrooms, and other foodstuffs gathered from the mountain-
sides to be used in cooking disappeared for two years because defoliants were
used to clear underbrush where guerrillas might be hiding in the mountains
north of the town near the more active area of Chichicastenango. Trips to
neighboring town markets were also dangerous because the military continually stopped and searched trucks and buses at mobile checkpoints.

Local organizations, with the exception of religious groups, stopped functioning because any meetings were viewed as potentially political and were finally banned by the government with the suspension of civil rights during the
state of siege. Cooperatives, which were key sources of credit for agriculture
and housing, ceased to function for several years during the height of *la
violencia* in the early 1980s.

It was clear to me as I interviewed people and followed public events in the
spring and fall of 1989 that *la violencia* had left deeper marks. For the people
of San Andrés, *la violencia* still comes up in every conversation, in every meeting or event. The intensity of violence that existed from 1978 to 1985 is used
by many Mayans as a temporal marker, like the 1976 earthquake—before *la
violencia*, after *la violencia*, during *la violencia*.[9] Yet, as one person put it, "*La
verdad es que la violencia siempre se mantiene*" ("The truth is that the violence
always continues, is always part of our lives").[10]

At the same time, there is great reluctance to discuss *la violencia* in any detail. "It's best to avoid the subject," one man explained, "because there might
be informers" (*orejas*, literally "ears"). So people usually respond to questions
from anthropologists and others with generalizations: "*Aquí no tuvo bastante
fuerza la violencia.*" "*No tuvo mayor fuerza.*" ("The violence wasn't so intense
here." "It didn't have great force.") It is as if denial and a low profile would
bring protection from a world that merits greater distrust than ever. The first
legacy of *la violencia* was silence.

The climate in San Andrés was one of tremendous uncertainty. When people talk about *la violencia,* they describe constant anxiety:

> You didn't have security in anything. There was terror at night, great insecurity.
> You didn't know which group might come to get you. There was fear of both
> sides. No one had tranquility. We say, "He who owes nothing, fears nothing"
> (*él que nada debe, nada teme*). We stayed in our homes.

You couldn't work well in the fields. To do so was to run a great risk because who knows who you would find yourself with, right? (*Al riesgo se corría porque no sabía uno con qué grupo ¿verdad?*) The order of the day was violence. So people tried to get work closer to town.

Most describe the situation as something rural communities were caught in but that was not of their making. One Trixano summarized the prevailing Kaqchikel views with these observations:

Not even we know much [about the roots of the violence]. There were confrontations the military (*el ejército*) had with the subversives (*la subversión*), but we never knew anyone from the subversives. You saw the climate of insecurity and from that time we couldn't do anything, just continue with our work. The reality is that it was a clash (*un choque*) of these two organizations, and this affected everyone.

At the same time, Mayans find an explanation for the genocidal intensity of *la violencia* in the deep fear *ladinos* have of the Mayan other:

There has always been a clash of classes here in Guatemala. Many have thought that some day the Indian (*el indígena*) would rise up. But many people misconstrued this, and their fear caused panic. Of course they were against the Mayans, thinking one day they would rebel. They thought the Mayans would exploit the opposition to the state that already existed. They believed Mayans were participants or were in the leadership. This is why they tried to eliminate, to kill the indigenous leadership.

The language is often veiled or oblique, often condensed into cryptic observations with unspecified agents. The listener is expected to fill in the obvious: that Mayans were involved in the opposition, that it was the government that was trying to eliminate the Mayan leadership. Those unable to deal with strategic ambiguities are by definition strangers with whom it would not be wise to share information.

Rural populations predict a difficult future for national governments if present-day problems are not dealt with adequately. For those who elaborated their views to me, the language of underdevelopment, class relations, and development projects—an interesting combination of rhetoric from the cooperative movement, progressive political parties, and historical-materialist critiques—captures rural claims on national society. Development-oriented Trixanos argue for economic assistance, access to the banking system for business loans, infrastructure, health, and peace so people can work without being disturbed. One activist in development projects concluded:

> If they are able to give these opportunities, there will be stability; they won't have a revolution. If they don't, there will be future instability. There has been support for the powerful; the wealthy exporters (*el exportador pudiente*) have everything. They don't give peasants (*el campesino*) access to loans. To avoid future problems, we need financial access, roads, schools, progress for the environment, health, water, help with diseases that are not known in other countries.

Most Trixanos, however, do not see the tension as existing between exporters and peasants; rather, they cast the conflict in ethnic terms as one between indigenous populations and *ladino* nationals.[11]

The subversives—the guerrillas—were greatly weakened by the counterinsurgency war as the 1980s wore on. The *Organización Revolucionaria del Pueblo en Armas* (ORPA) was active in the Sololá-Chimaltenango region. Apparently it saw itself as a special cadre—a secretive, militant opposition composed of radicalized *ladinos* and Mayans, without the primary goal of mass mobilization and education. In the face of clearly superior military forces, most people did not feel the guerrillas would be able to bring about the changes they sought. For some, the army won the war; for others, everyone ran out of steam in the mid-1980s. For still others, the guerrillas were not strong enough to protect Mayans from military reprisals no matter how true the opposition's critique rang. No one felt the underlying problems had been resolved.

Some Trixanos nevertheless had a romanticized image of the guerrillas, as they described guerrilla activities in other towns across Lake Atitlán:

> They swept down into other towns, coming out of nowhere. They were great orators, speaking in Mayan (*lengua*). They raised people's consciousness (*hace conciencia*), talking about the high costs of everything and why are we working for the benefit of the monied. Then they disappeared. The guerrillas are like supernaturals; they are special people. It was so exciting to actually see them.

Their leaders are called *canches* (the blonds), which refers to their uncertain origin. Perhaps there are some foreigners—mythic beings from outside the system—although there is no evidence that this is true.

People talk about the pervasiveness of surveillance and monitoring during *la violencia.* The word they use is *control.* Buses were stopped at roadblocks and passengers searched for evidence that they were involved with the guerrillas. It was dangerous to be carrying a walkman or cassette tapes—favorite items of Mayan youths—or the traditional black-and-white knit bag (*morral*) worn by the Mayan men of a more politicized Chichicastenango. In effect, it was risky to be too modern or too traditional. On a local level, people's comings and goings and connections with others were reported to the military by local military commissioners. Civilian patrols (*patrullas de autodefensa civil*) in San Andrés were in charge of protecting the town, monitoring movements, and reporting such movements to the military commissioner. People restricted their travels because they did not want others to misinterpret their actions and think they were participating in clandestine groups during absences from town. Those who lived in the greatest fear were the leaders of local organizations. In San Andrés, as in many towns, there were said to be lists of local leaders—teachers, bilingual instructors, catechists from Catholic Action, and officers of the cooperatives. As one person put it:

> One had to be very careful. If you were thought to be against the government, you were put on the list, and that was that.

To be on a list meant one was a marked person and was likely to be targeted for abduction and murder as a subversive. By definition, being a leader in the cooperative or a catechist in Catholic Action was suspect. Organizations that at one time had been promoted by the government to "integrate" Mayans into national society, channel their politics, and keep them from being radicalized were now considered dangerous and subversive by rightist political parties and the military (Bermúdez 1986; Warren 1989).

Respected adults in San Andrés were contacted by people in outlying hamlets who wanted them to advise people about what they should do in the climate of uncertainty and with which side they should ally themselves. Most leaders chose to curtail visits and remain in town because they felt all their movements were known in advance:

> The problem was that you never knew what kind of people would turn up, who you were talking to. (*Ya no sabía uno qué gente llegaba.*)

The town leadership felt increasingly insecure, and in 1980 it began to close local organizations. The housing cooperative was closed for three years in the early 1980s:

> We did it because we were concerned about working in the cooperative, because the truth is that one didn't know who might come by.

The situation of agrarian and housing cooperatives was particularly difficult. Their ideology was suspect because cooperativism was reconfigured into communism in the army's mind and the political loyalties of community leaders were in doubt. Local populations felt it would be suicidal to challenge the military's projection of these political labels and fears onto local organizations. People were unable to pay their loans, and no one—including the banks—wanted accumulations of money for fear of robbery. The regional bank in the neighboring state capital of Sololá was robbed and burned during this period. People still faced great financial hardships in 1984, when the cooperative was reopened. One agriculturalist offered this explanation of why it was impossible to repay loans:

> Even in 1984, people couldn't harvest their crops because of *la violencia*—they still couldn't work outside town. It wasn't safe; they didn't go to the fields. (*No había seguridad, no iban al campo.*)

The burning of the San Andrés municipal offices (*la alcaldía*) in 1981 was a turning point for the community. The town center was invaded by a force of around two hundred armed people who set up a machine gun emplacement on high ground and opened fire throughout the settlement with rifles and small arms. Everyone was terrified and hid in their homes. The invaders set fire to the municipal offices and a nearby shop, looted the general store at the cooperative, and tried to break down the doors of four carefully selected houses—all belonging to prominent *ladinos* with businesses and substantial landholdings. These families fled their homes, fearing for their lives. All four families left the town for good soon thereafter. Surprisingly, no one was killed that night.

One interpretation holds that the army attacked the town, demonstrating the anarchy of the moment:

> Ironically, the *ladinos* were chased away by the army. They must have felt the other side would hurt them, and if the military was out of control, there was no choice but to move to the city and—like many others—escape. So they left their lands rented.

But most people believe it was not *los palos* ("the sticks," as the army is sometimes called) but the guerrillas coming to punish.

The next day the most feared section of the armed forces, the *judiciales*, came to investigate. They called people to the plaza and interrogated them: "Why didn't you intervene? Why were *ladinos* the only ones sought out by the subversives? All of you must be involved." People realized that to proclaim their innocence or to point out that they had no arms with which to confront the invaders would only single speakers out for retribution. Finally, the military left. Thereafter life was increasingly militarized in San Andrés. A military outpost was established nearby; all adult men were forced to serve on civilian patrols; and the public telephone office, with its one line to the outside, was closed.

Ladinos, who had watched Mayans demand a greater voice in town affairs throughout the 1970s, were very distrustful. They felt the guerrillas had come to kill prominent *ladinos* and to destroy what they saw as "the society, the leadership" of the town. In fact, most *ladino* families had already begun to relocate. The younger generations of many old families had moved to the capital to prepare their sons and daughters for urban business and professions. Others migrated after the 1976 earthquake heavily damaged most homes and businesses in the town. The burning of the municipality completed the exodus, resulting in a town without powerful *ladinos.* Mayans successfully consolidated their control over local politics, development organizations, and the cooperatives in addition to the religious groups they had always run. *Ladino* land went on the market, and those Mayans who had the money acquired additional parcels; others planned to organize cooperative projects to solicit credits for land purchases. This was a dramatic change from the commanding position *ladinos* held in the town only a generation before when they owned all the major businesses and plantations (Warren 1989). Thus, one night of terror marked the culmination of a longer process of *ladino* outmigration and the beginning of what amounted to a localized agrarian reform.

The other event that is central to the way townspeople represent *la violencia* was the murder of a local schoolteacher who worked in a distant hamlet. As one Trixano narrated:

> One day it happened, according to the news we finally got. Every morning he went off to school; he lived nearby and walked to the hamlet. When he went, he was monitored (*controlado*). On his way that day, masked men intercepted him. I don't know if they had uniforms. They kidnapped him. This was five years ago. We didn't get any news of this then. The next day the school sent us a telegram saying that he hadn't shown up at school. We didn't do anything; we couldn't. His father tried to find out what happened, but he didn't learn anything. Shortly thereafter, they kidnapped another man who was also a bilingual promoter. They kidnapped him because he taught. For a time the teacher's wife went to the military post, but they didn't help her. They said, "There's no evidence he's dead. Maybe he's alive." But they kidnapped him.

Once again, however, there is a deeper message in this story. As one person explained:

> I believe some took advantage of the situation, some people who had personal differences. They used the opportunity to complain about others. There was much violence and many deaths because of this. It's possible this is what happened to the teacher. He was a good man, didn't even drink. It's possible that where he worked someone didn't like him or that someone didn't like his being a teacher. So finally something happened, the day came. Because of envy (*envidia*), there were personal differences over something, or perhaps it was simply that he wasn't from the place.

In these two examples we see the double-edged nature of *la violencia*. At the same time that Mayan agricultural communities were caught in a frightening national crisis over which they had no control, it was increasingly apparent that both the army and the guerrillas depended on local contacts for information. Thus, part of the world that was out of control, part of the insecurity and violence Trixanos experienced, was locally authored. This was the second legacy of *la violencia*. One Trixano illustrated the connection in the following terms:

> In one of the hamlets, a certain señor, they say, was collaborating with the guerrillas. The soldiers grabbed him, but they let him go—in exchange for whom, who knows.

Thus, people in the town became an integral part of national violence. They could act on personal animosities and *envidia* by denouncing fellow townspeople to either side, which was tantamount to a death sentence. In San Andrés, the process was felt to be driven by ethnic and individualized hatred; in other towns, existing factions or emerging power brokers turned on each other, resulting in widespread killings (cf. Paul and Demarest 1988).

San Andrés was not a place of innocence that was corrupted by external forces in the late 1970s. Nor was it a community in which preexisting factionalism escalated into self-destruction. An explanation of why some communities were massacred by the armed forces and others were not or of why some communities internalized violence by creating their own death squads and others did not is beyond the scope of the present ethnographic analysis. Let me nevertheless outline what I regard as critical structural dimensions of the wider conflict and the *municipio* of San Andrés that influenced local experiences and responses. First, the military did not consider this a major zone for confrontations with the armed opposition, although it was far from inactive. Second, guerrillas tended to concentrate their sustained activism in regions that were more remote and offered easier sanctuary than the largely deforested agricultural area immediately surrounding the lake. Third, historically, people from the *municipio* of San Andrés had come to terms with local religious factionalism in very specific ways. These groups had long been a major force in local Mayan politics. The civil-religious hierarchy–Catholic Action cleavage, which had troubled the town for years, was resolved without re-creating opposing factions when the traditionalist brotherhoods collapsed before *la violencia*. Catholic Action and the Evangelicals continued to have marked religious differences, but key members of the most powerful congregations had a twenty-year track record of supporting each other and fighting discrimination against Mayans in the cooperative, the elementary school, and the municipal government. These religious cleavages, which apparently channeled conflict in other rural communities, did not become the focus of internal tensions in San Andrés.

The most serious division, and the dimension of greatest distrust, was the bi-ethnic cleavage. *La violencia* hastened but did not determine the breakdown of the old bi-ethnic community and the establishment of greater Mayan local control. Although the fruits of the guerrilla invasion of San Andrés were not immediately available because of the suppression of local economic and political organizations, it was clear to many that additional lands and new powers would become available. Despite the central importance of these structural factors, they are only part of the explanation of why violence did not escalate within the community of San Andrés. They fail to convey how Trixanos represent the tragedy of local engagement.

BORROWING FROM THE PAST
TO REPRESENT THE PRESENT

In spring of 1989, I taped narratives told by several Trixano storytellers. In San Andrés these people gain a reputation for telling old tales late at night at wakes, after the serious part of the *velorio* is over and people struggle to stay awake for the all-night vigil with the body. Narratives are also told at home. In the past, fathers recounted these narratives to their children after the evening meal, and both mothers and fathers would discuss the moral of the story with their children. Today, they are shared among generations when extended families relax at home on Sundays and talk about what the town was like in the old days. They are meant to be interactive, with audience responses of laughter, questions, and comments during the telling. These narratives are Mayan histories, portraying events that are said to have happened in the town. They are also systematic expressions of Mayan cosmology and social ideology as practiced by past generations.

I was surprised by the interest local Catholic Action catechists expressed in these narratives. Although the Mayan catechists are critical of aspects of traditionalist religion judged to be incompatible with Catholic orthodoxy, they noted that the events in these traditionalist stories represent something that really happened: "This is really true, this really happened, Kay. My niece saw a woman as she was transforming herself." Why, I wondered, are those who appeared to have rejected traditionalist beliefs so intrigued with these narratives?

Let me present one of these narratives. An apt title for this story would be "Peel Off Flesh, Come Back On" for reasons that will be obvious.[12]

This story happened here in San Andrés. In the times of our grandparents, our fathers, there were many beliefs about spirits like the "master of the night" (called *rajav a'a'*, or *dueño de la noche*). These *rajav a'a'* have the freedom to walk about at night. They have this freedom the same as we do during the day. We have our work during the day, but when the night comes we rest. Now these people, for they are people, come out at night.

It is said that sometimes in a married couple, the woman turns out bad for the man. At first when the man [in this story] was married, the woman was just fine. No one was even aware that she was a *rajav a'a'* because, while the couple is still young, it seems *rajav a'a'* do not dedicate themselves to this work. But then when they get to be more than forty years old, they begin. Perhaps it's the destiny (*destino*) they have.

So this is what happened to this woman. The husband saw his wife every morning, all day, really sick. Totally sick with her head tied in a kerchief, with a shawl covering her. All of her body ached. The husband said, "Well what's wrong? You're always like this; I always see you with this thing."

"Yes, my body hurts, my head hurts. All my bones ache."

"Ah, you should prepare a sweatbath (*temescal*) so perhaps you can get better there."

Because in the past, the cure, the medicine was the sweatbath. So one sweated out all the sickness in this oven.

"That's fine," the woman replied obediently. Except the woman knew why she was in pain all the time.

Well, the man kept thinking, thinking, thinking: "What could be happening to my woman because she wasn't like this before? But now I only see her sick and exhausted." The man was always thinking of the woman at work.

Sometimes the woman came to leave him lunch, but she was always covered up, always sick.

"You came," he said. "How's your illness?"

"I can't shake it," she replied.

So this happened to the man. Time passed during which his woman wasn't dying, nor was she getting any better. But one day the man thought about how much he loved his woman. Well, they went to bed; it was time. But the man stayed awake for a moment. The woman had a mystery. She had the power to make him fall into a deep sleep when she wanted to go out because she was a *rajav a'a'*. The man did what he could to stay awake. Oh no, after trying so hard, in the end he didn't feel a thing. He was deeply asleep. This happened at midnight. The man stayed asleep but with the thought that he wanted to see if his woman really laid down to sleep with him or if she went out. The man thought something was happening. Well, when he finally woke up, the woman wasn't there. In her place, she left a long grinding stone in the blanket there beside the man because they slept together in the same bed.

"There he is alone, there he is alone," she said to herself.

But he felt the weight, saying, "What is this?" He lit a pine-pitch stick. Hah, here was the grinding stone. "Hah! This woman, she is doing something; she's involved me with this thing." And he heard throughout the town the noise of dogs barking. Ahhhhh, so it really was his wife who was going around disturbing the dogs. Then the man was wide-awake, wide-awake, wide-awake! One o'clock in the morning went by, then two, then three. It was 3:30 when he smelled a terrible odor. I don't know how the odor got into the house. Then once again he was lost in his dreams. That meant the woman entered without his being aware because he was asleep again. At five o'clock in the morning, the woman got up.

"You're there," he said.

"Of course," she said. "Get up, your tortillas."

Oh, but the man didn't say anything more to her. He thought, "With me you are not going to do this. With good reason you continue to be ill." Can you imagine why she continued to be in pain? The tremendous beating people gave her. People got up when the dogs barked, so she always took her blows. For this reason she was in pain all the time: because of the blows she received there in the town and because there are people who get up to look for the animal she became. Well, this happened. The man knew that this thing transformed itself. I don't know if it was in the form of a ram, a goat, or a dog. "Go on, you just wait, woman," he said to himself.

The next night she went out, and the man was ready to keep track of her return. But beforehand the man went to consult with a diviner. What was he to do to make sure the woman would fall into his hands? He consulted with an *aj q'ij*, a diviner of the day. The diviner said, "This is what you are going to do. You are going to get bunches of *puro*, with this plant they call rosemary and with fifty stems of cypress. But they should be hidden so you won't fall asleep again. Put them under your pillow so you will be aware when she gets up. This is the power that exists so she can't make you fall asleep." The man took all these things with him.

The woman didn't go out that night. She said to her husband, "Go to bed," and she embraced him. But the man didn't trust the woman now because he knew why she left the stone there. Well, the next night came, and she didn't go out. He felt the cloth. Then the third night, she began to stir again. But the man acted as though he were asleep. She threw the blanket over him. The man was playing dead. The woman got up. Like this, she left the blanket draped over the man's head. The husband was very, very alert. She entered the kitchen again to take out the grinding stone and leave it beside the man. Awake, the man thought, "Good, now I'm going to see what this woman is doing." Clearly, the woman had decided that tonight she was going out. He didn't lose consciousness again. "Now I'm going out," she said to herself. She went to the kitchen. And the man got up, staying low to the ground.

She opened the door and was transforming herself when her husband saw her. She was transforming herself, but she was there with four legs. Her hands served like another pair of legs, with four legs, like this. She was talking, talking, talking. But what was she saying? Now she was there half-changed, and the part below was what was left. The lower part with her feet was still human. It was as if the upper part were a ram. Now she had the upper body of a ram. But yes, she spoke. Then she was saying, "Peel off flesh, peel off flesh." Peel off means all of her body was coming off. When the man looked again, she was an animal. And off she went. What remained in a heap was the woman's body— that is to say, her flesh. She was an animal, a ram, a male goat. When the man saw her, the animal leaped twice and went off. It leaped over the enclosure. The man's hair stood on end: "And this woman!" Eshhhhh, she went, and her route was marked by the noise of barking dogs. "There goes my woman," says the man. (Laughter) "Oh, my woman," said the man, so sad. He went over to see the body of the woman, all the flesh there. What am I going to do with this? Well, the *aj q'ij* diviner says it will return at 3:00 a.m. or 3:30 a.m because at 4:00 a.m. the patrol goes out. The patrol of the spirits, as they say.

The man was playing dead under the blanket, waiting for his woman. He heard the noise of the dogs, he heard that something was coming. And her body, her flesh was already there. A long-haired ram entered. Then it leaped twice and said, "Come up flesh, come on up." First it was peel off, peel off. As it leaped, it took the form of a skeleton. It wanted to become a person once again. "Come up flesh, come on up," it said. Little by little the flesh rose up, and it became a woman. And the man in bed was playing dead. The woman entered, complaining, complaining, complaining as she came. Why? Because of the blows she received once again. Because people come out to look for it. Because this happens. She came in and the man turned over, as when one tires of sleeping on one side. The man was awake, and the woman embraced her husband. (Here the storyteller grimaced and laughed.) And the man with his hair on end was thinking, "This is a male goat." (Laughter) "Tomorrow you're going to drop off my lunch," he said, "How are you? How's your illness?"

"I'm sick, I'm sick," she said.

"Well," the man thought again, "This woman doesn't suit me; she's doing me bad."

The next night she went out again in the same form, in the same way. She transformed herself with the same words. And what happened? She left a mound of flesh again. "Well, I'm going to teach this woman a lesson. Why does she mock me? She looks me in the face, but she's really a spirit. That's not a woman." He began to say things, very nasty things about his woman. "Well, today I'm going to prepare ten pounds of salt. I'm going to be the assassin of this flesh. I'm going to salt this flesh."

The woman went off again, leaving her flesh there. Aaaaand the dogs were barking. He began to put salt on her flesh. Salt burns. What happened to the flesh? It dried out right then. It no longer had life. "I'm going to watch over this flesh to see what happens when she comes." Then, after the woman was finished, she leaped twice and said, "Come on up flesh, come on." But the flesh was dead, it was dry. She began to cry. She leaped up, left, and went off, and since that time the ram has never returned.

So ends the narrative. Edward M. Bruner (1986), I believe, is correct in suggesting that we may not do justice to the significance of narratives if we examine them as autonomous texts; rather, we must situate them in ways which demonstrate how they are historically contingent and how they are "reread" in different ways at different moments. Texts become significant as people bring them into tension with ever-changing contexts. Because narrator, audience, text, and context shape each other, we need to be concerned with how Trixano storytellers and their audiences understand this narrative, just as we need to be aware of our own preoccupations.

After hearing "Peel Off Flesh, Come Back On," many North American listeners appear compelled to ask about the significance of the gender imagery in this narrative: a man's anger and violence toward a woman and a woman's desire for autonomy but apparent lack of control over the consequences of her actions.[13] These themes resonate with the highly contested gender politics in our own society.[14] Yet, to understand Trixanos' current interest in this narrative, we need to find out whether the theme of gender politics is significant for them and, if so, what it represents for Trixano storytellers and their audiences in their contested present.[15] In fact, as this analysis details shortly, gender in this narrative is a complex theme, a field of meaning for the representation of the problematic nature of authority and cultural continuity. The gendered representation of these issues allows Trixanos to explore the intimacy of violence as they deal with other cultural paradoxes and tensions. The interplay of contingent issues that speak to the current political climate and tensions that are constructed as integral to Mayan culture are what I find most striking in these narratives. This convergence of tensions, neither of which can be reduced to the other, may explain the attraction and power of these narratives for people who otherwise present themselves as having rejected *costumbre*. Gender, however, is not the initial Trixano preoccupation in discussions of the narrative.

For the storytellers I talked to, the captivating aspect of "Peel Off Flesh, Come Back On" is the capacity of some, but not all, people to transform themselves. The *rajav a'a'* (masters of the night) are special beings who have human and animal transformations. Their identities are not generally known by others. During the day they present themselves as regular people, but at night they usher in another order in which spiritual forms dominate reality. This narrative catches transformation at its midpoint, dwelling on metamorphosis at the transitional, most abhorrent moment for Trixanos when the woman is half human and half magical animal.

These beliefs about the nature of the self are in fact variations on a theme common throughout Mesoamerica: that people have the capacity to transform themselves into animals and have animal counterparts. Scholars have traced these beliefs to preconquest cultures in central Mexico and to the interplay of Mesoamerican and Spanish understandings and misunderstandings of indigenous cultures (Foster 1944; Musgrave-Portilla 1982; Tranfo 1979). Called *nagualismo* (the phenomena of transforming witches or wizards) and *tonalismo* (the phenomena of companion animals or guardian spirits) in the literature, these conceptions are discussed by many anthropologists as part of a system of "multiple souls."[16] In the pre-Hispanic past, gods, charismatic leaders, and shamans had the capacity to transform themselves for good or evil. When the Spaniards conquered Mesoamerica in the sixteenth century, they brought their own beliefs in pacts with the devil and in transforming wizards (called *hechiceros* or *brujos*) that influenced missionaries' teachings and reactions to Mesoamerican religion. This complex of beliefs, then, represents an amalgamation of sixteenth-century indigenous Mesoamerican and Spanish religions.

In the present, Mesoamerican notions of transforming beings focus on the capacity of certain individuals to become spiritual animals at night, usually with malicious intents, frightening people or selectively pursuing those who are ill or who stand out as nonconventional consumers in their communities. Alternatively, they bring illness to other communities (Musgrave-Portilla 1982; Stratmeyer and Stratmeyer 1979). In some communities, individuals seek their powers through battles and pacts with the devil (Saler 1969).[17] Much of the Mesoamerican population also believes individuals have companion animals, or as Pitt-Rivers (1970) aptly puts it, "animal co-essences," whose form may be divined shortly after birth, may become clear in dreams, or may never be known to the individual (Gossen 1975). Generally, animal co-essences live lives parallel to their human counterparts and share their fate in life and death (Vogt 1970). In certain cases, parts of inner souls wander from human bodies at night during sleep or when a person is sick, has sexual intercourse, feels strong emotions, or dies. In some communities, the ancestors can punish individuals by knocking out part of an individual's inner soul and freeing their animal counterparts from the safety of their special sanctuaries (Vogt 1970). In other places, only powerful elders and healers have animal spirits they can use to bring disease to individuals as a punishment for social transgressions (Villa Rojas 1947). In cases of illness, healers diagnose the cause and direct social confessions that counteract the illness.[18]

The Mayans of San Andrés, as with many populations in the southern regions of Mesoamerica, have syncretized their own blend of these representations of the self: the belief that only certain individuals transform themselves into animals. The belief in the existence of companion animals has been merged with these beliefs about unstable selves. *Rajav a'a'* have an inner compulsion to wander at night, as in the narrative just presented. Other spiritual forms, called *rajav kab'il,* go out at night with the specific purpose of bringing sickness to neighboring towns. Other individuals gain their animal form when they are definitively transformed by the *rajav juyu*—the guardian of the wilds—who lives in a plantation inferno inside a sacred mountain. The *rajav juyu* transforms those who have made a pact with him, exchanging their labors after death for wealth during their lives. The *rajav juyu* also transforms those Trixanos who have committed incest or slept with *ladinos*. His animals suffer, only to be reborn as animals once again. Human-burros are fated to be burned as the hot fires of the volcano are stoked with bones they carry on their backs; human-pigs are raised to be slaughtered, only to be reborn and fattened once again.

When I listened to narratives such as "Peel Off Flesh, Come Back On" after hearing Mayan realist accounts of the violence in the town, I was struck by the ways these stories resonated with each other. I asked the storytellers if there was any connection, and the answer was yes, with an elaboration of intersecting themes. The significance of the narrative for them was that the man, who naturally assumed he knew his wife after so many years of living together, discovered that he did not know her. She was really a *rajav a'a'*, a master of the night, an awful animal who had power over him, and a powerful spiritual essence that violated their marriage and disrupted the town. Unlike normal humans, the animal-spirits are seen as unfeeling and *sin vergüenza* (without remorse), as driven to do what they must. There is a built-in antagonism between townspeople and the *rajav a'a';* people's anger is felt to be natural and justified when they encounter animals at night that are out of place in their town. A male goat should not be seen walking down the road alone at night, so it must be a *rajav a'a'*. In other narratives, people are shocked when they learn that the animal they have beaten is really a neighbor and that the neighbor is really a spiritual animal.

I would assert that for Kaqchikel Mayans, these accounts describe a world parallel to their current situation—one of betrayal and existential dilemmas. It is notable that the metaphor of betrayal is so often gendered as female. *Rajav a'a'* are frequently women. Moreover, those individuals who are punished in the parallel world of the sacred mountain for sleeping with *ladinos* are women. In both instances they have betrayed the authority of the males— fathers, brothers, and husbands—in their families. Women are powerful metonymic representations of community because they are felt to be central to the continuity of Mayan culture in their roles as the bearers of the next generation and the socializers of children in Kaqchikel culture. They stand for the essentialist construction of Kaqchikel identity—that there is an intrinsic uniqueness to being Kaqchikel—in the face of rapid social change. As Mayan men often put it (and even the urban ethnic nationalists assert this), it is more important for women to wear traditional dress than for men, who in many communities have adopted "ladinoized" clothing, because women perpetuate the culture.

Without the moral weight of their role, women are felt to have the potential to do great social harm by secretly becoming sexually involved with men other than their husbands. They are said to do so out of their own weakness in a world in which men are easily tempted to pursue, if not actively pursuing, other women. Trixanos describe the likely outcome as dangerously escalating family betrayals because suspicious husbands may seek vengeance by pursuing their own sexual affairs. The viability of the family and, by extension, of the community is threatened by anger and distrust, which are unleashed by challenges to male authority. Strikingly, these narratives and discussions represent the fragility of authority in a world in which men are supposed to be the unquestioned heads of their households.

When storytellers explained "Peel Off Flesh, Come Back On" and people told me of the violence, they described similar existential dilemmas. In communities in which people had lived together for generations, suddenly one did not know who was who. Some people were not who they appeared to be, but no one knew for certain who all the betrayers were. Trixanos feared *la violencia* would divide sons from fathers, wives from husbands as it unleashed different political sympathies, nascent envy, and distrust. For Kaqchikel Mayans in San Andrés, "Peel Off Flesh, Come Back On" and other related stories (cf. Warren n.d.) are reappropriated as alternative phrasings of contemporary dilemmas: Although we live together in the same community, can I really know who you are? Can I know your loyalties when appearances may be deceiving and alliances shifting? Can I trust you with my thoughts; can I know yours? How can we know if our children, our siblings are betraying us politically or if our wives are betraying us personally, culturally, sexually? Stories of the *rajav a'a'* express skepticism about social relations, loyalties, and the capacity to know those with whom one lives. Perhaps the storytellers have chosen the veiled language of these narratives, rather than a more explicit formulation, because mistrust has its own corrosive powers in a situation in which one needs to count on others for cues in order to survive the white waters of politics.

La violencia was not the point of origin for clashes of interest or *envidia* or of the ability of some to transform themselves into animals. But it did intensify and channel conflict, bring the coercive powers of the state and its political opposition—expressed in the capricious powers of particular soldiers, investigators, and guerrillas at moments that have become integral to the town's sense of its own history—into everyday life, and raise the stakes of social criticism and political action. Notably, stories of the *rajav a'a'* (and the *rajav kab'il*) are old and familiar languages of skepticism that individualize betrayal (and envy, although that is another story) rather than treating it as a collective act on the part of existing Mayan factions in the community. Perhaps here in the realm of representation we have identified another factor that has mitigated the internalization of violence in San Andrés.

SHAPES OF ANGUISH

La violencia has claimed many more victims than merely those who suffered physical harm (Simon 1987). The first dimension of anguish has been the silence imposed on rural populations who witnessed brutality and death but found themselves operating in a culture of terror in which they had to rephrase experiences into denials: *"Aquí no tuvo mayor fuerza la violencia."* Silence in this case is a denial of involvement, which ironically communicates the reality that there was little escape. Moreover, silence is continually subverted through cryptic public allusions to *la violencia* by the compelling desire to signal the influence of this period on the life of the town. It is as if people cannot dismiss what they feel they must deny.

Another dimension of anguish is represented as the arbitrariness of power, be it the military that largely controlled this region or the guerrillas when they were most active. Uncertainty and anxiety weighed heavily on Trixanos. There was no way of knowing if one might become a target of surveillance, when one might be singled out for detention and torture, and what might be considered evidence of subversive or collaborationist intentions. One did not know what would trigger the wrath of the *judiciales,* whether guerrillas were moving from strategies of recruitment to punitive actions, whether one's name might be on a list or which list it might be on, or whether a trip to the fields or the market would result in being caught in someone's sweep. In these representations of *la violencia,* the sources of discord are externalized to the world outside the community. Trixanos are rendered more passive than they actually were in these configurations of uncertainty. In practice, Trixanos recount small but astute efforts to send a message to the powers that be: They carried heavy loads of firewood on their backs, for example, with tumplines stretched across their foreheads to fields near the town to communicate that they were indeed hardworking peasants. They switched languages from Kaqchikel to Spanish so strangers from other Mayan language groups could understand the nonpolitical nature of religious meetings.[19]

Trixanos also represent violence as an internal matter. It is the product of ethnic hatred that denies Mayans their humanity, of interpersonal tensions experienced as angry *envidia,* and of betrayals for gain and vengeance in the climate of violence. This was another dimension of anguish, the existential dilemma expressed in the *rajav a'a'* stories. In practice it meant the blurring of the distinction between those one did not trust and those one might have trusted. Religious groups tried to counter the pressures of social fragmentation, as they had in the past, with expressions of solidarity and common purpose. However, the militarization of civilian life, with the creation of civilian patrols in 1982, forced all males to stand at the intersection of local and national violence. All had to face the double bind of being drafted officially "to protect and defend the town from outsiders" but, in fact, to monitor the activities of their own townspeople and families and report suspicious behavior to military authorities outside the town. In San Andrés, people tried to disengage themselves and to trivialize the duties of the patrols, which disintegrated soon after the 1985 election of President Vinicio Cerezo.[20]

Trixanos speak with carefully crafted ambiguity when referring to the perpetrators of violence: " *They* burned buses and shot the drivers and their assistants." " *They* killed the teacher." " *They* kidnapped people in a nearby town." " *They* aren't bothering people right now." There is most notably the illusion of safety for the speaker in the ambiguity of "they" because one does not have to reveal one's analysis or political sympathies. Armed groups are often described as having taken pains to disguise their identities and to mislead people about who they really were when they went out to kidnap or rob. The culture of terror creates a divided reality, one that balks at crediting any particular explanation of a violent act as definitive, even though people generally knew what happened.

Uncertainty, divided realities, and strategic ambiguities continue (cf. Taussig 1987, 1992; Bourque and Warren 1989). Buses are being robbed near San Andrés today on the back road through Godines to the Pan American Highway. Maybe the guerrilla is exacting a war tax. Maybe army soldiers are supplementing their incomes. Or perhaps it is *delincuentes* (highway robbers and muggers) who, like those with festering animosities and envy in the towns, are taking advantage of the confusion of the moment. As one woman recounted when describing how her bus had been intercepted, people searched, and some passengers robbed by people apparently in disguises: "You can look at their boots to really know, but we are so poor that it doesn't matter."

*   *   *

As Begoña Aretxaga recently pointed out to me, anthropologists are not exempt from the cultures of terror we live in and describe. Thus, it is important to stand back and reexamine my anthropological narrative of violence as a cultural form and a product of the fieldwork encounter. In significant ways, this analysis reproduces some of the same phenomena I encountered in my fieldwork: Like the Trixanos, I have found myself caught in the paradox of having witnessed something I cannot fully communicate. I recognize that there are limits to my abilities to translate between cultures, and there are horrors I know but cannot recount. This is anthropology's dilemma, and it is heightened when we study situations in which human rights are being violated. For many Latin Americanists, social research needs to address inequalities, local culture, and human rights. Our contribution is to give a voice to those who are muted by cultural difference and the politics of marginalization[21] and to explore the interconnectedness of U.S. and Latin

American political realities.[22] We also have moral commitments to the people with whom we work.

Flowing as they do from the paradoxes of our responsibilities, our analyses will embody some of the same silences, uncertainties, and ambiguities we document. The accounts we gather are products of dialogues, whether or not they result from formal interviews.[23] Sometimes we are chosen to witness the past; sometimes we are warned off; sometimes we are closed out; sometimes we are caught in an army sweep. Does our presence as outsiders—no matter how familiar—cause people to shift to a politically ambiguous language or to exaggerate uncertainty? Perhaps, although I found the constructions I have outlined here were pervasive in public meetings, in conversations over meals, in local histories written for other audiences, in accounts of discussions between people out of town, and in the press.[24] Are the silences we document in part the result of people's distrust of us as another kind of outsider? Of course they are, although Trixanos describe their own encounters with others' silence and their own desire to break through to find out what happened—especially in other, more militarized zones.[25] Perhaps we cannot recapture the immediacy of *la violencia* as it was initially experienced in the late 1970s and early 1980s, but we can work to understand the violence of memories only partially revealed and partially revealable.

NOTES

This chapter benefited from questions and comparative observations from colleagues at Brandeis, Harvard, Princeton, and SUNY-Albany where I presented earlier versions of the analysis. Special thanks go to my 1990 seminar on Culture and Conflict, especially to Begoña Aretxaga, Michael Hanchard, Davida Wood, and Henry Bienen. Also thanks to Jim Boon, Hildred Geertz, Jorge Klor de Alva, Ben Saler, Stanley Tambiah, Toni Morrison, Gananath Obeyesekere, Arcadio Díaz-Quiñones, and Joan Dayan. I owe great debts to the Mayans who helped me understand the terror. My research was supported by Princeton's University Committee on Research, Program in Latin American Studies, and Center of International Studies as well as the MacArthur Foundation.

1. Actually, "the terror" may be a more apt translation of *la violencia*.

2. See McClintock (1985) for the history of the state's war against communism and Figueroa (1991) on state terrorism.

3. The groups included the *Fuerzas Armadas Rebeldes* (FAR), the *Ejército Guerrillero de los Pobres* (EGP), the *Organización Revolucionaria del Pueblo en Armas* (ORPA), and the *Partido Guatemalteco del Trabajo* (PGT-*Núcleo*).

4. Translating *ladino* into English is particularly difficult because Guatemalan and U.S. ethnic systems are not counterparts of each other. I realize that "white" is a novel translation, but this may be a more appropriate metaphor in terms of the political association of *ladino* with mainstream, national culture versus Mayan communities that are constructed as marginalized minorities. Both U.S. whites and Guatemalan *ladinos* are *mestizos* by definition (as is everyone else). *Ladino* ethnicity is not created solely through the contrast with *indígenas* but also through their rebellion from the colonial Spanish past and the victory of New World nationalism in the nineteenth century. Ethnic passing, which deserves more subtle analytic attention for both societies, is common in part because some boundaries are fictitious in practice and ethnicity is situationally submerged.

5. Of course, they were not the first to do this. Mayans who migrated seasonally from the highlands to the coast for plantation jobs in the late nineteenth and twentieth centuries also found they had to learn Spanish in order to communicate across Mayan language groups.

There are complex conventions for language use in the bilingual community of San Andrés, where in 1970–1972 and 1989 I did the fieldwork on which this analysis is based. In practice a great deal of Spanish, including the term *la violencia,* has been absorbed into Kaqchikel, the region's Mayan language. Because of the gap between older Mayans whose Spanish may not be fluent and younger Mayans whose Kaqchikel may be limited, many events are held in both languages. My interviews were generally conducted in Spanish or, with help from research assistants, in Kaqchikel.

6. This is the community in which I researched Mayan ethnicity, religion, and political consciousness in 1970–1972 (see Warren 1985, 1986, 1989). My return to continue work on social change was undoubtedly smoothed by the presence of many of the people with whom I had worked long ago.

7. The implications of this irony are important. Catholic Action's rhetoric was oppositional, whereas in practice its relationship with the civil-religious hierarchy was a complex pattern of negotiation, appropriation, resistance, and reconciliation. A focus on practice rather than on sociological group formation explodes some of the scholarly myths about the alien nature of Catholic Action, Mayan essentialism, and cultural authenticity (see Warren 1992).

8. For a fuller explanation of the history and discussions of Mayan constructions of the process, see Warren (1989, n.d.).

9. Like "the troubles" in Northern Ireland or the *intifāda* in Israel, this term establishes both a periodicity and a politics that continue.

10. President Vinicio Cerezo Arévalo took office in 1986 as the first democratically elected civilian leader since 1970. Although hopes were high for a democratic opening and for reforms, Cerezo was candid about the continued powers and autonomy of the military. He was slow to change structures, unable to pursue human rights violators, and unsuccessful in taming the serious erosion in the value of the national currency, the *quetzal* (Painter 1987). Rural populations are skeptical of the ability of any president to reverse the institutionalization of monitoring and violence from the past. Se-

lective kidnappings and political assassinations—including the 1990 murder of the head of a major research institute in the capital—are still common in Guatemala (Americas Watch and the British Parliamentary Human Rights Group 1987).

11. In fact, Trixanos elaborated complex analyses of inequality, challenged their own constructions, experimented with alternative formulations that called for active challenges to racism in the community, and found it difficult to transform the local manifestations of a long history of discrimination no matter how egalitarian and universalistic the present policy (see Warren 1986, 1989).

12. This is a translation of the Spanish version of the narrative I taped in 1989. The problems of translation in this case, beyond the linguistic limitations of the analyst, have to do with important differences in Mayan Spanish and English. Markers of familiarity and hierarchy, which are elaborated in Mayan Spanish in pronoun and verb choices, are difficult to maintain in written English. Differences in tacit knowledge are bridged for the non-Mayan reader in the anthropological exegesis of the story, which parallels the Mayan practice of explaining the significance of the story through a series of summary retellings to conclude the performance. The written version, of course, suffers the restrictions of the medium. In practice, these stories are enacted with much body language, changes in voice and intonation to represent different characters, and much stylistic repetition. Although I have cut out standardized repetitions of phrases—something that is part of the enjoyable, energetic cadence of the telling—I have maintained the original metaphors and figures of speech. I have kept the word *rajav* or *dueño* (which can be translated as "master," "lord," "owner," or "guardian") in the original Kaqchikel to mark the fact that this concept has no easy counterpart in English, especially when talking about Mayan spiritual beings.

13. Steve Gudeman has also suggested to me that the story may represent a possible Mayan appropriation of a *ladino* archetype—the goat—for male philandering. The issues of the historical production of culture are briefly explored in this analysis through the discussion of the *nagual-tonal* complex. Clearly, much remains to be done to document the interplay of Spanish-*ladino* and Mayan systems of representation as they have influenced what was available for people to reproduce, appropriate, and subvert in local culture (cf. Warren 1989). On the issue of cultural production, identity, and conflict, see Stanley Tambiah's (1986) analysis of Sri Lanka, especially for ways in which such an analysis reveals the politics of ethnic difference and representation.

14. This is not just my construction but is what resulted as I read and circulated the narrative to various U.S. colleagues and audiences.

15. Unfortunately, I have not had the opportunity (taken the opportunity) to discuss these narratives with women, so other interpretations may remain muted in this analysis (cf. Bourque and Warren 1985).

16. In the literature on *naguales* and companion animals, the emphasis has been on animals as representations of social hierarchies, relative powers, life spans, and personality characteristics (cf. Gossen 1975; Musgrave-Portilla 1982; Pitt-Rivers 1970).

17. Structural functionalist explanations of *naguales* stress social control and the displacement of aggression from other spheres of life onto the transforming individual (Erice 1985).

18. John Watanabe (1989) explores distinctive constructions of the inner "soul" for Santiago Chimaltenango, Guatemala, and finds it to be an important aspect of commonality and ethnicity.

19. This happened in San Andrés when strangers from other Mayan language groups were in town. They were felt to be out of place and likely to be spies.

20. Elsewhere this was not possible. Patrols were sometimes directed to go on sweeps, and members were faced with orders from the military to kill their own townspeople who had been labeled as subversive or be killed themselves (Bermúdez 1986; Montejo 1987; Simon 1986). Terrible executions occurred when patrols mistook military patrols for guerrillas (Montejo 1987). In other cases, individuals misused their positions to enhance their own local powers, extort money or sex, and kill personal enemies (Paul and Demarest 1988; Simon 1986).

21. This calls for examinations of the interplay of ethnic, regional, class, gender, cultural, and religious cleavages, identities, and forms of domination.

22. For studies of U.S. policy and involvements, see McClintock (1985, 1992) and Americas Watch and the British Parliamentary Human Rights Group (1987).

23. Of course, anthropological accounts are mediated by additional narrative conventions. In this chapter, I found myself compelled to contextualize the analysis, to establish its scholarly scope and significance, through the conventions of an introductory overview and the brief historical treatment of the significance of transforming selves in Mesoamerica.

24. In the case of the press, this is a purposeful policy that is the result of intimidation, self-censorship, and a sensationalist style (cf. Americas Watch and British Parliamentary Human Rights Group 1987: 59–61).

25. See also Montejo (1987: 107).

BIBLIOGRAPHY

Americas Watch. *Guatemala: A Nation of Prisoners.* New York: Americas Watch, 1984.

Americas Watch and the British Parliamentary Human Rights Group. *Human Rights in Guatemala During President Cerezo's First Year.* New York: Americas Watch, 1987.

Anderson, Thomas. *Matanza.* 2nd ed. Willimantic: Curbstone Press, 1992.

Bermúdez, Fernando. *Death and Resurrection in Guatemala.* New York: Orbis Books, 1986.

Bourdieu, Pierre. *Outline of a Theory of Practice.* Cambridge: Cambridge University Press, 1977.

Bourque, Susan C., and Kay B. Warren. "Gender, Power, and Communication: Women's Responses to Political Muting in the Andes." In Donna Robinson Divine and Susan C. Bourque, eds., *Women Living Change: Cross-Cultural Perspectives.* Philadelphia: Temple University Press, 1985, 255–286.

Bourque, Susan C., and Kay B. Warren. "Democracy Without Peace: The Cultural Politics of Terror in Peru." *Latin American Research Review* 24, no. 1 (1989): 7–34.

Bruner, Edward M. "Ethnography as Narrative." In Victor W. Turner and Edward M. Bruner, eds., *The Anthropology of Experience*. Urbana: University of Illinois Press, 1986, 139–155.

Carmack, Robert M. *The Quiché Mayas of Utatlán: The Evolution of a Highland Guatemala Kingdom*. Norman: University of Oklahoma Press, 1981.

———. "The Story of Santa Cruz Quiché." In Robert M. Carmack, ed., *Harvest of Violence: The Maya Indians and the Guatemalan Crisis*. Norman: University of Oklahoma Press, 1988a, 39–69.

———, ed. *Harvest of Violence: The Maya Indians and the Guatemalan Crisis*. Norman: University of Oklahoma Press, 1988b.

Cojtí Cuxil, Demetrio. *Configuración del Pensamiento Político del Pueblo Maya*. Quetzaltenango: Asociación de Escritores Mayances de Guatemala, 1991.

Davis, Sheldon. "Introduction: Sowing the Seeds of Violence. " In Robert M. Carmack, ed., *Harvest of Violence: The Maya Indians and the Guatemalan Crisis*. Norman: University of Oklahoma Press, 1988a, 3–36.

———. "Agrarian Structure and Ethnic Resistance: The Indian in Guatemalan and Salvadoran National Politics." In Remo Guidieri, Francesco Pellizzi, and Stanley J. Tambiah, eds., *Ethnicities and Nations: Processes of Interethnic Relations in Latin America, Southeast Asia, and the Pacific*. Austin: Rothko Chapel/University of Texas Press, 1988b, 76–106.

Ehlers, Tracy. *Silent Looms*. Boulder: Westview Press, 1990.

Erice, Ana. "Reconsideración de las Creencias Mayas en Torno al Nahualismo." *Estudios de Cultura Maya* 16 (1985): 255–270.

Falla, Ricardo. *Masacres de la Selva; Ixcán, Guatemala (1975–1982)*. Guatemala: Editorial Universitaria, 1992.

Figueroa Ibarra, Carlos. *El Recurso del Miedo; Ensayo Sobre el Estado y el Terror en Guatemala*. Costa Rica: Editorial Universitaria Centroamericana, 1991.

Foster, George. "Nagualism in Mexico and Guatemala." *Acta Americana* 2 (1944): 85–103.

Gossen, Gary. "Animal Souls and Human Destiny in Chamula." *Man* 10, no. 3 (1975): 448–461.

Guidieri, Remo, Francesco Pellizzi, and Stanley J. Tambiah, eds. *Ethnicities and Nations: Processes of Interethnic Relations in Latin America, Southeast Asia, and the Pacific*. Austin: Rothko Chapel/University of Texas Press, 1988.

Handy, Jim. *Gift of the Devil: A History of Guatemala*. Boston: South End Press, 1984.

Hinshaw, Robert E. "Tourist Town Amid the Violence: Panajachel." In Robert M. Carmack, ed., *Harvest of Violence: The Maya Indians and the Guatemalan Crisis*. Norman: University of Oklahoma Press, 1988, 195–205.

Manz, Beatriz. *Refugees of a Hidden War: The Aftermath of Counterinsurgency in Guatemala*. Albany: SUNY Press, 1988.

McClintock, Michael. *The American Connection: State Terror and Popular Resistance in Guatemala*. London: Zed Press, 1985.

_____ . *Instruments of Statecraft: U.S. Guerrilla Warfare, Counterinsurgency, and Counterterrorism, 1940–1990*. New York: Pantheon, 1992.

Menchú, Rigoberta, with Elisabeth Burgos-Debray, ed. *I . . . Rigoberta Menchú: An Indian Woman in Guatemala*. London: Verso Editions, 1984.

Montejo, Victor. *Testimony: Death of a Guatemalan Village*. Willimantic, Conn.: Curbstone Press, 1987.

Montejo, Victor, and Q'anil Akab'. *Brevísima Relación Testimonial de la Continua Destrucción del Mayab' (Guatemala)*. Providence: Guatemala Scholars Network, 1992.

Musgrave-Portilla, L. Marie. "The Nahualli or Transforming Wizard in Pre- and Postconquest Mesoamerica." *Journal of Latin American Lore* 8, no. 1 (1982): 3–62.

Painter, James. *Guatemala: False Hope, False Freedom*. London: Catholic Institute for International Relations and Latin America Bureau, 1987.

Paul, Benjamin D., and William J. Demarest. "The Operation of a Death Squad in San Pedro la Laguna." In Robert M. Carmack, ed., *Harvest of Violence: The Maya Indians and the Guatemalan Crisis*. Norman: University of Oklahoma Press, 1988, 119–155.

Pitt-Rivers, Julian. "Spiritual Power in Central America: The Naguals of Chiapas." In Mary Douglas, ed., *Witchcraft Accusations and Confessions*. London: Tavistock, 1970, 183–206.

Saler, Benson. *Nagual, brujo and herichero en un pueblo quiché*. Guatemala: Ministerio de Educación, 1969.

Sam Colop, Luis Enrique. "Jub'aqtun Omay Kuchum K'aslemal—Cinco Siglos de Encubrimiento." *Seminario Permanente de Estudios Mayas Cuaderno No. 1*. Guatemala: Editorial Cholsamaj, 1991.

Sherman, William L. *Forced Native Labor in Sixteenth-Century Central America*. Lincoln: University of Nebraska Press, 1979.

Simon, Jean-Marie. *Civil Patrols in Guatemala*. New York: Americas Watch, 1986.

_____ . *Guatemala: Eternal Spring, Eternal Tyranny*. New York: W. W. Norton, 1987.

Stavenhagen, Rodolfo. "Classes, Colonialism and Acculturation." In Irving Louis Horowitz, ed., *Masses in Latin America*. New York: Oxford University Press, 1970, 235–288.

Stoll, David. "Between Two Fires: Dual Violence and the Reassertion of Civil Society in Nebaj, Guatemala." Ph.D. diss., Department of Anthropology, Stanford University, March 1992.

Stratmeyer, Dennis, and Jean Stratmeyer. "El nawal jacalteco y el cargador del alma en Concepción Huista." *Guatemala Indígena* 14, nos. 3–4 (1979): 102–129.

Tambiah, Stanley. *Sri Lanka: Ethnic Fratricide and the Dismantling of Democracy*. Chicago: University of Chicago Press, 1986.

Taussig, Michael. *The Nervous System*. New York: Routledge, 1992.

_____ . *Shamanism, Colonialism, and the Wild Man: A Study in Terror and Healing.* Chicago: University of Chicago Press, 1987.

Tedlock, Barbara. "The Role of Dreams and Visionary Narratives in Mayan Cultural Survival." *Ethos,* in press.

Tedlock, Dennis. "Torture in the Archives." Unpublished manuscript, n.d.

Tranfo, Luigi. "Tono y Nagual." In Italo Signorini, ed., *Los Huaves de San Mateo del Mar, Oaxaca.* Mexico: Instituto Nacional Indigenista, 1979, 177–210.

Villa Rojas, Alfonso. "Kinship and Nagualism in a Tzeltal Community, Southeastern Mexico." *American Anthropologist* 49 (1947): 578–587.

Vogt, Evon Z. "Human Souls and Animal Spirits in Zinacantan." In Jean Pouillon and Pierre Maranda, eds., *Echanges et Communications.* The Hague: Mouton, 1970, 1,148–1,167.

Warren, Kay B. "Creation Narratives and the Moral Order: Implications of Multiple Models in Highland Guatemala." In Frank Reynolds and Robin Lovin, eds., *Cosmogony and Ethical Order: New Studies in Comparative Ethics.* Chicago: University of Chicago Press, 1985, 251–276.

_____ . "Capitalist Expansion and the Moral Order: Anthropological Perspectives." In David Krueger and Bruce Gruelle, eds., *Christianity and Capitalism: Perspectives on Religion, Liberalism and the Economy.* Chicago: Center for the Scientific Study of Religion, 1986, 161–176.

_____ . *The Symbolism of Subordination: Indian Identity in a Guatemalan Town,* 2d ed. Austin: University of Texas Press, 1989.

_____ . "Transforming Memories and Histories: The Meanings of Ethnic Resurgence for Mayan Indians." In Alfred Stepan, ed., *Americas: New Interpretive Essays.* Oxford: Oxford University Press, 1992, 189–219.

_____ . "Each Mind Is a World: Dilemmas of Feeling and Intention in a Kaqchikel Maya Community. " In Lawrence Rosen, ed., *Other Intentions.* Cambridge: Cambridge University Press, in press.

Watanabe, John. "Elusive Essences: Souls and Social Identity in Two Highland Maya Communities." In *Ethnographic Encounters in Southern Mesoamerica: Essays in Honor of Evon Zartman Vogt, Jr.* Albany: Institute for Mesoamerican Studies, 1989, 263–274.

Wilson, Richard. "Machine Guns and Mountain Spirits: The Cultural Effects of State Repression Among the Q'eqchi' of Guatemala." *Critique of Anthropology* 11, no. 1 (1991): 33–61.

2 Culturalism Versus Cultural Politics: *Movimento Negro* in Rio de Janeiro & São Paulo, Brazil

MICHAEL HANCHARD

Afro-Brazilian social movements of the 1970s greatly altered the course of Brazilian racial politics. For the first time in the history of the Brazilian republic, black activists and militants publicly denounced racially based inequalities and violence imposed on Brazilians of African descent and refuted accommodationist tactics employed by previous Afro-Brazilian associational groups. They organized and sought to coalesce mass numbers of militant Afro-Brazilians with divergent regional, socioeconomic, and ideological backgrounds—to the consternation of white elites.

Their activism precipitated coercive and preemptive acts by the state apparatus to repress Afro-Brazilian protest. The dynamic relationship between Afro-Brazilian protest and state-led reforms and controls led to new laws and social practices. It also led to new modes of consciousness for many Afro-Brazilians who discovered within the concept of an African diaspora racial self-identification and an awareness of other peoples and struggles.

The process of *distensão* (decompression) initiated by the Geisel military regime (1974–1979) resulted in the relaxation of military restrictions imposed on civil society, such as the banning of political protest, organization, and assembly. Thus, it was no accident that the late 1970s brought civic resurgence in the form of political parties and social movements. Afro-Brazilians, however, had to contend not only with the precarious, orchestrated cessation of the military dictatorship but also with the legacy of another subordinating process—racial domination.

Racial domination in Brazil has assumed myriad forms that have similar expressions in other multiethnic polities. Quantitative analysis of census data has revealed that when controlling for educational levels and regional, age, and gender differences, race is a determining factor in life expectancy, physical health, housing, and employment (Hasenbalg and do Valle Silva 1988; Lovell 1991).

Racial democracy as the ideological manifestation of Brazilian racial hegemony, however, is peculiar to Brazil, not only as an ideological construct but also in its use by white and nonwhite Brazilians. It has been both colloquially and academically known as the myth of racial democracy, largely because of the discrepancies between its ideological construction and social realities. Racial hegemony is hereby defined as a process of socialization that generates and reproduces racial discrimination and inequality while simultaneously denying its existence by promoting a false premise of racial egalitarianism.

What further distinguishes Brazilian racial politics from other examples in this volume as well as from politics of other multiethnic and multiracial societies is the absence of the historical moment—an instance of direct confrontation involving dominant and subordinate racial, ethnic, or national groups such as can be found in South Africa and Northern Ireland. This absence has also contributed to the paucity of scholarship on Brazilian racial politics.

There is substantial literature on the myth of racial democracy, the false premise of racial equality codified by Gilberto Freyre (1946) in the 1930s, and its consequences in the preempting of conflicts surrounding ongoing practices of racial discrimination within the Brazilian polity by both mass citizens and elites. There is virtually no scholarship, however, on the responses by black citizens to various modes of racial domination—the ideology of racial democracy being just one facet of the process of racial hegemony.

Using a neo-Gramscian approach to analyze Brazilian racial politics, I explore the process of racial hegemony as it relates to the articulation of Afro-Brazilian social movements in Rio de Janeiro and São Paulo in the 1970s. Although much of the literature on the myth of racial democracy and the realities of racial oppression in Brazil addresses both the form and the process of racial discrimination, few works address the *contents* of racial dynamics in Brazil—particularly Afro-Brazilian resistance to discrimination and violence.

Afro-Brazilian sociopolitical formations in Rio de Janeiro and São Paulo did much to alter the manner in which Brazilians of African descent thought about themselves as well as the ways in which many white Brazilians perceived Afro-Brazilians. Yet the discursive and practical articulation of Afro-Brazilian dissent also revealed certain problematic aspects of Brazilian society and culture that were internalized by activists of the *movimento negro*.

One of the principal ideological and cultural effects of the racially hegemonic process in Brazil has been the neutralization of racial identification among Afro-Brazilians, making race an improbable point of mass mobilization for nonwhites in the country. Furthermore, the relegation of Afro-Brazilian social and political practices to the realm of culture has presented Afro-Brazilian activists with a major paradox: How do subordinate individuals and groups forge counterhegemonic values out of values that reaffirm the dominant social order? Can the process of subversion avoid reproducing those prevailing values, at some level, in new forms? Clearly, these were the two overarching predicaments for Gramsci and the Italian Communist party during the rise of Fascism in the 1920s and for Afro-Brazilian militant organizations of the Left during the period of *abertura*—the reopening of civil society—in the 1970s.

Unlike the United States, South Africa, or Great Britain—where there is an uneasy recognition of African and African-inflected presences—Brazilians have long celebrated African and African-American figures within their midst. The nation's folklore, anthropology, and religions are replete with Afro-Brazilian figures. As Peter Fry (1982) has noted, the artifacts of Afro-Brazilian culture are transformed into national symbols devoid of racial-political content. In the attempt to reverse this process of symbolic depoliticization, Afro-Brazilian activists of the 1970s attempted, and were often successful in, infusing new meanings into old Afro-Brazilian symbols and cultural practices.

The consequences of the infusion of new, racially charged meanings into national discourse were ambiguous. Although this infusion did lead to new expressions of solidarity and organization among Afro-Brazilians, it resulted in the use and appropriation of cultural practices as ends in themselves rather than as means to broader, more comprehensive ethico-political activities. Culture often became equated with material objects and symbols as the expression of an Afro-Brazilian, Afro-diasporic way of seeing rather than as merely one facet of comprehensive political and economic mobilization.

This reification and commodification of culture left many Afro-Brazilian social formations without ideological direction or strategies. When combined with the intense pressures placed on the articulation of Afro-Brazilian dissent by civic elites and the state apparatus, many of the movements and organizations did not survive the decade. In their wake, two questions arise that have implications for future prospects—and study—of Afro-Brazilian social movements.

First, how does one distinguish cultural politics from culturalism in formations such as those of the *movimento negro?* Second, given this distinction, what are the potentially useful ways in which the term *culture* can be reconceptualized with respect to the discipline of political science? The answer to the first question is found in the analysis below of three separate politico-cultural developments among Afro-Brazilian *militantes* of Rio de Janeiro and São Paulo in the 1970s: the *Africanistas* versus *Americanistas* in Rio de Janeiro; the

Black Soul movement of Rio de Janeiro and São Paulo; and the development of Afro-Marxism and the *Movimento Negro Unificado* in São Paulo. The response to the second question, clearly an exceedingly ambitious one to formulate, will be attempted in the conclusion of this chapter. Before proceeding to the three historical moments noted above, a brief account of their genesis is in order.

BRIEF HISTORICAL OVERVIEW

Afro-Brazilian political activity and Brazilian cultural practice have been inextricably linked since the third decade of the twentieth century, since Gilberto Freyre's anthropological reading (1946) of Afro-Brazilian religions and mores into the matrix of emergent national identity known as *The Masters and the Slaves* (*Casa Grande e Senzala*). One of the marked ironies of Brazilian racial politics has been that the paternalist, functionalist glorification of Afro-Brazilian culture as well as more radical uses of that culture emerged from the same source—the recognition that Brazil was as much an African nation as it was a country of the New World. As a response to the Modernist impulses that were emerging among bourgeois artistic circles in São Paulo and other parts of the country, Freyre sought to institutionalize his appreciation for things that were Afro-Brazilian and to emphasize the regional peculiarities of traditional, preindustrial Brazil (Levine 1973).

Freyre along with white and nonwhite intellectuals created the first centers and institutes for the study of Afro-Braziliana in the 1940s. Mario Bick and Diana Brown (1987) have noted how *candomble* and *umbanda,* African- and Afro-Brazilian-derived religious practices, were frowned on by whites until the 1940s as forms of religious worship. The academic and artistic production of these intellectuals became the basis for the study of African cultures and peoples in Brazil as well as grounds for the critique and subsequent dismissal of these studies by later generations of scholars and activists.

Within this quasi-academic realm, scholarly and political debates about Afro-Brazilian cultural practices first emerged. Those debates led subsequently to the creation of institutes and community organizations by Afro-Brazilians themselves. It could be said that Afro-Brazilian social movements after the 1940s sprang from the academy as opposed to the *suburbio* or the *favela.* These origins would become one of the recurrent problems intrinsic to Afro-Brazilian political development throughout the 1970s.

The psychic and geographical distance from the mass of Afro-Brazilians, coupled with the tendency—first generated by intellectuals—to treat the problems of Afro-Brazilian subordination and marginalization as academic rather than politico-strategic issues, has led to a proclivity toward culturalism within the *movimento negro*. Culturalism as it is used here refers to the abstraction, reification, and commodification of artifacts and expressions of a particular social collectivity for the purpose of projecting the image of that collectivity as a whole. This process hypostatizes, or freezes, cultural practices, divorcing them from their histories and from the attendant modes of consciousness that brought them into being. This obviously limits the range of alternative articulation and movement by Afro-Brazilian peoples.

The second feature of Afro-Brazilian political and cultural practices has been the need to veil explicit religious, artistic, cultural, and political expressions that presented critiques of the dominant social order. This is not unique to blacks in Brazil and has been well documented about blacks in other parts of the New World.

Until the 1970s, most Afro-Brazilian leaders emerged from *samba* schools, cultural and religious organizations, and athletics. In the period between 1945 and 1970, Afro-Brazilians were either accommodated through patron-client relationships or banished altogether from the system of political favors. In fact, corporatist accommodation of Afro-Brazilian protest predates the aforementioned period by eight years. The demise of the Black Brazilian Front—the first civil rights movement in Brazil—occurred when Getulio Vargas outlawed all political parties. The more conservative members of the front joined the ranks of the Integralists, Vargas's political party (Hasenbalg and do Valle Silva 1988; Mitchell 1977).

One can well comprehend the necessity for Afro-Brazilian activists to couch various forms of expression in narrowly culturalist terms, ones that would not bring the attention of the state or of white elites in civil society. With virtually no representation in the academy, national or local politics, or the military, Afro-Brazilian activists have operated through an aesthetic web even when presenting social-economic or political concerns.

White Brazilians in turn have largely interacted with Afro-Brazilians within these parameters, as has the state—which under various regimes has exercised its political and coercive powers through interventions into Afro-Brazilian organizations in order to repress, control, and alter counter-hegemonic tendencies. This mirrors Gramsci's interpretation of totalitarian rule in which party and state are conflated and represent the sole channels of formal political participation. In such societies, a political party's functions

are no longer directly political, but merely technical ones of propaganda and public order, and moral and cultural influence. The political function is indirect. For, even if no other legal parties exist, other parties in fact always do exist and other tendencies which cannot be legally coerced; and against these, po-lemics are unleashed and struggles are fought . . . it is certain that in such parties cultural functions predominate . . . political questions are disguised as cultural ones, and as such become insoluble. (Gramsci 1971: 149)

Further complicating matters has been the tenuous relationship between the *movimento negro* and the Brazilian Left. Until the late 1970s, the rather ossified brand of Brazilian Marxist-Leninism consistently maintained that "the social problem" is one of class and labor, not race or gender. As recently as 1990, a Worker's Party (PT) militant Pedro Wilson Guimaraes, talking to a U.S. audience in Philadelphia, Pennsylvania, responded to a question about the party's stance toward racial and gender issues by stating that "these issues are important, but we have our priorities. We are primarily concerned with the social problem of working class exploitation in Brazil."[1]

Guimaraes's narrow understanding of the social problem begs a simple question: Does racial- or gender-based discrimination—indeed, any form of discrimination—exist outside of a social context? If not, then such forms of discrimination are part of the social problem as well, inasmuch as blacks and women carry their "secondary" forms of discrimination with them into labor markets. Guimaraes's comments, taken representatively, point to two major problems the Brazilian Left has had historically with interpreting racially based mechanisms of exploitation in civil society and with the subsequent re-production of such exploitation in leftist intellectual circles.

Afro-Brazilian activists set out on distinct paths of cultural and political engagement during the process of *abertura* in the 1970s, autonomous from both conservative, authoritarian and "radical" leftist formations that relied on reductionist interpretations of race. In doing so, they took their cues from their "brethren" in the Caribbean, the United States, and Africa.

The "new" character of the black movement in Brazil was in fact an old, latent trait that was developed and pronounced in the 1970s. This trait was leftist radical discourse, which had trudged along in fits and starts at the fringes of several black organizations since the 1940s but, as implied above, was a residual[2] element in black political culture. What was unprecedented about the upsurge of groups and protest organizations during the 1970s was the confluence of race and class-based discourses within the black movement. Activists and followers alike abandoned the accommodationist and social mo-bility credos of the 1930s and 1940s, respectively. By the end of the 1970s, those two forms of political discourse were discredited and marginalized within the black movement. Both came to be associated with statist, elitist values and counterproductive practices. Evidence of this ideological reversal can be found in numerous conferences and publications of this epoch.

With the offer of political amnesty to those in exile in 1979 and the increase in the number of students allowed to enter colleges and universities in 1975, both new and old activists of the center-Left had more room for private debate about new tactics and public criticism of the slowness of the decompression process. Former exiles who gained political insights in encounters with New Left groups in Western Europe, the United States, and other parts of Latin America shared these insights with the insurgent generation of activists and with the remaining militants of the pre-1964 era.

The New Left in Brazil attempted a more coalitional politics, one that paid attention to issues such as race, ecology, and gender. Thus, it is no accident that when political parties on the Left were reconstituted in Brazil, most had greater heterogeneity in terms of popular support and organizational agendas than those parties before 1964.

Another external tributary that influenced the black movement was the proliferation of nonwhite, or Third World, insurrectionist movements in Asia, Africa, Latin America, and the Caribbean. This greatly influenced the tone and rhetoric of black activists in Brazil, although no one sought to replicate the full-scale revolt found in Third World scenarios or the militarist tactics occasionally employed by such groups as the Weathermen and the Symbionese Liberation Army in the United States.

Masses of black Brazilians, who had never before gathered around a single racially rooted issue, were attracted to the Brazilian versions of Negritude and Black Soul in the 1960s. At the organizational level, black militants created institutions—some ephemeral—that represented a path between extant party politics and organizations on the Left and the more traditional organizational resources of black communities that survived the coup and subsequent dictatorship, but with a nonideological or statist character.

Another internal tributary flowing into these cultural and political reservoirs was black college-educated professionals. Many black professionals who became militants for the black movement first increased their awareness of racial politics not through the movement itself but through student activism and personal circumstance. As Carlos Hasenbalg (1979) acutely notes, this segment of the *movimento negro* turned to activism when it became clear that race, not training and education, was the principal key or impediment to socioeconomic advancement. One of the first manifestations of this phenomenon in Brazil in the early 1970s was the development in Rio de Janeiro of *Africanista* and *Americanista* factions among Afro-Brazilian student activists.

AMERICANISTS VERSUS AFRICANISTS

By the 1970s a wave of protest movements had developed in Africa, the United States, the Caribbean, and South America. These movements employed the rhetorics of Pan-Africanism, Negritude, and Black Power, among others, to express solidarity with Afro-diasporic peoples and to highlight the similarities of particular struggles involving people of African descent against colonialism, imperialism, and apartheid-like conditions in nation-states in which blacks were citizens. By 1970 there had been a Black Power movement in Trinidad (Oxaal 1982; Ryan 1972), the appropriation of reggae and Black Power protest songs and slogans in Great Britain (Gilroy 1987), the emergence of a Black Consciousness movement in South Africa, and a Black Soul movement in Brazil. The transnational dimension of these various movements and moments hints at the interactive facet of Afro-diasporic peoples and the ability of their cultural processes, at an epistemological level, to organize people across national boundaries.[3]

In Brazil, Afro-Brazilian activists were attracted to ideational developments on the African and North American continents and showed some interest in the Rastafari movement in Jamaica. These developments were melded into an Afro-Brazilian constellation in an attempt to apply their concepts and practices to Afro-Brazilian social realities. Although activists in Rio de Janeiro, São Paulo, and other parts of Brazil looked to outside "Third World" struggles for reference, those struggles provided only clues, not answers. Neither a national liberation struggle in an anticolonial sense nor a national push for civil rights among nonwhite citizens occurred in Brazil. Many activists in fact lamented the absence of open confrontation among racial groups because they felt clearly defined antagonisms would breed greater alliances among blacks.

With neither broad alliances nor stark, unambiguous oppression, activists tried to forge identities and strategies for a mass-based black movement in Brazil with situational templates from the United States and Africa. In Rio de Janeiro and São Paulo, many activists hoped to apply the lessons of civil rights and anticolonial struggles to Brazil.

One cadre of Afro-Brazilians in Rio de Janeiro combined Black Power and Black Panther ideologies with the more integrationalist agenda of civil rights activists. This group—which believed boycotts, sit-ins, and protests against specific acts of racial exclusion could work in Brazil—was known as the *Americanistas,* or the Americanists. In purported contrast were the *Africanistas,* the Africanists, who advocated a more transformative sort of black movement in Brazil based on anticolonial movements in Africa. In practice, no clear line separated the two groups; in fact, several individuals had a sort of dual membership. It was difficult to correlate political affiliations with political language and action. Yet the divide existed insofar as it led to the formation of group clusters predicated on perceived differences. There were similar divisions in São Paulo among groups such as *Centro de Educação de Cultura e Arte Negra* (CECAN) and the *Movimento Negro Unificado* (MNU), but these were not formulated along Africanist and Americanist lines.

The Africanists were in some ways more easily identifiable than the Americanists because after an initial period of group affinity, the Africanists situated themselves in opposition to Afro-Brazilians who advocated such things as black capitalism and equal opportunity. Africanists saw themselves as part of the revolutionary wave that undulated across the African continent in the 1950s, with its ebb and flow of national liberation and then of neocolonialism. For Africanists, it was not enough to sit alongside white Brazilians in bathroom and restaurant dining facilities (which in theory nonwhites could always do). The integration of public space, they argued, would not solve the deeply rooted problems of racial dominance in Brazil. In addition, only by the most conservative estimates were blacks a minority group in Brazil as they were in the United States. Black Brazilians, the Africanists suggested, should make demands on the state and on civil society as a majority group.

Discussions between Africanists and Americanists took place at three principal locations: Candido Mendes University, then in Ipanema, which housed the Center of Afro-Asiatic Studies (CEAA); the Institute for the Research of Black Culture (IPCN), created in 1975; and the Society for Brazilian-African Exchange (SINBA), created in 1976. Candido Mendes University was the original site for meeting. After differences emerged, the Americanists met at IPCN, the Africanists at SINBA.[4]

Yedo Ferreira, one of the founders of SINBA, discussed the rationale for its creation:

> We were interested in the liberation movements in Africa and most of all the work of Frantz Fanon. We were observing the black movement in the United States and found black Americans also looking for a historical referent in Africa . . . for us it was very easy to have a great cultural identification with Africa. We were returning to Africa, not the United States.[5]

Africa signified a place of origin and return, or more precisely, a site to be symbolically retrieved by members of SINBA in the quest for a political compass. Unlike IPCN and CEAA, SINBA did not receive funding from U.S.-based institutions and considered this a sign of autonomy. But with few resources, members could only manage to publish a journal and hold meetings and small conferences through the mid-1970s. IPCN and CEAA, on the other hand, used their funding to provide assistance to Afro-Brazilians in the form of small scholarships, legal advice, and institutional support. Both organizations exist today, whereas SINBA does not.

Ideological cloudiness contributed to SINBA's demise. Its push for an Afro-centric position alienated the leadership from some of its founding members and compounded the leaders' inability to make alliances with Americanist or other groups. Several members decided that merely assuming an oppositional stance to all things American and an attraction to the African continent would not suffice as a strategy for effecting change in Brazil. Two founding members cited the increasingly narrow ethnocentrism as a principal organizational flaw.[6] Ferreira, in retrospect, admitted this during an interview about his own position when he and several others decided to create the organization:

> I had the desire to create an institution, but without a formulation of political struggle . . . no one stopped to reflect on this . . . so the institution remained, just like this, without being able to advance more than where we were at the start.[7]

Without ideological-strategic clarity there was no balance between issues and praxis. As with many other groups of the era (and today), the organization followed the path of unchartered culturalism in search of the elusive African essence. The absence of demarcated ideological positions also suggests a reactive, day-to-day tendency of a social movement that has existed without a firm grounding in party politics along the left-right continuum. Without a competing ensemble of beliefs, values, and ideologies to mediate the relationships between leftists and conservatives, between Afro-Brazilian and Afro-diasporic realities, the likelihood increases that activists will employ commonsense understandings of race and politics that are congruent with those already in existence that affirm, rather than overturn, meanings of a dominant social order.

The Africanists and Americanists also exemplified the academicist tendencies within the *movimento negro*. Both were spawned in intellectual environments where, for the most part, they remained. Their differences were based on vaguely ideational constructs grafted from various external sources rather than on distinct interpretations of the violence and inequalities affecting Afro-Brazilian peoples.

BLACK SOUL: A THREAT TO THE NATIONAL PROJECT

Another, more popular attempt at the formation of racial identity in the 1970s was a movement called Black Soul, which started in Rio de Janeiro. Black Soul was another instance in which blacks from one cultural and national context appropriated some of the symbolic and material forms of black expression from elsewhere for the purpose of affecting a two-tiered discourse—among black social groups with differentiated histories on one level and among blacks with common national or cultural origins. In one of the few existing analyses of Black Soul, anthropologist Peter Fry (1982: 15) posited that

> The proliferation of Afro-Soul dances in São Paulo and Rio are instances in which black Brazilians create new symbols of ethnicity, in accordance with their social experience. Although some people believe these phenomena are examples of "cultural dependency" or of the capacity of the multinationals to sell whatever product, I have no doubt that, just the same, they represent a movement of major importance in the process of identity in Brazil.

In contrast, Pierre-Michel Fontaine (1985) downplays the movement's significance because Black Soul had its genesis in the United States, not in Brazil. Fontaine argues that the importance of a movement such as Black Soul is based on its "authenticity," its originary gestation within a Brazilian cultural matrix.

My interpretation of Black Soul parallels Fry's initial observation. Primary materials, leading figures, and events of the Black Soul movement provide ample evidence to suggest that the movement had as much to do with the process of identity creation among blacks in Brazil as with the alleged importation of cultural symbols. In fact, Black Soul, like Negritude, was a catalyst for an identity-based politics that continues today in the African Blocs and in several other organizations. "Filo," one of the leading protagonists of the movement, stated, "Black [Soul] was not a fashion; it had an origin. A fashion does not last for fifteen years."[8] Filo was referring to the reconstitution and survival of many of the themes and rallying points of Black Soul in the phenomena of Funk and Charme, forms of dance and musical celebration that emerged in the 1980s that carried Black Soul's imprint—all of which have a basis in a racialized Afro-Brazilian identity.

There is no official date for the start of the Black Soul movement, but its emergence was precipitated by the nascent popularity of U.S. "soul music" in Brazil. A white Brazilian disc jockey known as Big Boy is credited with first playing soul music on commercial public radio in 1967 on a show called *O Baile da Pesada*. The music first attracted the attention of black Brazilians from Rio de Janeiro's *Zona Norte*—a poor, predominantly black area of the city.

Dance and party organizers in the zone began playing soul. People such as Osseas "Mr. Funk" Santos, considered the originator of Black Soul, and Filo developed reputations as able purveyors of this music and of its attendant dances, styles of dress, and symbolic modes of protest. For many followers of Black Soul, James Brown was the principal interlocutor of this form of musical expression with songs such as "Say It Loud (I'm Black and I'm Proud)," which was a major hit in the United States and among Black Soul participants in Brazil.

The music soon found its way into more traditional *samba* clubs and neighborhood associations and ultimately into the Renascença Clube—Rio's answer to the *Aristocrata Clube* in São Paulo—an exclusive club for middle-class blacks. By 1970 the club's membership had changed greatly. It was no longer an enclave in which working-class and petit bourgeois blacks with middle-class aspirations socialized. Clubs such as Renascença had to adapt to new social realities, *abertura,* and increased racial identification.

Filo and others began organizing soul music dances known as *Noites do Shaft* (Shaft's Night), named after the well-known 1974 U.S. film, at the club two years before Black Soul in Rio was reported on as a social phenomenon by major daily newspapers such as *Jornal do Brasil* and magazines such as *Veja*.[9] According to Filo, the influx of black Brazilians into the Renascença Clube with Afro hairstyles, high-heeled shoes, and other reified elements of the U.S. black experience during this period caused some dissonance among many of the club's leaders. This was due in part to the generational differences between Black Soul participants and the black petit bourgeois establishment of Renascença. Yet the signifying forms of Black Rio were unprecedented and thus may be a more important reason for the dissonance.

Never before had black Brazilians identified with cultural forms that were black but neither African nor Brazilian, the two categories through which sputterings of racial consciousness had occurred in *escolas de samba* and houses of worship. In many instances, this process of identification had do-

mestic repercussions in homes in which black identity and consciousness
were negated or repressed. The young women and men who participated in
Black Soul often found themselves in conflict with their parents or as cata-
lysts for family members who had never confronted issues of racial oppression
and identification. Thus, hair and clothing styles became important not only
in their symbolic representations but in their association with other cultural
practices, suggesting autonomy from predetermined modes of racial identification in Brazil.

Dances organized by Mr. Funk or Filo in *Zona Norte* often attracted three
thousand to ten thousand people. The popularity of these dances soon expanded beyond the confines of the Renascença Clube. The organizers of the
dances at Renascença left the club to form their own group, Soul Grand Prix,
and held parties in various parts of Rio. Soul Grand Prix soon became a television show.

Soul Grand Prix also developed into a traveling multimedia event with
slide presentations filled with racially specific imagery; it appeared at various
clubs in the city. Pictures of U.S. blacks in protest and self-adulation were
abundant, which pleased many black participants but offended some whites.
Grand Prix members thus altered the slides to suit the audience, deleting racial content from visual presentations in white clubs.

In situations in which the constituency was overwhelmingly black, however, the Afro-centered slide presentations were a success. Newspaper report-
age and interviews with party goers from this era confirm gestaltlike revela-
tions by many individuals. Scenes of black people crying while viewing the
slides and U.S. movies such as *Wattstax* and relating the imagery of blacks in
the United States and elsewhere to their own experience were common in
clubs and dance halls in which Soul Grand Prix produced events.

This facet of what came to be known as Black Soul caused consternation
among both military and civilian elites. It must be remembered that Black
Soul as well as the proliferation of Afro-Brazilian groups in general coincided
with the most profoundly repressive phase of the military dictatorship
(1969–1975). At the level of propaganda and communication, a dissemi-
nated image of national unity was paramount, and any mention of racial discord—either within or outside of Brazil—was prohibited. As part of the censorship criteria, film censors were instructed to assess whether a film depicted
racial problems in Brazil or if it dealt with the Black Power movement in the
United States (Pierce 1979: 37). In an example of race-specific censorship in
print journalism, one sentence of a reprinted article on chess from Britain's
Manchester Guardian was censored because it read: "The whites have great

material advantage while the blacks have almost no legal opening" (Pierce 1979: 33).

By the time Black Soul received media coverage in the late 1970s, it was criticized by the military government, which sought to invoke the increasingly bankrupt ideology of racial democracy, and by civilian elites who opposed the dictatorship but who nonetheless believed the exponents of Black Soul were fomenting racial hatred and conflict. Both cadres viewed Black Soul as a phenomena that needed to be brought under control.

Because it was independent of white elite definitions of both national "Brazilianness" and Afro-Brazilian cultural practice, Black Soul was subject to criticism and ultimately to repression. In a *Jornal do Brasil* article on Black Rio in 1977, the municipal secretary of tourism in Rio de Janeiro stated that "Black Rio is a commercial movement with a racist philosophy," with its development attributable to "a sociocultural problem."[10] He added that the movement lacked any trace of authenticity.

Also on the question of authenticity, a report was published in *Folha de São Paulo* regarding a teacher's denunciation of "external" musical influences in Black Rio that sullied Brazil's musical heritage of Afro-Brazilian music:

> What is most tragic, above all, is that they are imposing a rhythm, a harmony, and a sound that has nothing to do with *our* musicality. Worse still they are deceiving a band of innocents, who cannot evaluate the importance of our musical treasure which has an African heritage.[11]

Criticism such as this was symptomatic of the emergent tensions between practitioners of Black Soul and the many arbiters, white and black, of nationalized Afro-Brazilian culture. As a representation of the unification of national and international dimensions of Afro-Brazilian consciousness, Black Soul also signified a weariness with existing modes of cultural practice that had become commodified and, in an existential sense, deracinated. *Samba* and *umbanda* had become so nationalized that large segments of the white middle classes had claimed them as their own, in contrast to earlier points in the twentieth century when *samba* was considered the domain of the lower classes—black as well as white (Hasenbalg 1979; Schwarcz 1987).

Several prominent *Sambistas* and *escolas de samba* opposed Black Soul because of their perception that this import was invading their own shrinking islands of cultural autonomy. This was an ironic stance on the part of the more conservative *samba* schools in light of the fact that it was commonplace for police to enter these schools during this period and indiscriminately arrest up to two hundred young black males at a time in the middle of the dance floor. As criticism intensified, it became clear that Black Soul could not coexist with "national" culture.

The reason for this was based only minimally on the musical and symbolic innovations of Black Soul practitioners. The critiques were arguably only a pretext for the more significant concern of white elites, both civil and military, that Black Soul was the harbinger of a protest movement by black Brazilians. For such a movement to occur, black Brazilians would have to develop forms of critical consciousness and organization that were specific to them and that therefore were not national, inasmuch as *national* signified the repression of racial identities and race-specific claims. To allow such a process to occur would be to admit nationally to both racial discrimination *and* racial identification.

Gilberto Freyre sounded the alarm against Black Soul for precisely these reasons. In a 1977 article published in *Diario de Pernambuco,* Freyre warned his fellow nationals of the threat Black Soul posed to both national identity and security:

> Perhaps my eyes are deceiving me? Or did I really read that the United States will be arriving in Brazil. . . . Americans of color. . . . Why? . . . To convince Brazilians, also of color, that their dances and their "Afro-Brazilian" songs would have to be of "melancholy" and "revolt"? And not, as it is today, . . . *samba* which are almost all happy and fraternal. If what I have read is true, it is once more an attempt to introduce into a Brazil that is growing fully, fraternally brown—what appears to cause jealousy in nations that are also bi- or tri-racial—the myth of negritude, not of Senghor's type, of the just valorization of black or African values, but that which brings at times that "class struggle" as an instrument of civil war, not of the lucid Marx the sociologist but the other: the inspirator of a militant Marxism with its provocation of hatred. . . . What must be made salient, in these difficult times which the world is living in, with a terrible crisis of leadership. . . . Brazil needs to be ready for work being done against it, not only of Soviet imperialism . . . but of the United States as well.[12]

Note the links Freyre's critique of Black Soul makes with denunciations of Negritude, Marxism, and two imperialisms. For Freyre, Negritude is mythical when emphasis is placed on militancy—protest—and not on the valorization of African culture. When the former is highlighted and not the latter, Freyre sees overdetermined class struggle and ultimately militant Marxism lurking behind it.

Freyre was not alone in this belief. The widespread repression in the mid-1970s of even liberal critiques of the dictatorship, well documented in the São Paulo archdiocese report on torture in Brazil after 1964 (1988), confirms that the anti-Communist hysteria of the time was such that any dissenting voice was perceived as part of the broader Marxist conspiracy. Consequently, any group or individual—Communist or not—protesting against the military regime and the environment of terror could have been and often was subject to censorship or physical repression. Thus, members of Black Soul in Rio de Janeiro and São Paulo whose activities included passing around copies of Stokely Carmichael's *Black Power* or Frantz Fanon's *Wretched of the Earth* for group discussion were (mis)identified as part of the conspiracy theory propagated by civilian and military elites. No documentation is available on the surveillance and perceptions of Black Soul and the black movement in general during this period due to the nature of the regimes during the dictatorship; however, a high-ranking official of the National Information Service (NIS)—the resourceful intelligence arm of the state—confirmed during an interview that several black activists were closely monitored in the 1970s because of the state's belief that they were cogs in the ever-turning wheel of Communist conspiracy. [13]

As for Freyre's criticism of Negritude, two things should be noted. First, Negritude took hold in a very diffuse way among individuals and groups in Brazil, mostly as an attitude rather than a movement with a clear politics. Negritude as a belief system was one facet of a wider insurgent recognition of things African, or of the diaspora. Ironically, it was originally conceived by Leopold Senghor and Aime Cesaire as a blend of Pan-Africanism, socialism, and psychoanalysis; thus, in this sense both Freyre and mild followers of Negritude in Brazil were off the mark in their separation of Negritude from a political and a social movement.

Second, regarding the recurring construction of authenticity in Brazilian culture, Freyre's and other criticisms neglect the fact that the "authentic" *samba* most Brazilians had come to know and exercise was a *samba* that had been appropriated by the white middle classes and elites in the post–World War II period when it was discovered by these social groups as an inexpensive means of leisure. As Peter Fry (1982), Diana Brown (1979), and others have shown, this form of Afro-Brazilian cultural expression was considered a lower-class practice reserved for very poor whites and for Brazilians of African descent. Therefore, the appropriation of the practices relating to Black Soul by Afro-Brazilians was no less authentic than the elite appropriation of *samba* that can be vividly witnessed in the annual competitions and spectacles of *Carnaval*. In this sense Black Soul can be seen as a counterbricolage to extant constructions of Afro-Brazilian, and therefore national, identity.

Moreover, many Black Soul dances were held in *samba* schools, due largely to the high cost of renting dance halls and the reluctance of many white owners to allow throngs of black Brazilians into their buildings. Once inside, *samba* and Black Soul enthusiasts interacted—in music and performance— without conflict. Indeed, in some cases this intersection also led to new, more experimental *samba* compositions.

Although Black Soul did have its political moments, it was largely a culturalist and a musical phenomenon. The principal figures of Black Soul in Rio de Janeiro were considered too Americanist and were disparaged as crass materialists by several factions of the black movement. This image was confirmed, according to its critics, by the involvement of Filo and others in the production of several commercial record albums and the organization of concerts featuring black U.S. soul performers.

Part of the difficulty in bridging the chasm between political and cultural practices was the incorporation of Black Soul by the Rio de Janeiro tourist and entertainment industry, which soon became a more than able competitor for the handful of black production companies that were turning a small profit. Monsieur Lima, a white Carioca club owner who sponsored *bailes soul* in *Zona Sul* (Botafogo) by contracting groups such as Black Power and Soul Grand Prix, went so far as to suggest that the dances were not only commercially viable but were forms of social control as well:

> If not for these dances, what would the mass of people do on Saturdays and Sundays? How would they enjoy themselves? If they didn't have this I guarantee there would be a great increase in assaults on the weekend by these people who have nothing to do . . . the government must encourage it [the dances]. [14]

Thus, the sixteen- to twenty-year-olds who flocked to the weekend soul festivals were viewed as a criminal element despite the fact well-documented by Hermano Vianna and others[15] that drugs, alcohol, fighting, and other forms of social disturbance were absent from these events.

In São Paulo, several activists of the mid-1970s mentioned during interviews that unlike the Funk and Charme parties of the 1980s, Black Soul events were fertile occasions for pamphleteering and disseminating information regarding marches, discussions, and other events pertaining to the black movement. The Chā Bridge (*Viaducto de Chā*), a major thoroughfare in the center of São Paulo, was the meeting place for "blacks" (i.e., those of the *movimento black*) and blacks who directly participated in the full spectrum of sociopolitical positions of the center-left in the 1970s. Although Black Soul promoters and disc jockeys were perhaps sympathetic to the covert political activity during this period, they were not agents for such activities. This was unlike the instances of the use of soccer matches in public stadiums in South

Africa or of funerals or other public forums at which African National Congress members met to strategize during numerous cycles of repression in the 1970s. Despite their symbolic repercussions, the parties were ends in themselves—hence the division between political and cultural practices of Black Soul and other more explicitly political Afro-Brazilian groups of the period.

This view is echoed in the work of Carlos Benedito Rodrigues da Silva (1983) in one of the few scholarly analyses of the Black Soul phenomenon. Focusing on the emergence of Black Soul in Campinas, São Paulo, after 1978, Rodrigues da Silva posits that its appearance there represented a process of ethnic identification as well as the material production of leisure. The impresarios of black Campinas were the offspring of the traditional middle-class black families well represented in *samba* schools and social clubs for upwardly mobile *paulistanos negros*. Although their activities within the soul movement were in some respects counter to the traditional assumptions about black elites forgetting their ethnic and African origins, their functions belied the impresario's middle-class origins. There was an implicit acceptance of white bourgeois values, evidenced in the preoccupation of both organizers and party goers with *comportamento*—being well-groomed—and a desire to occupy a social space that heretofore had been denied them in high culture (Rodrigues da Silva 1983).

In contrast, Mr. Funk, Filo, and many other figures of Black Soul–Black Rio were from poor backgrounds and built a following in the predominantly black north section of the city before attracting the attention of the mass media. Filo and Carlos Alberto Medieros wrote a newspaper column pertaining to Black Soul events under the pseudo-acronym J.B. to disseminate information about Black Soul to the public.

By 1978, however, the attacks and discrediting in the mass media coupled with the rising popularity of disco music had noticeable effects on Black Soul. The parties, newspaper columns, record contracts, and television specials waned. Funk and Charme, dance hall phenomena in the 1980s with their basis in black U.S. music, were reminiscent of Black Soul but without glimpses of alternative forms of racial identification found in the slide presentations, films, and literatures circulating in and around their predecessor (cf. Vianna 1988).

How, then, do we assess Black Soul? Rodrigues da Silva is correct in asserting that final judgment of its merits is not an either-or proposition—that is to say, a matter of determining whether either the commodification of leisure or racial identity formation was predominant in the movement. Both are clearly evidenced in the discussion above, with each made prominent in particular moments. Perhaps the most important barometer of Black Soul as a critical instant of racial consciousness in Brazil is the reaction it evoked in white elites. They recognized a dangerous undercurrent to the images projected of black social protest elsewhere and its impact on black Brazilians. Here is where the significance and the incompleteness of the Black Soul movement lie—in its valorization of forms of self-expression and identification that were previously repressed or denied by both whites and nonwhites in Brazil.

That these new ways of self-expression and identification did not materialize into something broader reflects the boundaries imposed by white elites on Black Soul as well as its limitations. Raymond Williams (1977: 113) persuasively characterizes this facet of alternative cultural emphases and the challenges understudied "fashions" such as Black Soul often inadvertently pose to the status quo:

> Alternative political and cultural emphases, and the many forms of opposition and struggle, are important not only in themselves but as indicative features of what the hegemonic process has in practice had to work to control . . . any hegemonic process must be especially alert and responsive to the alternatives and opposition which question and threaten its dominance. The reality of cultural process must then always include the efforts and contributions of those who are in one way or another outside or at the edge of the terms of the specific hegemony.

THE *MOVIMENTO NEGRO:* NEW ORGANIZATIONS, THE *MOVIMENTO NEGRO UNIFICADO*

Black Soul and the diffusely applied concept of Negritude did not exist in a vacuum. New Afro-Brazilian organizations, both political and cultural, existed during the period of Black Soul. Their proliferation signaled the emergence of a new generation of black intellectuals in major cities such as Rio de Janeiro and São Paulo and also in Salvador, Brasilia, Recife, and Minas Gerais. In the age of emerging democracy, Afro-Brazilian activists did not want to regress to the previous limitations of either leftist economic determinism or the patron-clientelism of the right.

Paulista militants and groups appeared to be far more comprehensive and ambitious in their attempts to project the black movement onto a national stage than were activists in Rio de Janeiro. Although the *Movimento Negro Unificado* (MNU) was the most obvious manifestation of this difference, there were important precursors. *Grupo Evolução,* formed in 1971 in Campinas by *Carioca* Thereza Santos and the São Paulo intellectual Eduardo Oliveira de Oliveira, infused political and ideological issues into its cultural presentations—plays, poetry readings, dances, and festivals. Its use of culture, namely performance art, as a pedagogical and political device to educate blacks greatly influenced future leaders of MNU—such as Hamilton Cardoso, Vanderei Jose Maria, and Rafael Pinto—who saw this practice as a powerful distinction between the culturalism that plagued the movement up to that point and cultural practices linked to party or organizational politics.

The *Centro de Educação de Cultura e Arte Negra* (CECAN), in which Santos and Oliveira de Oliveira were also involved, served a similar purpose for militants emerging from the shadows of political repression with yet-undecided political affiliations in the new age of democracy. Other organizations and events attempting a cultural-political synthesis were the *I Encontro de Entidades Negros de São Paulo* and the *I Semana do Negro do Arte e na Cultura Negra de São Paulo* in 1975; the *Associação Casa de Arte e Cultura Afro-Brasileiro* (ACACAB), founded in 1977; and the *Festival Comunitaro Negro-Zumbi*, known as FECONEZU, which was first held in Araraquara, São Paulo, in 1978 in commemoration of the death of Zumbi, the leader of Palmares. Newspapers such as *Jornegro* and journals such as *Avore de Palavras* and *Cadernos Negros* undertook similar campaigns.

As noted earlier, most black protest in the country had been limited to relatively isolated individuals and associational groups of lower-middle-class origins. As a consequence, undertakings on a national level were highly uncoordinated and even contradictory; this did not change in the 1970s. What was needed was an organization with the structure of a political party but with modes of outreach like those of a social movement.

In 1978 the *Movimento Negro Unificado Contra Discriminação Racial* (which later became MNU) was created by militants from Rio de Janeiro and São Paulo in response to the torture and murder of Robson Luz, a black taxi driver, by São Paulo police in April of that year. This was not the first or the last act of violence perpetrated by the state against one of its citizens, but it served as a catalyst for social and political mobilization.

MNU's first public act was an organized demonstration on July 7, 1978, in front of the municipal theater in downtown São Paulo, where the creation of MNU was first announced to the Brazilian public (Gonzalez and Hasenbalg 1982). Approximately two thousand people attended the event, during which various activists decried police brutality and the overall state of authoritarianism during *abertura*.

Soon afterward, *Centros de Luta* (CL) were formed in Salvador, Bahia, Porto Alegre, and Espiritu Santu. The organization made inroads into coalitional politics with various other social movements: syndicates, unions, and gay rights and feminist organizations. The ambitious motivating principle of MNU was to operate as an overarching entity for all black militant organizations in the country. It was organizationally biased against political conservatives and liberals of any color, who were less visible and self-congratulatory after the failures of the economic miracle and quasitotalitarian policies of the mid-1970s.[16]

MNU's view of supporting political parties was that of an independent. Although many of its members were part of the Worker's Party (PT) by the time of MNU's founding in 1980, MNU operated separately from PT and other parties. MNU aided only those parties and individual candidates whose stance on race and other issues was congruent with its own. Its support of individual candidates, however, appears to have had little bearing on the outcome of elections, given the overall weak presence of blacks in electoral politics. With the exception of the 1988 election of Luiza Erundina as mayor of São Paulo, few candidates backed by MNU have been voted into public office.

MNU, like many organizations of the movement, has displayed a penchant for extended, rather academic debates over ideology and "proper" politics in lieu of organizational discussions of broad strategy within civil society. Gonzalez (Gonzalez and Hasenbalg 1982) notes how discussions centered around the flaws of *Quilombismo*—Abdias do Nascimento's purportedly scientific explication of communalist practices of quilombo slave societies—as well as other issues of ideology, not of practice. This tendency, also found in MNU, has also been detrimental to the group's outreach to people for whom running water, housing, and food are more pressing issues than the merits of *Quilombismo.* This is not to suggest that these issues remain muffled but that they need to be placed in their proper perspective.

After the initial fervor of the late 1970s and early 1980s, MNU—although still black—no longer seems a viable movement or organization. Ambitious at first, the centers of struggle vary widely in activity and influence in communities nationwide (Gonzalez and Hasenbalg 1982). They are active in areas where the black movement in general is visibly operative but are just another thread in a crowded mosaic of groups. Simply put, there were too many groups, often with competing programs, for any single organization to function in umbrellalike fashion. By the mid-1980s MNU had become just one organization among many rather than the overarching entity it had hoped to be.

IMPLICATIONS FOR COMPARATIVE STUDY

The Africanists and Americanists, Black Soul, and the MNU were three distinct instances of cultural and political activity in the 1970s. Although each had its epochal moment in terms of culturalist or political mobilization, only MNU made an organizational effort at broader coalitional politics. This effort was hindered by limited resources and also by strategies that often emphasized academic debates at the expense of community outreach. Likewise, the Africanists and the Americanists exposed their quasi-academic pedigrees by distinguishing themselves in relation to each other and their perceived attitudinal differences rather than through their relationships with constituencies in the poor, predominantly Afro-Brazilian communities of Rio de Janeiro. Black Soul, although a more popular manifestation of identity politics and cultural articulation, never really left the confines of the dance hall. Thus, it was both an expression of resistance and a form of commodified leisure that was ultimately appropriated for mass production, circulation, and consumption.

Yet it would be an error to regard these instances as absolute failures. As examples of politico-cultural imagination, they helped spawn the *Blocos Afros* (African blocs), the "race-first" entities that came to dominate cultural-political activities in the northeast in the 1980s. The modes of racialized consciousness that emerged from the *Africanistas* and *Americanistas,* Black Soul, and MNU revitalized various spheres of Afro-Brazilian cultural production with a racially cognitive dimension that had been erased by the process of deracination that occurs in the transformation of racial or ethnic symbols into national symbols in Brazilian society.

Thus, although these movements had their shortcomings, each represented significant advances from previous generations of Afro-Brazilian activism, which relied heavily on the patron-clientelist matrix of traditional Brazilian politics for individual favors and advancements. At the same time, however, the fetishization of cultural artifacts and expressions, which characterized previous generations of Afro-Brazilianists at varying points on both racial and ideological continuums, was reproduced in both the national and international tiers of Afro-Brazilian racial consciousness in the 1970s.

This is most evident in the Black Soul and Africanist-Americanist phenomena, where Afro-Brazilians internalized the symbolic aspects of Afro-diaspora that were most easily translatable—the artistic and ideological expression by blacks of the New World and of Africa. The practical dimensions of this expression, those of community and politics, were largely ignored. More important, there were no Afro-Brazilian versions of boycotting, sit-ins, civil disobedience, and armed struggle in their stead.

The absence of these forms of struggle in the Brazilian context highlights the culturalist tendencies of the *movimento negro* of the 1970s and indeed the 1980s as well. The extraction of artifacts and expressions from outside social and cultural totalities is not unique to Brazilian racial politics or Afro-Brazilians. Almost any interaction between individuals or social groups from distinct collectivities will entail such activity in one form or another on a continual basis. Yet norms, values, and practices for political ends that are distinct from the dominant social order in which they are encased must be part of entire social processes—at once ideological, cultural, and material—in order to have coherence.

Perhaps this partially explains the contradiction between Black Soul and Africanist-Americanist nationalization of the transnational rhetoric and symbolism of the Afro-diaspora and the inability to nationalize organized resistance based on Afro-Brazilian mobilization and concerns in Rio de Janeiro, São Paulo, Salvador, or Bahia. Although the movement had the ideational space to incorporate discourses of Negritude, Pan-Africanism, or Black Power, it did not have the practical space to accommodate forms of "peopled resistance"—the historical moments of rebellion and revolution from which such artifacts and expressions came. It could be said, then, that these appropriated discourses were bled of their historical content and functioned as myth rather than history at a general level of Afro-Brazilian political thought and activism.

Once the historical content was bled, the presence and prospect of struggle in the Afro-diaspora and in Brazil itself vanished. A gap existed between the circulating products of cultural and political production, whether indigenous to Brazil or not, and the processes of cultural and political activity peculiar to the movement itself. Several São Paulo activists interviewed in the 1980s perversely lamented that although numerous Afro-Brazilians had died from malnutrition, violence, and police brutality, not one had died in the name of the *movimento negro*.

This leads directly into what I consider to be the most significant tension for Afro-Brazilian movements from the 1970s to the present—the tension between forms of struggle and meanings of struggle and the need for activists to distinguish one from the other. This is not, as some may conclude, an ex-

cessively formalist exercise but one that is inextricably bound to the conceptualization of practical activity within the *movimento.* Admittedly, social
movements are replete with narratives and signification—those generated by
movements as well as those attributed to them. In this sense, the relationship
is indivisible. Yet on another level, which I relate shortly, they can be distinguished.

The residual effects of the U.S. civil rights movement can be found not
only in contemporary U.S. racial politics but in the feminist and gay rights
movements as well. Civil disobedience and songs such as "We Shall Overcome" are just two of numerous echoes from a previous era of black activism
that resonate within other, more recent paradigms of political struggles involving subordinate groups. The songs from that era have reappeared in
everything from angry "rap" songs conveying recalcitrance to television advertisements hawking leisure, teenage sexuality, and the awakening of the
U.S. libido.

South African apartheid has often appeared in dramatic form for foreign
consumption. The film *Cry Freedom* and plays such as *Sarafina!* and *Master
Harold and the Boys* represent very palatable depictions of a situation that for
many remains unpalatable.

All these permutations suggest and share with the culturalist tendencies of
Afro-Brazilian activists the fact that *all* forms of expression, along with the
meanings first attributed to them, can be appropriated and rearticulated by
either dominant or subordinate groups. Thus, it was no accident that Black
Soul was both a moment of racial identification and a conversion of Afro-
diasporic expression into commodified leisure. In each national context, there
appears to be a correlation between the degree of popularity and socialization
of a creative practice peculiar to a subordinate racial group and the likelihood
that this practice will be repressed or rearticulated by the dominant racial
group. In national contexts where the most powerful members of a dominant
racial group seek to lead as well as to rule, the process of rearticulation is crucial to the maintenance of racial hegemony—whether to present alternative
or insurgent practices as things to be accommodated or conversely as figures
to be worn down. In both scenarios such practices must be managed and
dealt with.

What resists rearticulation is social struggle encapsulated in movement, in
the sense that movements can be interpreted in innumerable ways but cannot
be reproduced in the same way in which they first appeared. Attempts at either reviving preexisting political practices or retrieving them through histori-

ography entail reliving those practices, which for both historiographers and common folk is an impossibility.

Objects, gestures, and antics from one era can be glorified or caricatured in another and re-presented in subsequent eras as a history writ large. Such activities, however, are based on norms and intentions steeped in the present. They can never alter what occurred in the past but can only change the meanings attributed to it. Meanings of the past become politically viable only when they intervene in debates and practices rooted in the continuous present. This type of intervention, so crucial for subaltern historiographers who want to affect the politics of their own era, has been undertaken by Afro-Brazilian activists with only limited success.

In Brazil, South Africa, and the United States, intellectuals of subaltern groups have utilized history—in one form or another—to contest the fragmented rearticulations of the dominant group that are presented as whole. Steven Biko had to die before a movie such as *Cry Freedom* could be made about Donald Woods; yet the film does not alter his death. In the chapter on Northern Ireland in this volume, Begoña Aretxaga observes how the meanings, both derogatory and laudatory, derived from the death of Bobby Sands are not the same as his actual demise. His death amid the nationalist struggle of Northern Ireland provided the basis for debate over his death's meaning.

The distinction between meanings attributed to social struggle and meaning enveloped by social struggle is consequential for the *movimento*. The internally and externally produced meanings interpreted and circulated by Afro-Brazilian militants cannot supplant *praxis,* no matter how much they allude to, talk about, commiserate with, and reminisce about social struggles in Brazil or elsewhere. Language and signification are indissoluble elements of cultural and material life; yet unless they are bound up with nondiscursive practices, they are politically self-limiting. It is from this necessary distinction that practical activity within as well as comparative analysis of Afro-diasporic social movements may begin.

CONCLUSION

This chapter sought to provide an overview of three moments in the history of Afro-Brazilian social movements in Rio de Janeiro and São Paulo in the 1970s. In doing so, I highlighted the culturalist tendencies of the *movimento negro* and subsequently distinguished culturalism as a social practice from the ethico-political activities of cultural politics. In conclusion, I turn to this chapter's second purpose and use the three moments analyzed to emphasize the necessity of reconceptualizing culture and racial politics within the discipline of political science.

The term and field known as political culture has left an ambiguous mark on political science in the United States. Although the works of Gabriel Almond and Sidney Verba, Edward Banfield, Mary Douglas and Aaron Wildavsky, and others have made the discussion of norms, motivations, and values fairly commonplace within the discipline, the very notion of what constitutes culture and its importance in understanding power relations among individuals and groups in a given polity has been greatly simplified.

As has been noted elsewhere, the corpus of political culture literature has defined culture as either dependent or independent variables: "subjective" dimensions of politics and power relations that only clouded social realities or, as in *The Civic Culture,* an ill-defined, nebulous sphere of social interaction that democratic polities had and antidemocratic polities lacked. Philippe Schmitter (1974) has referred to these uses of culture as a "spigot variable," one to be turned on and off whenever first- or second-order explanations of political processes proved unsatisfactory. The term *culture* therefore carried with it a pejorative connotation whereby it was used as an explanation for phenomena that could not be explained otherwise.

It is hoped that this chapter has contributed to the consideration of culture, conceptually and historically, as a social and interactive process. Similarly, racial difference and its political repercussions reflect deeply social processes that unfold and change over historical time. For Afro-Brazilians and their "brethren" and "sistren" of an Afro-diaspora, the intersection of these processes undergirds the formulation of racial consciousness, politics, and social movements that seek to affect change.

NOTES

This research was supported by the MacArthur Foundation. Special thanks to Kay Warren, Henry Bienen, and Begoña Aretxaga for discussions of these issues.

1. Pedro Wilson Guimaraes, a PT intellectual and *militante,* stated this during a question-and-answer session of the Brazil Network organizational meeting on January 13, 1990. He was questioned on this point by the author and by a black woman activist, Joselina da Silva, from Rio de Janeiro, and repeated his position in Portuguese, thereby refuting the claim made by one organization member that the meaning of Guimaraes's comments was lost in the subtleties of translation.

2. Residual, as employed here, alludes to Raymond Williams's (1977) explication of a cultural form that lies embedded in dominant cultural practices.

3. For a discussion of racial consciousness and the transnational features of Afro-diasporic experiences, see Michael Hanchard (1991).

4. For an account of the early days of SINBA, IPCN, and other happenings of the black movement in the early 1970s, see Lelia Gonzalez and Carlos Hasenbalg (1982).

5. Interview with Yedo Ferreira, Rio de Janeiro, 1989.

6. Both Carlos Alberto Medeiros (Americanist) and Togo Ioruba (Africanist) stated during interviews that the ethnocentrism of SINBA diminished their interest in the group.

7. Yedo Ferreira interview.

8. Interview with "Filo," Rio de Janeiro, September 22, 1989.

9. Lena Frias provided the first extensive media coverage of the Black Soul phenomenon in *Jornal do Brasil,* July 17, 1976, in an article entitled "O Orgulho (Importado) de Ser Negro No Brasil."

10. Pedro de Toledo Pizza, then-secretary of tourism, quoted in "Turismo ve so comercio no Black Rio," *Jornal do Brasil* (Rio de Janeiro), May 15, 1977.

11. Julio Medaglia, quoted in Antonieta Santos, " 'Black Rio' assusta maestro Julio Medaglia," *Folha de São Paulo,* June 10, 1977.

12. Gilberto Freyre, "Atenção Brasileiros," *Diario de Pernambuco* (Recife), May 15, 1977: "Opinião" section, A-13.

13. Interview with NIS official (name withheld), Rio de Janeiro, November 5, 1989. Although both Filo and Mr. Funk stated during their interviews that they never experienced or knew of overt actions taken by the military (shutting down parties, for example), Filo alleged he was kidnapped for several hours in Rio de Janeiro by several men who first placed a hood over his head so he could not identify anyone. While being held against his will, Filo stated he was asked several times to explain why the Central Intelligence Agency (CIA) had given him $1 million to create the Black Soul movement in Brazil. Although this may appear farfetched on first reading, it is useful to remember that scare tactics such as these were used by the military during this period. The alleged kidnapping could also have been done by others interested in Black Soul's demise.

14. Monsieur Lima, quoted in "O Soul, Do Grito Negro a Caderneta de Poupanca," *Jornal do Brasil,* Caderno B (Rio de Janeiro), August 3, 1976.

15. In *O Mundo Funk Carioca,* an anthropological study of the funk music and dance phenomena in Rio de Janeiro, Hermano Vianna (1988) notes the nonpoliticized nature of the Funk craze in contrast to Black Soul as well as the noted absence of criminality during Funk and Black Soul eras.

16. For a more detailed account of the formation and evolution of various black organizations, including MNU, see Gonzalez and Hasenbalg (1982). For more specific material on MNU, see Movimento Negro Unificado (1988).

BIBLIOGRAPHY

Archdiocese of São Paulo (Brazil) Catholic church. *Torture in Brazil.* New York: Vintage Books, 1988.

Bick, Mario, and Diana DeG. Brown. "Religion, Class and Context: Continuities and Discontinuities in Brazilian Umbanda." *American Ethnologist* 14, no. 1 (February 1987): 73–93.

Brown, Diana DeG. "Umbanda and Class Relations in Brazil." In Maxine Margolis and William E. Carter, eds., *Brazil: Anthropological Perspectives, Essays in Honor of Charles Wagley.* New York: Columbia University Press, 1979, 270–304.

Fontaine, Pierre-Michel, ed. *Race, Class and Power in Brazil.* Los Angeles: Center for Afro-American Studies, UCLA, 1985.

Freyre, Gilberto. *The Masters and the Slaves.* New York: Alfred A. Knopf, 1946.

Fry, Peter. *Para Ingles Ver.* Rio de Janeiro: Zahar, 1982.

Gilroy, Paul. *There Ain't No Black in the Union Jack.* London: Hutchinson, 1987.

Gonzalez, Lelia, and Carlos Hasenbalg. *Lugar do Negro.* Rio de Janiero: Editora Marco Zero Limitida, 1982.

Gramsci, Antonio. *Selections from the Prison Notebooks of Antonio Gramsci,* Quintin Hoare and Geoffrey Nowell-Smith, eds. New York: International Publishers, 1971.

Hanchard, Michael. "Racial Consciousness and Afro-diasporic Experiences: Antonio Gramsci Reconsidered." *Socialism and Democracy* edition no. 14, vol. 7, no. 3 (Fall 1991): 83–106.

Hasenbalg, Carlos. *Discriminação e Desiqualdades Raciais no Brasil.* Rio de Janeiro: Graal, 1979.

Hasenbalg, Carlos, and Nelson do Valle Silva. *Estructura Social, Mobilidade e Raça.* São Paulo: Vertice e IUPERJ, 1988.

Levine, Robert M. *The Vargas Regime: The Critical Years, 1934–1938.* New York: Columbia University Press, 1970.

_____ . "The First Afro-Brazilian Conference: Opportunities for the Study of Race in the Brazilian Northeast." *Race* 2, no. 15 (1973): 185–193.

Lovell, Peggy. "Development and Racial Inequality in Brazil: Wage Discrimination in Urban Labor Markets, 1960–1980." Presented at *The Peopling of the Americas Conference,* Veracruz, Mexico, May 1991. Mimeographed.

Mitchell, Michael. "Racial Consciousness and the Political Attitudes and Behavior of Blacks in São Paulo, Brazil." Ann Arbor: University Microfilms, University of Michigan, 1977.

Moore, Barrington. *The Social Origins of Dictatorship and Democracy.* Boston: Beacon Press, 1966.

Movimento Negro Unificado. *1978–1988 10 Anos de Luta Contra o Racismo.* São Paulo: Movimento Negro Unificado—Seção Bahia, 1988.

Oxaal, Ivar. *Black Intellectuals and the Dilemma of Race and Class in Trinidad.* Cambridge, Mass.: Schenkman, 1982.

Pierce, Robert. *Keeping the Flame: Media and Government in Latin America.* New York: Communication Art Books, 1979.

Piven, Frances Fox, and Richard A. Cloward. *Poor Peoples Movements.* New York: Pantheon, 1977.

Rodrigues da Silva, Carlos Benedito. "Black Soul: Aglutinação Espontanea ou Identidade Etnica." In Luiz Antonio Machado da Silva, *Movimentos Sociais, Urbanos, Minorias Etnicas e Outros Estudos.* Brasilia: Associação Nacional de Pos-Graduação e Pesquisa em Ciencias Sociais, 1983, 245–262.

Ryan, Selwyn D. *Race and Nationalism in Trinidad and Tobago.* Toronto: University of Toronto Press, 1972.

Schmitter, Philippe. "Still the Century of Corporatism?" In Frederick B. Pike and Thomas Strich, eds., *The New Corporatism: Social Political Structures in the Iberian World.* Notre Dame: Notre Dame Press, 1974, 85–131.

Schwarcz, Lilia Moritz. *Retrato em Branco e Negro: Jornais Escravos e Cidadoes em São Paulo no Final do Seculo XIX.* São Paulo: Companhia das Letras, 1987.

Vianna, Hermano. *O Mundo Funk Carioca.* Rio de Janeiro: Jorge Zahar Editor, 1988.

Williams, Raymond. *Marxism and Literature.* New York: Oxford University Press, 1977.

Wolf, Eric. *Peasant Wars of the Twentieth Century.* New York: Harper and Row, 1968.

3 Politics of Identity in a Palestinian Village in Israel

DAVIDA WOOD

For most people in the United States, and even for many Israelis, the term *Palestinians* refers to the inhabitants of the West Bank and the Gaza Strip, to refugees in Lebanon, and to those displaced by wars who have found homes in other parts of the world—the Palestinian diaspora. Ironically, until very recently the people who managed to remain on their land in the part of Palestine that became Israel (see Fig. 3.1) have not been thought of as Palestinians but as "Israel's Arab citizens" or "Israeli Arabs." When Israel was established in 1948, approximately 156,000 Palestinian Arabs found themselves within the borders of the Jewish state and for the next eighteen years were controlled by a military administration. Although they were granted citizenship and the right to vote in national elections, in the eyes of the state the status of Israel's Arab citizens has been contradictory. The status of citizen implies a shared political identity with the Jewish majority: Israeli identity. It also assumes a basic loyalty to the state. By this logic, the differences between Jewish and Arab Israelis must be ethnic or religious but not national—that is, differences that can be contained within the existing political framework. Thus, just as Palestine ceased to exist in 1948, so the Israeli Arabs were legally severed from any political identification that had been meaningful prior to that date. As a group, however, these citizens were viewed as potential enemies of the state. Even after the military administration was officially dismantled in 1966, Israeli domestic intelligence continued intensive surveillance in the Arab sector. Despite official equality with fellow Jewish citizens, an extensive range of jobs was closed to Arabs for security reasons. Because of anticipated conflicting loyalties, Arabs were exempted from army service. Rather than integrating the Arab sector into national structures, special Arab departments were created in each government ministry. Although Arabs were allowed to vote, political movements or parties that advocated a secular state (as opposed to a Jewish state) were quickly suppressed.[1]

88

Figure 3.1
MAP OF ISRAEL SHOWING CONCENTRATION OF
ARAB VILLAGES IN THE GALILEE

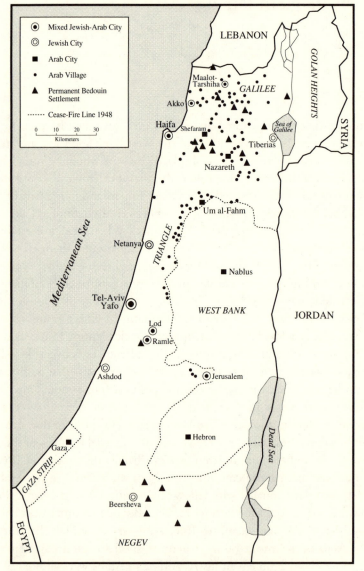

Adapted and reprinted from Joseph Ginat, *Blood Disputes Among Bedouin and Rural Arabs in Israel* by permission of the University of Pittsburgh Press. Pittsburgh: University of Pittsburgh Press, 1987.

"LOCAL CULTURE," STATE CONTROL, AND THE POLITICS OF IDENTITY

In this context, the state definition of Israeli Arabs as an ethnic minority is part of a discourse that makes possible statements such as the following:

> The Arab minority (whether Muslim or Christian) had no distinct cultural Israeli or even Palestinian identity, except on the local, traditional level which had survived through centuries of conquest (S. N. Eisenstadt, quoted in Asad 1975: 281).

From the point of view of the state, the construction of *local tradition* defined not only the cultural identity but also the newly invented political identity of Israeli Arabs. Cultural differences and especially political systems associated with cultural otherness were the rationale behind the distancing of Israeli Arabs from a national identity, be it Israeli or Palestinian.[2] The first local councils set up in the villages were appointed by the military administration, continuing the Ottoman and British policies of appointing local governments from above. In 1946, however, only twenty-four Arab villages had local councils. [3] After Israel was established, the Ministry of the Interior introduced a program to extend the institution of village councils. Yet despite the stated modernization goals of the program, council members were appointed with the aim of representing each traditional unit of social organization[4]—that is, in villages in which two or more religious groups resided (e.g., Muslim, Christians of various denominations, Druze), representation followed sectarian lines; in religiously homogenous villages, council members were appointed as representatives of 'patrilineal clans,'[5] or *ḥamūlas*.[6] As Talal Asad (1975: 274) has argued:

> The *ḥamūla* of Israeli Arabs was the ideological resolution of a Zionist problem—for it constituted a mode of control and an imputed identity for the only political existence allowed to Arab villagers in Israel.

On the national level, no Zionist political parties included Arabs as full members or as candidates on their main election lists.[7] If Arab candidates were listed at all, it was on separate minorities lists whose members were recruited into patron-client relationships on the basis of their regional, religious, and kin support. In other words, the lists were not organized on the basis of a political program but on the assumption that they would bring in the Arab vote based on *ḥamūla* solidarity.[8]

There is, then, an intersection of political aims and the construction of ethnicity that unavoidably implicates any cultural analysis an anthropologist might produce. Beginning in the mid-1970s, a body of scholarship emerged that avoided the issue of local constructions of identity and concentrated instead on state manipulation and suppression of any form of Palestinian identification.[9] Underpinning this approach was a trenchant Marxist critique of "ethnicity" as an analytical category. By privileging ethnicity, the argument goes, one implies a cultural and political autonomy that exaggerates the ability of tradition to provide forms of resistance on the one hand and minimizes the inequality of power between the villagers and the state on the other. Rather than isolating an ethnic group as a unit of analysis, research should examine the larger structures in which such groups are embedded and that determine their mode of social organization.

Although I agree with much of this critique and regard the research on the role of the state as invaluable, such an approach ignores the fact that the categories of identity as conceived by the villagers are not necessarily congruent with those the state attempts to impose. By attributing the creation of categories of identity to the state, the legitimacy of any local constructions of identity is precluded. Nevertheless, local constructions of identity do make up an important part of the conceptual world of the people in question, shaping their experience and thus their political thought and actions; any analysis of identity must take these categories seriously. To deny that 'kinship' is significant in Palestinian political life or to claim that such categories are merely imputed by the state, is to suggest that the Israelis have been successful in completely defining the terms of consciousness for Arabs. The problem is not that the state imposes categories that have no bearing on the reality of Palestinian Arab social organization in Israel but that the state has *appropriated* these categories and has reified and frozen them in an attempt to exclude the possibility of any other form of political identification. The task of the anthropologist as I see it is to recover the dynamic character of identity (on the theoretical level) and to research the terms of the struggle for the reappropriation and construction of Palestinian identity (on the political level).

If, then, we are to have any understanding of the Palestinian struggle toward class, nationalist, or any other consciousness in the context of Palestinians' ambiguous status as Israeli Arabs, we must move the analysis to the conceptual world in which the changing constructions of identity take place.

Such an analysis must address the *multiplicity* of identities meaningful for Palestinians in Israel as well as the dynamic ways in which these identities are continually constructed and reconstructed. 'Kinship,' nationalism, and class are not categories that necessarily exclude one another, either logically or chronologically; rather, they are frames of reference that may coexist or conflict not only within the politics of a community but also within the identity of individuals.

In Palestinian Israeli society, I argue, two disparate concepts of power and political authority are intertwined. The authority of a *ḥamūla* elder, based on personal and 'family honor,' originates in a radically different discourse than the authority of a party leader, which is derived from the votes of those who support an ideological position. In practice, however, the adoption of one political discourse—that of nationalism and the political party—does not automatically exclude the continued significance of the other—that of 'honor'[10] and the *ḥamūla,* especially when the two coexist in the uneasy terrain of Western dominance. The transformation of consciousness, after all, is not a state of mind that can be induced by merely proving the existence of heretofore-unperceived structures such as nation or class. Rather, it involves shifts in the conceptualization of power and authority, shifts that can only be the outcome of political—often conflictual—processes.

A study of these processes, then, would focus not only on resistance to external domination but also on the internal political dynamics involved in the process of transformation. This chapter is an attempt to examine the meaning of being both "ethnic minority" (with local as well as state concepts of political power) and "terrorist enemy" (existing in an ungovernable space that must be dominated and controlled) for the construction of Palestinian Israeli identity. I begin by outlining the emergence of Palestinian nationalist movements in Israel on the organizational level and argue that although co-optation has become increasingly difficult, state practices of repression and infiltration have created a culture of skepticism that poses severe constraints on the ability of these bodies to develop the moral authority necessary to transform local political structures. The core of the chapter is an ethnographic example of this political culture on the local level—illustrating increasing resistance to Israeli domination, the coexistence of both the national community *and* the patriarchal *ḥamūla* as meaningful political concepts for Palestinian Israelis, and the potential for violence created by the manipulation of ambiguous identities. This analysis is based on thirteen months of fieldwork in a Palestinian village in the Galilee between December 1987 and January 1989—the first year of the *intifāḍa.*

THE TRANSFORMATION OF POLITICAL CONSCIOUSNESS: CONTINUITY, DISCONTINUITY, AND SKEPTICISM

Even as arguments were being made about why the Palestinians apparently acquiesced to becoming Israeli Arabs, there was evidence of an increasing Palestinian national consciousness. March 1976 marked a turning point in the history of the Palestinian minority's relationship to the state with the protest of the planned expropriation of land in the Galilee. Although the state had declared that the land would be used for development projects to benefit both Jews and Arabs, the Palestinians interpreted the initiative as part of the Judaization of the Galilee project, a project designed to attract more Jews to the area to balance the high percentage of Arab inhabitants. A protest strike named Land Day was called for March 30; six people were killed by the Israeli army on this day of demonstrations, which has since been commemorated in annual Land Day demonstrations.

Much of the groundwork for the protest had been laid by the Israel Communist Party (ICP),[11] which had formed the National Committee for the Defence of Arab Lands in late 1975. The Communist party has played a special role in the history of the Palestinian Israelis since 1948.[12] Shortly after the establishment of the state, the ICP went into opposition as the only anti-Zionist political party. Although recognizing the state of Israel, the party rejected its characterization as a Jewish state and thus became the principal defender of the rights of Palestinian Arabs in Israel. For years, it was the one political party to which Arabs had direct access. For this reason, a vote for the Communist party came to constitute the protest vote against governmental policy toward the minority population.

On the village level, the Communist party was again the only countrywide party to systematically nominate candidates to the local council across 'clan' lines. Yet only in the elections following Land Day did the party gain significant influence on the local councils. In this context, the party was marginalized as *ḥamūla* leaders competed for the power and prestige of council membership and for the favors first of the Military Administration and later of the various governmental departments on Arab affairs.[13] In addition, and especially in the early days of local-level organizing, fear of government retaliation was translated into a diffuse fear of association with the Communists.[14] Gradually, however, the Communist party succeeded in challenging the moral authority of these leaders, who increasingly came to be seen not as legitimate representatives but as hypocritical collaborators in a regime that sought to control and isolate the Palestinian population.

In the elections following Land Day, support for the Communists rose dramatically. Riding the crest of success, the Communist party was able to form an electoral alliance with some non-communist Arab mayors, who usually ran strictly as *ḥamūla* personalities, as well as non-communist Jewish groups (most notably the Black Panthers with its Moroccan Jewish constituency). In the 1977 national elections, this alliance—the Democratic Front for Peace and Equality (DFPE)—won an impressive 49.4 percent of the Arab vote. The DFPE is popularly known as the *Jabha,* the Arabic word for front, and I henceforth refer to it by this name.[15]

Percentage of the Arab Vote for *Rakah* (Communist Party)[16]

Year	Percent
1965	23.6
1969	29.6
1973	37.0
1977 (with the *Jabha*)	49.4

Yet some radical Palestinians opposed the coalition with the *ḥamūla*-based politicians. Also in the mid-1970s, a radical nationalist movement called Sons of the Village, or *Abna' al-Balad,* was formed. Rejecting the Israeli parliamentary framework altogether, this group sought political guidance from George Habash's Popular Front for the Liberation of Palestine (PFLP), a leftist group within the Palestinian Liberation Organization (PLO). Although it does not participate in national elections, it organizes through networks of local groups that do submit lists in elections for the local councils.

In 1984 a second party was formed that participated in national elections and fully integrated Palestinian Israelis. The Progressive List for Peace (PLP),[17] although intended to be an integrated Jewish-Arab movement, attracted mostly Palestinians and was led by a lawyer who had once been a member of Al-Arḍ—a nationalist movement that had been banned in 1964. Both the Communist party and the PLP endorsed a two-state platform (i.e., recognized Israel and agreed to a Palestinian state alongside it in the Occupied Territories), yet the PLP aligned itself with—and indeed won the endorsement of—*Fatah,* the mainstream nationalist component of the PLO headed by Yāsir 'Arafāt.[18] An alternative to the Communist party, the new party attracted many who for various reasons had not supported the Communists and had previously abstained from voting or had voted for Zionist or Zionist-sponsored lists.

Finally, the 1980s witnessed an Islamic revival as a way of expressing political and cultural identity. Whereas an older generation of religious functionaries had been easily co-opted by the Ministry of Religion and the religious parties, a younger generation of sheikhs—educated in the West Bank cities of Jerusalem, Hebron, and Bethlehem since the 1967 occupation—was more nationalistically oriented.[19] In the earlier part of the decade, the Islamic Association (*Al-Rābiṭa Al-Islāmiyya*) focused on community work and the building of mosques and kindergartens. By the 1989 elections, however, it had made significant inroads in local politics, most notably in the communist strongholds of Nazareth and Umm Al-Faḥem.

The context for these developments includes the transformation of Israeli Palestinian village society from peasant to proletarian with the more recent emergence of a small professional class (Rosenfeld 1964, 1979); the complex relationship with Jewish-Israeli society; and the Israeli occupation of the West Bank and Gaza in 1967, which reopened the issue of the relationship with the more than one million additional Palestinians now under Israeli rule (Flores 1983). Thus, notwithstanding the official categorization of Israeli Arabs as loyal citizens, by the time the *intifāḍa* (uprising) in the West Bank and the Gaza Strip began in December 1987, there was considerable concern on the part of Jewish Israelis as to who the Israeli Arabs really were. In operational terms, this translated into the question of whether this population would actively join the Palestinian uprising. News articles began to appear questioning the existence of the Green Line separating Israel from the Occupied Territories and declaring that the term Israeli Arab had become totally meaningless.[20] Depending on the politics of the writer, this could either mean a recognition of the Palestinian identity as Israeli Arabs or a warning of the dangers posed by an alien population within the borders of the state.

As it turned out, support for the *intifāḍa* remained limited mostly to legal demonstrations, solidarity strikes, and food and financial support drives. But within this context of legal protest, the Labor Party's Arab Knesset member—'Abd Al-Wahab Darāwsha—resigned in January 1988 because of that party's repressive response to the *intifāḍa*. The new Arab Democratic Party (ADP) that he formed was the first all-Arab political party that had been allowed to exist since 1948.

Despite the initial acquiescence to being defined as an Israeli ethnic minority, then, Palestinian identity in Israel has been shaped not only through

state policy and the actions of the dominant parties but also through its reinterpretation by the Palestinians themselves. But if the state has not been om-
nipotent, neither have the Palestinians had complete autonomy in shaping
their political identity; indeed, repression and infiltration have had profound
implications not only for freedom of organization but also for the moral authority that might serve as a basis for the transformation of political structures. Although I have narrated these developments as if they reflect a linear
strengthening of nationalist organization, other interpretations contest the
authenticity of these parties and movements, arguing that they simply represent more sophisticated forms of collaboration.[21]

At the same time, although a variety of movements and organizations articulating a nationalist consciousness have come into being, *ḥamūlas* have
continued to have political relevance. Indeed, as local personalities have become members of actual political parties rather than minority lists, *ḥamūla*
and party politics have become interwoven in even more complex and subtle
ways. If an argument could have once been made that *ḥamūla* politics dominated the local elections whereas individual interest was more likely to direct
support in the national elections, this distinction is now difficult to make.

In analyzing the origin and spread of nationalism, Benedict Anderson
(1983: 33) borrows Foucault's concept of "discontinuity of consciousness" in
order to describe the advent of a new style of imagining community. For Anderson, the distinguishing characteristic marking the break is that whereas social ties were once imagined particularistically—"as indefinitely stretchable
nets of kinship and clientship"—the only link among members of the national community is their common embeddedness in an abstract "society."
Whereas the fundamental conceptions about social groups were once hierarchical, the decline of the religious community and the dynastic realm in
Western Europe made it possible to conceive of a fraternal society of equals.
Thus, "regardless of the actual inequality and exploitation that may prevail in
each, the nation is always conceived as a deep horizontal comradeship"
(1983: 16). Further, one of Anderson's central theses is that the concept of
the nation is a "modular" one; that is to say that although specific historical
circumstances facilitated this style of imagining, once conceived, the concept
of the nation was capable of being transplanted to all societies—thus precipi-
tating the above-mentioned abrupt "discontinuity of consciousness."

This argument, however, fails to address the putative decline of concepts
of hierarchical political authority in the societies to which the national model
is transplanted. Do all other concepts of political authority simply lose their
grip once nationalism appears, regardless of the power relations specific to

each circumstance?[22] Is this "decline" uniform through all sectors of society and in all contexts? If not, what are the implications for political transformation? In other words, does the ability to imagine a horizontally linked society necessarily imply the exclusion of other concepts of power and authority? What I am questioning, then, is how enlightening it is to use Foucault's concept of discontinuity to talk about the transformation of discourses of power in colonial and postcolonial contexts.

The context of colonialism represents a distinct case in that under colonialism, the discourse of nationalism is imposed—that is, it is perhaps the only discourse that can be adopted in order to legitimize claims for independence. Nevertheless, despite the articulation of a plurality of Western secular ideologies in the course of liberation struggles, local concepts of authority have in fact continued to play an important role in informing the polities of postcolonial nation-states.

In my view, Anderson's tendency to privilege the concept of the egalitarian nation as the contemporary "fundamental conception" of the social group is misleading. In studying political and cultural transformations of both Western and non-Western societies, we need to examine the *interaction* between horizontal and hierarchical concepts of authority.

In the Israeli Palestinian case, *ḥamūla* 'honor' and nationalist ideology are simultaneously significant and are manipulated by a range of actors that include local Palestinian activists of a variety of political persuasions as well as Israeli intelligence officers. Rather than being characterized simply as a single, clean break, shifts in discourses of power are processes that must also be studied for conceptual continuities and the skepticism with which claims to a new basis of authority may be greeted.

AN ETHNOGRAPHIC EXAMPLE:
PARTY, *ḤAMŪLA,* 'HONOR,' AND
COLLABORATION IN THE VILLAGE OF ANJAD

The Israel Communist party, then, has been portrayed in the literature as the spearhead of Palestinian nationalism in Israel. Ostensibly, to vote for the Communist party meant recognition of an identity transcending that of the *ḥamūla,*—that is, a national identity. It was to study this Palestinian national consciousness that I chose the village of Anjad,[23] which had a long history of Communist-organized resistance and which was popularly known as Red Anjad.

This section has three parts. The first is an overview of the history of village politics since 1948 from the perspective of local Communist and *Jabha* supporters. The second part is a study of the internal politics of a particular *ḥamūla*, in which the interweaving of the political cultures of the 'clan' and party is described. The third part examines some of the ways in which the respective logics of these political cultures are manipulated by local actors to make sense of the unfolding of village politics in a context of skepticism of claims to authority.

Village Politics: The Party Line

Located in the Lower Galilee, in 1985 the population of Anjad was 10,600 and was predominantly Muslim. As with most Palestinian villages in Israel, since 1948 its economic base has been transformed from agricultural self-sufficiency to wage labor in nearby cities.

Before 1948, the main social cleavages were along *ḥamūla* lines, with the two most powerful *ḥamūlas*—the Yasārs and the Kuttabs—vying for control of the village. In the 1950s, the Communists' first battles to eradicate the significance of the *ḥamūla* in local politics were waged against the *mukhtārs*,[24] or 'headmen,' of these *ḥamūlas*, who sought to maintain their position through the cultivation of patron-client relationships with the Israeli authorities. A Communist man in his forties, whose father had been a contemporary of the *mukhtārs* of that time, described the situation to me in the following terms:[25]

Fawzi Yasār was the stick in the hands of the authorities. Especially after the occupation, he was extremely unhelpful in mediating the relationship between the authorities and the villagers. At that time, people needed permits to travel outside of the village, and he would delay granting these until he had extorted as much as he possibly could from the poor people. These he would term "gifts." And if a villager was too poor to present the *mukhtār* with anything at all, the *mukhtār* would agree to having his wife come and serve his own wife, scrubbing and cleaning for his household. And so it was with any sort of permit or official paper the peasants required. Even before the Israelis, in the time of the British, Fawzi Yasār would often refuse to give the tenant farmers their due. The Kuttab *mukhtār* would go as far as extorting peasants' land. [Here his mother, a woman in her eighties, added that the *mukhtār* in the time of the Turks would search out young men who were hiding in order to escape conscription into the army.] Fawzi Yasār would also denounce people, including his best friends—one of whom was my father—for having illegal goods, such as tobacco or arms. So although he was superficially a generous man, this was all to serve his own interest so people would admire him despite his oppressive behavior toward them. So with the *mukhtār* collaborating with the authorities, what was left was the Communist party.

Abū Ibrāhīm, one of the first to join the party in Anjad, put it this way:

> With the establishment of the Communist Youth, the confrontations began to increase between us and those we would call "the authority's men" or "the authority's collaborators," which made up the leadership of the *mukhtār*. . . . The Communists in that period, through their journalism and their meetings and the lectures they would offer, through all these things and their daily social relationships with the people, wanted to preserve the national identity of the Arab people inside the country; and it is clear that it earned them the respect, it earned them the trust of the people. That is why the situation started to change after that. Those who cooperated with the authorities began to be ashamed of themselves, and it stopped being how it was—that they were proud or would show off, that they were of the authority's men. At that stage they began to be isolated, and this group became limited, despised among the people for collaborating with the authorities.

The first local council in Anjad was appointed by the Israeli government in 1964. 'Abdallah Yasār—Fawzi Yasār's successor—was named head of the council, and each *ḥamūla* was represented by a council member regardless of its local power. Subsequent councils were to be elected. When the first election was held in 1968, the Communists tried to build a coalition to run against the slates nominated by the *ḥamūlas* (the family lists). In this period, then, in the context of an election in which all the *ḥamūlas*—not only the most powerful—would participate, the opposition was deflected from the *mukhtār* to the family lists, which in turn were linked to the Zionist parties through patron-client relations. The Communists thus called for the creation of a local front that would run against the family lists. In that election and in the one that followed, the front won two of the nine council seats, and the family lists won one each of the remaining seven. However, according to the villagers, it was difficult to recruit candidates who were prepared to run purely on the basis of the political platform of the party and not to exploit their position in the Communist party in order to consolidate their personal status within their *ḥamūlas*.[26] Nevertheless, the Communists gradually began to have a greater impact on local politics. Abū Ibrāhīm elaborated:

> Today, the situation is beginning to change. Before, in those first and second elections, you would find only the Communist people who were really conscious of their role and their responsibility prepared to stand up to the families

from within. Me, for example: My brother ran on a family list, and I was in a confrontation and struggle with him. I refused to vote for my brother because he hadn't reached the same conclusion about the unity of the people in the framework of the front, and therefore I worked against that list that was led by my brother. Today the people have begun to see as a result of a special situation that is now developing, and you will find many whose *ibn 'amm* or *ibn khāl*[27] or I don't know which relative takes one approach [to politics] and he takes another. That is, in one way or another, the front and the party played a role in order to separate politics so it would not be on a family basis. . . . [The front] tries to implant in the souls of the youth and the people in general the basic and genuine thing—that is, the labor problem, the peasant problem, the problem of the teachers, the problem of the students, and also the problem of our people, the Palestinian problem, and the right to self-determination of the Palestinian Arab people.

Communist supporters in the village thus paralleled the academic portrayal of the Communist party as the key proponent of Palestinian national identity in opposition to 'clan' politics. Yet I found a number of problems with this formulation: First, *ḥamūla* and national identities were not so diametrically opposed as they appear to be when used as analytical categories. In the case of Anjad, the Communist party did enjoy a massive increase in support after 1976, but this support came in the form of an alliance with the Yasārs, one of the largest *ḥamūlas* in the village—the same *ḥamūla* that had provided generations of *mukhtārs*. Despite the importance of Land Day as a pivotal event, Palestinian consciousness in Anjad clearly was not born overnight as a result of the Land Day incident but had existed before and was not unproblematic afterward. The candidate of the Yasār *ḥamūla*, Abū 'Isām, had run for the council on a family list in previous elections;[28] yet in the elections after Land Day, he joined the Democratic Front for Peace and Equality (the *Jabha*)—the Communist-dominated alliance that became a nationwide coalition party in 1978. On the local level, Abū 'Isām was placed as the first candidate on the *Jabha* list. At the time of my fieldwork in 1988, which was another election year, he had been the head of the council for twelve years. When I interviewed him about his political career, he was very candid about the fact that he had been approached by the Communists before 1978 but had refused them because he had no need of a coalition and in fact stood to lose *ḥamūla* votes through such an association. Only after Land Day, with the increased popular support for the Communist party, did he think the *ḥamūla* would support this decision.

Thus, the following apparent paradox presents itself: Although there is a heightened nationalism, this nationalism is channeled *through* the *ḥamūla*. I think it is significant that the Yasārs did not vote independently for the Communists; rather, they voted for their own candidate and the *Jabha* simultaneously. I want to examine this issue of holding *ḥamūla* and nationalist consciousness simultaneously—and the different concepts of power and the person they imply—more closely by looking at the internal dynamics of particular *ḥamūla:* the Nasīm *ḥamūla.*

Internal Ḥamūla *Politics*

In 1988 both the *Jabha* and the Progressive List for Peace were functioning in Anjad. Also operating in the village was the Sons of the Village Movement, or *Abna' al-Balad.* This group had some support in Anjad but not enough to win a seat on the local council. Another political force was the Islamic Association, which in 1988 had little influence in Anjad and did not even attempt to win a council seat.

All of the major political forces in the village—the *Jabha,* the PLP, and *Abna' al-Balad*—were represented in the Nasīm *ḥamūla.* Furthermore, this *ḥamūla,* although not one of the largest, had produced leading figures in each of these groups: Fu'ād Nasīm was a high-ranking party official in the local Communist party branch and was a prominent member of the countrywide Committee for the Defense of Arab Lands; Abū Muṣṭafa Nasīm, one of the most educated men in the village, was a leading member of the local branch of the Progressive List for Peace; Yiḥye Nasīm was one of the leaders of the local *Abna' al-Balad.*

The extended family with which I lived was very strongly Communist or, if not card-carrying members, supported the *Jabha.* At first, the fact that the *ḥamūla* did not vote as a unit was presented to me purely in terms of differences in ideological conviction and as evidence that the *ḥamūla* was rapidly disintegrating as a significant idiom of political organization. As far as the Jabhawi Nasīms were concerned, the PLP had been created by the state for the sole purpose of destroying the *Jabha* by posturing as a nationalist party. On the national level, evidence for this belief lay in the Koenig memorandum that was leaked to the press in September 1976, six months after the Land Day confrontation. In this memorandum, the district commissioner of the Ministry of the Interior for the Galilee, Israel Koenig, referred with alarm to the increasing mass support for the Communist party and proposed, among other measures, the creation of a new political force in the Arab sector that the government would "control" by means of a "covert presence."[29] On the local level, evidence for the fraudulent nature of the PLP lay in the moral character of its supporters, many of whom, they argued, had been known collaborators before the inception of the party in 1984. Moreover, much of its support came from the large Asmar 'clan,' who, they claimed, were the most politically and socially "backward" people in the village. As for *Abna' al-Balad,* members were portrayed as violent criminals whose radical politics were irresponsible and ultimately detrimental to the national cause. This group also conspired to subvert the *Jabha* effort.

In listening to speeches at public meetings and rallies of the Communist party, both in the village meetinghouse and at the regional headquarters in Nazareth, it became apparent that the informal commentary of the Jabhawi villagers about rival political organizations approximated the party line and tactical sensibilities. On the local level, however, social relations were also bound up with a sexual politics—a dimension absent from the party rhetoric and the official explanation of factionalism. In the case of the internal politics of the Nasīms, ideological differences were not the only political differences within the *ḥamūla;* concurrent with the partisan rivalry was a 'blood feud' involving a sexual transgression, the politics of which were at once an affair of the *ḥamūla* and of the party.

At this point the cultural and political concept of 'honor' and its relationship to the *ḥamūla* needs to be introduced. For the purposes of this chapter, I deal primarily with that aspect of 'honor' that is linked to sexuality—a privileged subset of 'honor' known in Palestine as *'ard,* in Turkey as *namus,* and in Algeria as *ḥurma.* It should be understood, however, that 'honor' in its broader meaning (*sharaf*) refers to other moral values, including autonomy, bravery, and generosity. Similarly, *ḥamūla* politics cannot be reduced to or equated with sexual politics. Nevertheless, because the significances of *'ard* and *sharaf* shade into one another, I have chosen to gloss the concepts with the English word 'honor.'

The interconnectedness of sexuality and politics is not unique to Arab society or even to non-Western patriarchies. Rather, gender (like class and race) is a cultural category through which power relations are generally constructed.[30] Given this understanding, we can say that the meaning and organization of sexuality and politics are elaborated differently across cultures and societies. In the Middle East, the concept of 'honor' expresses the relationship among these categories. Yet we can be even more specific because social organization and cultural meanings are not homogeneous here either, and the meanings of 'honor' are intertwined with local political concepts.[31] Further, because of the political character of 'honor,' its meanings are challenged and contested—and are thus multiple—even within particular societies.

In Palestinian villages, the meanings of 'honor' share much with those of other Middle Eastern societies, but they are shaped by the specific structure of the *ḥamūla*.[32] As in Turkish 'clans' (Meeker 1976), Egyptian Bedouin 'tribes' (Abu-Lughod 1986), and Algerian 'lineages' (Bourdieu 1977)—to cite just three examples—'honor' links the moral worth of men to the sexual behavior of the women under their charge. Because moral worth is the basis of authority, challenges to the ability of men to control female sexuality threaten their positions in the sociopolitical hierarchy. To restore 'honor' lost in this way, men must respond by showing their ability to reestablish control, which may be expressed by the threat of physical violence or even 'honor killing.' The question, then, is: Which men are obliged to respond to such challenges? Specific to *ḥamūla*, sexual politics is the continued linkage of the 'honor' of brothers (and other male natal kin) to the behavior of their sisters, even after the latter have married. The disgrace or slander of a married woman affects the 'honor' of her husband only in the sense that it disrupts the transmission of 'honor' to his sons. The 'honor' of her brothers, however, is directly affected; thus, it is they who are obliged to actively respond.

As Richard Antoun (1968) has discussed, 'honor killings' in fact occur only in highly circumscribed contexts. Sexual transgressions only threaten male 'honor' if they become public knowledge, and if at all possible, violations are concealed. Even if they become known, nonviolent solutions are preferred. These include elopement, banishment, compensation, or any combination of these. But some circumstances make these solutions difficult to resort to. These include pregnancy, the woman's prior betrothal to another man, and the high status of her natal kinsmen. To this I would add that status in the *ḥamūla* is not a static quality of an adult male. On the contrary, this is a political status that must be understood in a dynamic, historical context of local personalities building their careers, the flux of the meanings of 'honor' and *ḥamūla*, and changing broader political circumstances. It is in this historicized sense that the strategies of "challenge and riposte" (Bourdieu 1977) should be understood.[33] In the example of the Nasīms that follows, a nonviolent solution to a sexual transgression was chosen despite the publicity of the scandal, the woman's pregnancy, and her prior betrothal. The violence that ultimately ensued can only be understood as part of a historical, political process. Moreover, because of the contested nature of the 'honor killing,' it originated a 'blood feud' that became an inseparable part of the assertion and reassertion of power in village politics.[34]

Who were the non-Jabhawi Nasīms of whom my adoptive family spoke with such contempt? Because the 'feud' was conceived on one level as a *ḥamūla* issue, I first describe the structure of the *ḥamūla* (see Figure 3.2). The genealogy of the *ḥamūla*, calculated patrilineally, ultimately traces its

Figure 3.2
SIMPLIFIED KINSHIP DIAGRAM OF THE NASĪM *ḤAMŪLA*

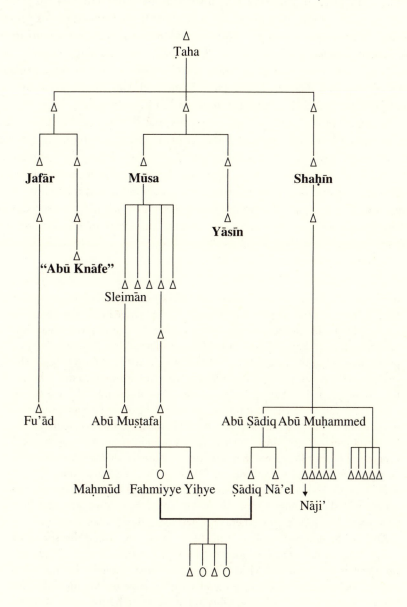

Bold names = names of 'subclans.'

roots to Omar Ibn Khatab—the second of the four rightly guided caliphs who conquered Jerusalem in A.D. 638, coming from the Arabian peninsula and bringing Islam to Palestine. The history of the Nasīms in Anjad is traced to an ancestor—Taha, son of Nasīm—who came from Transjordan six generations (about 250 years) ago.[35] The descendants of this ancestor constitute the Nasīm *ḥamūla* in Anjad today. Currently, the genealogy depicts five 'subclans,' each named for an ancestor who lived either two or three generations ago: Shahīn, Sleimān Mūsa, Jafār, Yāsīn, and Abū Knāfe. They are the great-grandfathers of the current household heads.

The origins of the 'feud' go back to approximately 1965 to a secret love affair between a Mūsa woman and a Shahīn man. The following narrative was told to me by a scholar from another *ḥamūla* in the village. His narrative is different from what I was told by the Nasīms because most of them assumed I knew the story and thus only referred to fragments of it as it related to some other issue. For the sake of clarity, I present the native scholar's interpretation before discussing the continuing relevance of the event in the lives of the Nasīms.

The following is taken from my notes.

It all started with a love affair between Nā'el's brother Ṣādiq and a woman named Fahmiyye (see Figure 3.2). Fahmiyye was engaged to a Kuttab at the time, and her relationship with Ṣādiq was a secret. Fahmiyye was from a poor, low-status family named Naṭūr in the Mūsa 'subclan.' When Fahmiyye became pregnant, she hid the pregnancy until the end. After the child was born, she confessed that it was Ṣādiq's. The child was given up for adoption in the hospital. Fahmiyye's father, having little status in the village and only two young sons, could not do much about this shame; and so he opted for Ṣādiq to marry his daughter, and Ṣādiq agreed. But Abū Muṣṭafa, the leading figure in the Sleimān branch of the Mūsa 'subclan' [and a prominent member of the local Progressive List for Peace in 1984], objected because the shame reflected on his family as well as on the protectors of Fahmiyye, who had, according to him, been 'raped.' Abū Muṣṭafa, you see, regards himself as the bearer of Arab values, including 'family honor.' So Ṣādiq 'kidnapped' Fahmiyye, and they went off to live in Nazareth, where they married and had other children.

And this became the gossip of Anjad for years—how would this shame be avenged? In the meantime, Fahmiyye's little brothers Yiḥye and Maḥmūd grew up, and Yiḥye married Abū Muṣṭafa's sister. Everybody thought that this was a strange marriage, because Yiḥye could have done better for himself. This woman was considered ugly, and Yiḥye was a successful businessman, was well liked, and could have married whomever he wanted.[36] So it seems there was more to this closing of ranks between Yiḥye and Abū Muṣṭafa. Next the two brothers approached Nā'el, Ṣādiq's brother, and demanded that he give his sister to them so they could 'rape' her as 'revenge' for the 'rape' of their own sister. The plan was for Nā'el to take her to the fields where his father had a tent and leave her there. Nā'el refused. The Shahīns were so angered that they invited Ṣādiq and Fahmiyye back to Anjad to live under their protection deliberately to provoke the Mūsa's—or, more specifically, the Sleimān Mūsa's, because Abū Muṣṭafa was seen as the behind-the-scenes director of the 'revenge.'

So Ṣādiq and Fahmiyye came back and lived in the same house where Nā'el lives to this day. This meant Fahmiyye's brothers had to find another means of 'revenge.' The solution, to kill the couple, was several years in the planning and involved the establishment of connections with Beduin working in the Israeli army, from whom the brothers purchased a bomb. This they kept for around two years, waiting for the right opportunity. And finally, one summer evening in 1974 while Ṣādiq and Fahmiyye were asleep, Maḥmūd, one of her brothers, tossed the bomb through the window. Ṣādiq was killed instantly, but Fahmiyye was only injured in the leg; miraculously, the children were not hurt. Fahmiyye was rushed to the hospital and never returned because by this time the Shahīns had had enough. They had never wanted Fahmiyye in the first place, and now that Ṣādiq was dead, the children were theirs;[37] there was no reason for Fahmiyye to return. Today she lives in Jerusalem. After the murder, the brothers were taken to court, and Yiḥye was given nine years [in jail] and Maḥmūd twenty-five.

This is not the only version of this story; other people stressed different aspects, displayed different biases, and offered additional or contradictory information. My point, however, is that both the 'rape' and the murder are acts of political violence insofar as they had a profound impact on the social order of the *ḥamūla*. In the context of Arab culture, acts that are interpreted as 'rape,' for example, include not only the coercion of individuals but also assaults on 'family honor,' which is collective. Note that the terms 'rape' and 'kidnapping' in this instance do not consider the volition of Fahmiyye herself; what is relevant to the moral order is that the sexual transgression is seen as an assault on the family and an encroachment on its sphere of autonomy in terms of authorizing the legitimacy of sexual relationships. It is in this sense that the control over sexuality is a political issue, symbolizing a domain of authority and with it, 'honor.'

The relationship between Fahmiyye and Ṣādiq was also political in the sense that it was the site of conflicting interpretations of the nature of the transgression and of appropriate responses to it. Just as 'honor killing' is not an inevitable response to illicit sexual relations, so there are no preexisting cultural solutions to be applied mechanically. On the contrary, violations of 'honor' present moral dilemmas in which the outcomes are not clear. On the political plane, violations of honor are similarly indeterminate: They are challenges to which cultural actors bring to bear what power they have to ensure that their interpretations become the defining ones. Solutions are never inevitable or predictable; they may also be temporary and are always subject to contestation and redefinition.

In the Nasīm case, there were three major areas of contestation. The first concerned the decision to opt for elopement as a solution to the scandal. Despite the fact that a reconciliation ceremony (ṣulḥa) took place and compensation money changed hands, many villagers did not recognize the peace as valid—or at least were persuaded over time that it was not. Countering the attempt to cast the relationship of Ṣādiq and Fahmiyye as a legitimate marriage was the charge—most significantly from Abū Muṣṭafa—that a 'rape' had been committed and that compensation was not sufficient to restore 'honor.'

The second contestation was a disagreement over the proposal that a brother make his sister available to be 'raped' in order to avenge a previous 'rape.' The suggestion that this might happen with the consent of a brother was considered to be insulting—so insulting that it prompted the Shahīns to risk inviting the couple back to the village despite the danger to their lives this entailed. Again, there was no consensus as to the morally appropriate course of action.

After the killing of Ṣādiq, there was another attempt at reconciliation. Once more there was disagreement over the moral value of the act of vengeance. Although the Mūsas were prepared to pay blood money and had sold land to raise the funds, they refused the second condition of reconciliation laid down by the Shahīns: that Yiḥye be banished from the village for one year in addition to the time spent in prison.[38] Negotiations for the ṣulḥa broke down, and the 'blood feud' remained unresolved.

It is at this point that it is impossible to extricate the politics of the ḥamūla from that of electoral politics. In the wake of the murder, Abū Muṣṭafa rose to political prominence at the village level as part of the major opposition to the incumbent Jabha, and for the Shahīns his career became a reflection of their own status and identity. The more political power Abū Muṣṭafa and the PLP gained, the more the 'honor' of the Jabhawi Shahīns was threatened. But as long as the Jabha remained in power, the urgency for the Shahīns to assert their strength in response to the killing of Ṣādiq was tempered.

The respective affiliations of the Shahīns and the Sleimān Mūsas before the murder are difficult to trace. Until the 1974 election, Abū Muṣṭafa was aligned with his former school friend AbuʻIsām Yasār, who, as mentioned above, at that time was running as head of a ḥamūla-oriented faction. In the 1974 election, after the murder, he first headed his own list—forming a coalition with the Asmar 'clan,' which, although large, had no strong leadership.

According to Abū Muṣṭafa, in the Nasīm ḥamūla, only Dār Jafār was Communist before the murder because of Fuʼād Jafār, who became active in the party at a very young age. After the murder, the Communists exploited the 'feud' and were able to draw in half of the Shahīns and also half of the Abū Knāfe, who are genealogically close to Dār Jafār. Yāsīn, however, which is genealogically closer to Dār Sleimān, remained loyal to Abū Muṣṭafa. Interestingly, Abū Muṣṭafa denies having been behind the murder, claiming that those Shahīns who remained with him knew he opposed it.

But the Communist Nasīms tell a different story, claiming vigorously that they were all with the Jabha from the beginning and in fact that Dār Sleimān were party supporters before Dār Shahīn were. Fuʼād Jafār, for example, recalls that in 1954, during a showdown between the old elite and the Communist party, Dār Sleimān—under the leadership of Abū Muṣṭafa's father—came to the defense of the Communists and protected them from being beaten. This interpretation of events stresses the 'kinship' priorities of Dār Sleimān, who are said to have left the party as a result of the 'feud' to rally around Abū Muṣṭafa. These 'kinship' priorities are counterposed with the ideological steadfastness of the Jabha supporters: "Those Shahīns who are currently with the party—Nāʼel and Abū Muḥammed and his brothers—were with it before and after the murder; they did not change," Fuʼād Jafār insists.

Nevertheless, concurrent with the strength of their ideological convictions, the way in which the ardent nationalism of the Jabhawi Nasīms was expressed was also necessarily constrained by the context of the 'feud.' Note that the enmity of the Shahīns became focused on the Sleimān Mūsas, even though Fahmiyye and her brothers were from a different branch of this 'subclan.' Because Abū Muṣṭafa was such a prominent personality his status became the major political threat. Thus, especially for those Shahīns closest to Sādiq, the competition between the Jabha and the PLP was also a rivalry between themselves and the Sleimān Mūsas.

Before I present a series of examples that illustrate this intersection of political consciousness, I must add one more layer of complexity. What of Fahmiyye's brothers? After serving only six years, Yiḥye was released from prison and became a leading figure in the local Abnaʼ al-Balad. This further constrained the political choices of the Shahīns in expressing Palestinian identity because Yiḥye's presence in this more radical movement precluded their allegiance to it. Thus Shahīn youth, no matter how impatient they may be with the moderate stance of the Communist party, cannot contemplate endorsing radical nationalism.[39]

Yet the situation is even more complicated because many people in Anjad suspect Yiḥye of collaboration with Shin Bet (the Hebrew initials for the Security Service, the Israeli internal intelligence). This is the case because he got out of prison early and he also came out with a pistol, which has become a common sign of collaboration because access to arms comes with a Shin Bet job. Again, collaboration with the security forces was turned back on the villagers and specifically on Yiḥye's enemy the Shahīns, a fact that became public knowledge. As for Yiḥye's brother Maḥmūd, he got out of jail after only four years, but his whereabouts are unknown. He is rumored to be working as a double agent for Syria and Israel.

I now turn to specific examples of the way in which the local 'feud' shapes the way the Shahīns identify as Palestinians. These are the experiences of the family I lived with: The father, Abū Muḥammed, is Ṣādiq's father's brother and the children are Ṣādiq's parallel cousins, which in terms of Arab 'kinship' makes them his closest relatives. The mother's natal family is in the *Jabha* side of Abū Knāfe so the affinal kin are in the same political camp.

The first incident occurred on Land Day in the early 1980s and was related to me by Nāji', one of Abū Muḥammed's sons—a young man in his twenties who is very active in the Communist party. That year a Land Day memorial rally was held in Anjad, and he was working as an organizer for the party. One of his duties was to keep the rally peaceful and particularly to make sure the Palestinian flag was not raised, an act certain to provoke a confrontation with the Israeli army. This issue of the flag raising is a hotly contested point among Palestinians who debate about how best to serve the national cause. The Communist party, committed to working within the legal structures of the state, officially argues that raising the flag is counterproductive and is constantly blaming *Abna' al-Balad* for subverting activities sponsored by the party by giving the security forces an excuse to harass its members and repress its activities. In this context, the act of raising the flag (as distinct from the flag itself) has become a symbol of who is controlling the type of statements that are being made and thus becomes an area in which the power as well as the politics of the party are challenged.

In the domain of the 'feud,' tensions had already arisen during the weeks prior to Land Day, when Nāji' had been preparing his little cousin—a daughter of the slain Ṣādiq—to recite a poem at the Communist-organized rally.

Yiḥye—who was out of prison by now—had objected to this but was power-less to prevent her participation despite being her mother's brother. Finally, on the day of the rally, all the dimensions of the conflict crystallized in a mat-ter of moments. In the midst of the ceremony, Yiḥye showed up with some others from *Abna' al-Balad*—"not to see it but to cause problems." Mean-while, also present at the rally with an ulterior motive was Nāji's paternal un-cle, Ṣādiq's father. For him, this was an opportunity for vengeance by killing Yiḥye and melting away in the crowd of fifty thousand. When Yiḥye and his friends tried to raise the flag, they were immediately attacked by some party members, and a struggle over the flag ensued.

At this point Nāji' could no longer ignore the contradiction between the dual identities of 'clan' and party. When the fight broke out, Abū Ṣādiq ex-pected Nāji' to kill his cousin's murderer. Nāji' knew this, yet the party re-quired him to avert violence and maintain a peaceful rally. Nāji's decision to be loyal to party policy and try to avoid the 'blood feud' so angered his uncle that the latter came up and struck him. For Nāji', who was nineteen at the time, this conflict of loyalties provoked an emotional crisis. It was one of the few times he has cried, and he went home and slept for two days. To this day, he and his father debate as to whether the practice of *thār* ('revenge') should continue.

Nāji' thus vehemently denies that his hatred for *Abna' al-Balad* is based on the 'feud.' However, not all the Shahīns put party loyalty above that of 'family honor,' or, more accurately, not all of them are willing to redefine the notion of 'honor' in the way encouraged by the party. This is not a generational dif-ference, a contrast between father and son, because Nāji's brothers and cousins continue to plot their 'revenge.'

The second example is from a context in which violence had quite a differ-ent meaning. As Land Day of 1988 approached, four months after the *intifāḍa* had begun, tension mounted as both Palestinians and Israelis specu-lated about whether Palestinians inside the Green Line would now join the uprising. As a symbol of the Palestinian Israelis' resistance to alienation from their land and their Palestinian identity, the annual commemoration of Land Day was always conceived as a decisive moment for how solidarity with Pales-tinians in the West Bank and Gaza would be expressed. In this atmosphere, graffiti began appearing on the walls of Anjad in support of the *intifāḍa,* and during the month of March the security forces made a series of arrests as a warning against increased involvement. The week before Land Day, the Communist newspaper *Al-Ittihād* (the Union) was closed down by the authorities and its license suspended until after the event was to take place. Talk began to circulate in the village about the possibility of the reimposition of a military government on the Arab sector.

In this situation, Nāji's brother received word that the Shin Bet were waiting for an excuse to arrest one of the Shahīns. Yiḥye had apparently decided to use the political climate to focus police attention on the Shahīns and had complained to the Security Services—by whom it was believed he was employed as an informer—that his life was in danger. This prompted a heightened anxiety within the family, and Nāji's father warned him against getting involved in clashes with the police. From this perspective, the political activity of the Shahīns was doubly constrained. Not only was the danger in their becoming more radical now increased because they were under surveillance, but their arrest would signify a victory for Yiḥye—this time not in the guise of a political activist in *Abna' al-Balad* but in his role as police informer. Just as identification with *Abna' al-Balad* would have dual significance because of Yiḥye's involvement, so their arrest would have contradictory meanings when considered in terms of national and local politics. That is to say, although being arrested might be positive as a symbol of nationalist commitment, it would be negative when seen as a triumph for one's rival in a 'clan feud' and the success of a collaborator.

The Knesset elections of November 1988 provide the arena for the third example of the interlocking of local and national politics. On the day of the election, Abū Muḥammed again became extremely anxious, pacing up and down and reminding his sons of the way their participation in party politics affected the status of the family. The issue this time was the flamboyant display of their party allegiance, decking their van with red flags and *Jabha* posters and blaring cassettes of *Jabha* songs through a megaphone as they drove around the village ferrying the older men and women to and from the polling booths. Both Abū Muḥammed and his older sister Ammt Juheina warned them against such a display until the results of the election were known. Nāji' explained that all eyes were on the Shahīns, who would have to bear the snickers of the Sleimān Mūsa's—whose neighborhood they had to pass through to get to the center of the village—if the PLP increased its support at the *Jabha's* expense. In spite of himself, Nāji' became subsumed in the concerns of his family. Once again caught in the contradictions implicit in his dual loyalties, the consequences of the possible shaming of the 'subclan' were for the moment more salient than the corresponding political loss for the party. But this was a momentary lapse because as soon as the results came out—in the *Jabha's* favor—Nāji' rushed off to celebrate the victory with his

Communist youth friends. To my remark that now the Shahīns could relax, he replied on his way out the door that he was no longer thinking about that.

Thus, the identity of the family had become wrapped up with that of the party, and the entire 'honor' of the Shahīns seemed at that moment to depend on a *Jabha* victory. In one sense, the parties had become the personal symbols of the factions, and the two idioms of political power were fused at that moment in the struggle for authority. Yet as we have seen, they were not always fused. Despite the superficial compatibility of 'clan' and party loyalties, their respective concepts of authority were based on very different principles. Just as Nāji' attempted to devalue the importance of 'family honor,' preferring to celebrate with a group of friends that seemingly cut across 'clan' lines, so his father—as the next example shows—was not always content to let the fate of the party determine his social position in the village.

The final example is taken from the elections for the local council, which were held in February 1989—three months after the Knesset election. This time the protagonists were slightly different. Abū Muṣṭafa had stepped down from the leadership of the PLP acknowledging that a personality from the Yasār *ḥamūla* might be more successful at bringing in votes. Moreover, he was not running as a candidate for a seat on the local council. As a result, the worry that Abū Muṣṭafa's party might provide the next mayor was relieved for the Shahīns. However, *Abna' al-Balad* was running a list of its own on which Yiḥye was a candidate. This provoked much bitterness among the Shahīns, particularly the young men who had to face challenges from *Abna' al-Balad* supporters. But the starkest expression of outrage came from Abū Muḥammed himself.

Up to this point, my communication with Abū Muḥammed had been rather limited. Although there was a mutual affection, our relationship was constrained by our structural differences and by his own preoccupations, including unemployment and taxes. We had had perhaps three or four extensive conversations; more often, acknowledgment of my presence came in the form of a mutter ordering me to make coffee for his guests. We had never even approached discussing as personal an issue as the 'feud.' But on this night, two days before the local elections, he initiated a different relationship. I had been to the PLP's preelection rally and returned to the house fairly late—around 10:30—a time when he would normally be asleep. But that night as I passed his *dīwān* ('guest house'), the door opened and he invited me in. As I expected, he wanted to hear about the rally, so we talked about that for a while. From there, the conversation drifted to other political issues, and I was moved by his devotion to the *Jabha*. Because he was out of work, he had

occupied himself by unofficially campaigning for this coalition, using his social connections to go from house to house not only in Anjad but in neighboring villages as well. As his face lit up with pride, I was struck again by how
the *Jabha* seemed to have become a symbol of his own identity.

At some point I got up to leave, assuming that now that he had heard my
news about the rally, staying longer would be an intrusion. But he insisted
that I stay, seeming anxious to talk more. He began telling me how optimistic
he was about the election and how he had been calculating the votes every
day, and he went into some detail about the factors he took into consideration. But after a short pause, he said, "I hope there won't be any problems on
the day of the elections." When I asked what he meant, he alluded to Yiḥye's
presence at the polling station (the way the voting system was set up, all the
Nasīms cast their ballots at the same polling station). I decided to be direct
with him:

"Do you mean because of 'the blood?' "

"So, you've understood."

I told him I had known for a long time. Then I pressed him to be more
specific about what he feared would happen if he and Yiḥye faced each other
at the polls:

"Will Yiḥye make trouble?"

"No, it might come from me."

Now Abū Muḥammed began to get extremely excited, drumming his feet
on the ground. I was faced with the dilemma of being chilled to the bone and
trying to figure out the appropriate anthropological response to the confidence that he was contemplating a murder. To me it seemed that the idea of
restoring the 'family honor' at this moment was a form of compensating for
the humiliation of his economic problems. In an effort to dissuade him from
acting out this impulse, I hesitantly told him my interpretation. He rejected it
out of hand, but a moment later he said that after the elections he might go
away.

"Where to?"

"Just go and keep going."

I was not sure if he meant this as an alternative to killing Yiḥye or if he
would leave subsequent to it, but I told him that no matter how bad things
were now, they would be much harder on his family if he left. He kept silent.
I asked if there was no work for him at the local council. He mentioned the
possibility of a job as a guard at the school.

I left shortly, both of us embarrassed after the moment of intimacy had
passed. Two days later the election took place. Although some confrontations

between rival groups did occur, there was no incident involving Abū Muḥammed and Yiḥye.

Interpretive Frameworks

Finally, the outcome of the local 1989 election is an appropriate starting point to discuss the way in which the respective logics of *ḥamūla* and party politics provide interpretive frameworks that, as on the level of praxis described above, are sometimes complementary and sometimes contradictory. It is important to stress that it is not structural rifts that are exploited by the "authorities" but rather a conceptual framework of divisiveness and betrayal that has been elaborated in the context of infiltration. Rejecting the 'clan' as a political unit would not simply mean abandoning a corporate group.[40] Rather, it would mean reinterpreting an elaborated cultural concept of 'honor' in which gender relations are used as a model to construct concepts of the person, authority, and identity.

The *Jabha* lost that election. For the first time in twelve years, the Communists would not be a part of the ruling coalition on the local council. For Nāji', for whom the epithet Red Anjad had summed up the entire being of the village, the whole world had been turned upside down. This perception was clearly one the party had fostered. Nāji' had first heard the epithet when it was used by a Communist MK (member of Knesset, the Israeli parliament), when he had visited the village during a previous election campaign. How was the party going to explain this sudden change of face?

Before the party had a chance to offer an analysis and while its leadership was still stunned, local interpretations immediately began to spring up. The dominant theory was that critical votes had been lost because the Yasārs had "betrayed" Abū 'Isām. Because the opposition had run a candidate from the same *ḥamūla,* Abū 'Isām had been unable to deliver the support of all his kinsmen. Thus, whereas for Nāji' the defeat was a blow to both his personal and national identities, for his mother it was simply a Yasār *ḥamūla* affair: "So they betrayed each other; what concern is that of ours?" Those more cynical about the party blamed the defeat on the hypocrisy of forming an alliance with a personality whose support was based on 'kinship' ties, rather than on shared ideology.

Such an analysis, however, was clearly not one with which the party could be comfortable. By the next day, the party had come up with an alternative explanation: The Shin Bet had had a hand in the elections; certain people who had previously supported the PLP but who had publicly changed their allegiance to the *Jabha* in this election had been put up to this by the Security

Services, to whom they would pass campaign information about who had been canvassed. This information would in turn be passed back to the PLP, which would quickly recanvass the same people and give them "stronger incentives." This interpretation served to mediate the contradiction between the perception of Red Anjad and the cold fact of the Progressive victory in a way that was consistent with the image of the antagonism between the nationalist Communist party and the state security: The party's official position argued that the opposition candidate had *not* drawn a significant percentage of the Yasār vote. The defeat was a result of defections that had been far more evenly spread and that had been organized by Shin Bet infiltration. In this way the issue was redefined as one of national loyalty, not factional allegiance.

For Communist party members and some of its supporters, the party line thus provides an interpretive framework with which to make sense of political events. As Nāji' explained, "We don't know what the truth is until the party tells us." But most people do not rely uncritically on the party line because it is not exempt from the charges of lying and misrepresentation.

For many villagers, including *Jabha* and Communist supporters, judgments about the political integrity of people and the parties to which they belong are bound up with terms of judgment about their 'honor,' which is closely linked to sexuality. In this way, assertions about political integrity and leadership ability were linked to a sexual idiom. Thus, for example, for those who saw Yiḥye as a collaborator, this evaluation could not be separated from their contempt for his idea of avenging his sister's 'rape' with another 'rape.'[41]

On the local level, in villages inside the Green Line, redefining the ideology of 'honor' has been problematic in the context of skepticism about the political integrity of the new leadership and in general of the people with whom one lives. There is a heavy sense of disjuncture between appearance and reality that provokes uncertainty about the ability to judge the trustworthiness of those with whom one lives, and I would suggest that one of the dominant cultural dilemmas of Palestinians in Israel is to devise paradigms with which to interpret political developments.[42]

FINAL OBSERVATIONS

In presenting this case study, I am not arguing that 'clan' politics subsume the national question—that is, that local politics are of more importance to Palestinians and therefore subvert the formation of a national consciousness. People such as Nāji' and his father are concerned with and constantly discuss issues of discrimination and land expropriation inside the Green Line, the occupation and the *intifāda* in the territories, the bombing of refugee camps in Lebanon, and the Palestinians' right to a state. The Sleimān Mūsas are no less concerned with these issues despite the fact that this concern is not expressed through participation in Communist-sponsored marches and demonstrations. In both cases, there is a deep sense of shared experience and common destiny with people to whom they are not related either through kin or faith: the Palestinian people—*al-sha'ab al-filastīnī*. The state's manipulation of *ḥamūla* cleavages thus has not resulted in the desired opposition of nationalists versus 'clan' members, in which the former are an isolated minority. Instead, the result has been the formulation of multiple ways of identifying as Palestinian.

What I *am* arguing is that local politics, in its specific idiom of 'kinship' and 'honor,' is nevertheless integral to the way one's national consciousness is constructed and articulated. Nor is this multiplicity of identities peculiar to Palestinians. More generally, to abstract the concept of nation from the matrix of categories in which it is embedded is to risk reifying it. Although Anderson's analysis of the emergence of nation as a cultural concept was pathbreaking, the challenge is to study it ethnographically as well as textually, in practice rather than as an isolated discourse. The experience of years of police surveillance and co-optation by the Shin Bet and the unresolved ambiguity about what it means to be a Palestinian in Israel have posed serious problems for the politics of nationalism. "Deep horizontal comradeship" can be imagined, certainly, but it exists in tension with 'clan' and personal rivalries, the protagonists of which are often recruited to play the dual roles of blood enemies and national traitors.

Under such circumstances, it is perhaps easy to see how a protracted confrontation with the state, such as the current *intifāda,* would be accompanied by an escalation of internalized violence. Although this chapter does not directly address the situation in the West Bank and the Gaza Strip, it may shed light on the increased number of assassinations in those areas of those suspected of collaboration with the occupation army. As Joost Hiltermann (1990) has pointed out in his excellent article, the Western and Israeli media have decontextualized this violence, recasting it as "intercommunal strife" among "Arabs."[43] But as Hiltermann documents, the "intra-fada" cannot be understood in isolation from the tactics of the military and the Shin Bet— ranging from recruitment of informers based on a knowledge of local politics to the distribution of forged leaflets—which aim to blur the identities of moral offenders, collaborators, and nationalist activists. In an attempt to counter this situation with clear lines of leadership, the Unified National

Leadership of the Uprising and the PLO issued directives forbidding the killing of any agent in the absence of a central decision. Nevertheless, to the extent that the internalized violence has spilled over from strictly nationalist assassinations to local retribution, the system has functioned to diffuse and decentralize moral and political authority.

NOTES

I would like to thank the people with whom I lived and worked in Anjad who stood by me through times of skepticism and without whom my research would not have been possible. A concern for their privacy prevents me from naming names. I would also like to thank Muslih Kanā'ane for long and patient discussions that were the source of many of the ideas in this chapter. I am especially indebted to Kay Warren, who believed in this project when it was barely formulated and who read and commented on numerous drafts. The analysis owes much to the participants in her spring 1990 seminar on Culture and Conflict, particularly Begoña Aretxaga and Clarissa Bencomo with whom I shared many inspiring moments. I also benefited from the guidance and comments of Lila Abu-Lughod, Elissa Sampson, Abdellah Hammoudi, Elias Sanbar, Joost Hiltermann, Zachary Lockman, and John Kelly, who read earlier drafts. Profuse thanks go to Pauline Caulk, who put up with my unending questions about word processing and who generated the kinship diagram. My research was funded by the Center of International Studies, which received support for a comparative project on Culture and Conflict from the MacArthur Foundation, a Princeton University scholarship, and a Fulbright Israel government scholarship.

1. See also Anton Shammas's (1988) discussion of the ambiguous nature of Israeli identity cards and the implications this has for Arab citizens.

2. At the same time Zionist discourse assumes that the Palestinian population is indistinguishable from "Arabs" in general, except for local tradition, and hence that its members could easily make their homes in any Arab country.

3. At that time there were also twenty-six municipalities—twenty-two Arab, two Jewish, and two mixed—and eleven Arab local councils (Rosenfeld and Al-Haj 1990).

4. The program for the establishment of local councils in Arab villages was introduced by the Ministry of the Interior after the establishment of the state of Israel. The target of the program was threefold: "(1) to form councils which would in the course of time, bring the level of Arab local government to the level of the Jewish and thus serve as a suitable link between the villages and the central State authorities; (2) to create tools to assist economic development, by giving the villagers a representation capable of acting in their best economic interests, negotiating loans, etc.; (3) to serve as a sort of safety valve for long-standing envy and strife as well as for the feelings of frustration caused by sudden transformation into a minority" (Landau, quoted in Nakhleh 1975: 503). See, however, Henry Rosenfeld and Majid Al-Haj (1990) for a critique of

the program, in which the authors argue that it has militated *against* the modernization of political representation, exacerbated existing differences, and instilled systematic budgetary discrimination.

5. Following Michael Meeker (1976), single quotation marks signal the use of an English term to gloss a cultural category in Palestinian society, thus underscoring the disjunction between the two discourses.

6. The Arabic plural for *ḥamūla* is *ḥamāyil*. To avoid confusing the non-Arabic-speaking reader, however, the anglicized plural will be used. The transliteration system used in this chapter is guided by that of the International Journal for Middle East Studies.

7. A partial exception to this is MAPAM (United Workers Party).

8. For more details on the use of affiliated Arab lists by Zionist parties, see Sabri Jiryis (1968: 121–127), Abner Cohen (1965: 153–157), and Ian Lustick (1980: 137–140 and 203–208).

9. The relationship between political practice and academic theory in the Palestinian-Israeli context—that is, the unconscious ideological underpinnings of scholarship—is masterfully detailed in Talal Asad's critique (1975) of Abner Cohen's *Arab Border Villages in Israel*. Early Marxist analyses include those of Henry Rosenfeld (1964a, 1964b, 1968). Perhaps the most comprehensive analysis of the state apparatus is that of the political scientist Ian Lustick (1980). Other examples of top-down anthropological and sociological analyses are those of Khalil Nakhleh (1975) and Elia Zureik (1979).

10. I discuss below the decision to use the English 'honor' rather than the Arabic terms.

11. More precisely by the New Communist List, or *Rakah* (its Hebrew acronym), which had split from the ICP in 1965 over the issue of Palestinian rights and was recognized by Moscow as *the* Communist party in Israel in 1967. For a detailed history of this split, see Sondra Miller Rubenstein (1985: Chapter 16).

12. For the origins of the Communist party in Palestine before 1948, see Musa Budeiri (1979) and Sondra Miller Rubenstein (1985).

13. Namely the Office of the Adviser to the Prime Minister on Arab Affairs and the respective Arab departments of the Labor Party, the Histadrut (the umbrella trade union), and the Ministries of the Interior and of Education. By participating in elections and the council as a 'clan' personality, a leader could gain control of campaign funds, award contracts for public works, hire and fire schoolteachers and administrators, and allocate municipal taxes. See Ian Lustick (1980: 205–206).

14. One informant, recounting attempts in the 1950s to sell the party newspaper, expressed this fear with the vivid comparison of the paper to a snake. Other villagers systematically explained misfortunes—political and otherwise—as government retribution for alliances with the Communists.

15. The full Arabic name is *Al-Jabha Al-Dimūqrātiyye Li'l-Musawā Wa'l-Salām*.

16. From Lustick (1980: 331).

17. In Arabic, *Al-Qā'ima Al-Taqadumiyya Li'l-Salām.*

18. The PLO is made up of four major political groups: *Fatah,* the Popular Front for the Liberation of Palestine, the Democratic Front for the Liberation of Palestine, and the Palestine Communist party.

19. Ironically, religious education and organizations in the Occupied Territories were encouraged at first by the Israeli government.

20. See, for example, Meron Benvenisti (1987) and David Rudge and Ken Schachter (1988).

21. Darāwsha, for example, was accused of feigning the split from the Labor party in order to recapture the Arab vote, which he would later deliver by rejoining the party. Although this interpretation was fostered by the Communist party, which was obviously threatened by the new party, many others simply could not trust a man who had worked with Labor until as late as 1988. The other parties are discussed more below.

22. In Clifford Geertz's language, does everybody simply become "religious-minded" rather than "religious"—and in all contexts, political and other? For an example of the coexistence of secular nationalism and religious images of power in the West, see Begoña Aretxaga's chapter in this volume.

23. The name "Anjad" is a pseudonym, as are all the names of individuals and 'clans' referred to in this chapter.

24. Although the term *mukhtār* is often used to refer to the traditional leader of a village, the position was in fact created by the Ottoman authorities in 1864 in order to facilitate contacts on the local level. Moreover, there was no single position of authority in the village; instead, dominant *hamūlas* controlled the village, and the leadership of these *hamūlas* had to support the appointment of the *mukhtār* in order for the system to work. Thus, in many cases there was more than one *mukhtār* per village, depending on the number of dominant *hamūlas*. The position might be held by the head of the *hamūla* himself, but as Nakhleh puts it, the *mukhtār* could also be the "lackey" of a particular kin group. In Anjad, however, the term is popularly used to refer to the head of a *hamūla.*

25. The following is a reconstruction from my field notes.

26. Criticism of Communist personalities, both past and present, often takes the form of an accusation that they either misunderstood what the party was about, interpreting it as a new vehicle for *hamūla* politics, or else willfully attempted to subvert it to their personal ambitions. Although the former is usually cited with respect to the early days of the party in the village and is intended to belittle those perceived as slow to comprehend the new political climate, the latter continues to be the idiom with which to discredit those claiming to have village or national interests at heart.

27. These are the Arabic names for male parallel and cross cousins, respectively.

28. Although Abū 'Isām managed to consolidate Yasār support, the Yasārs had suffered from internal fragmentation in previous years. In 1972, for example, four lists were headed by Yasār men, each of whom recruited support from other 'clans.' All of the lists did poorly, and 'Abdallah Yasār—the incumbent mayor—lost his place on the local council. As we will see, this potential for disarray resurfaced in the 1989 local elec-

tions. For an analysis that argues that village politics in general shifted from corporate-based to faction-based conflict after incorporation into Israel, see Kahlil Nakhleh (1975).

29. See Ian Lustick (1980: 68–69) for further discussion of this document.

30. For theoretical elaboration, see, for example, the work of Joan Scott (1988). For the relation of gender and nationalism in particular in colonial discourse as well as in that of the colonized, see Cynthia Enloe (1991) and Ann Stolar (1991).

31. See Michael Meeker's (1976) framework for the comparative study of 'honor.' The following description of the specific relationship between 'honor' and the *ḥamūla* in Palestinian society follows his analysis.

32. Later we see that Palestinian discourses on nationalism also reinterpret the meaning of 'honor,' thus underscoring that aspect of 'honor' that is the standard distinguishing the identity of the community.

33. Although Bourdieu appears to introduce a temporal element in his theory of practice, his notion of time is strangely ahistorical, as if it were merely the elapsing of time itself—a time devoid of events and changing circumstances, that is significant in cultural exchanges.

34. By 'blood feud' I mean a homicide that must be avenged in order to restore the 'honor' of the victim's group. As in the case of the inability to control women, it is the perception of weakness that demands that power be reasserted.

35. Transjordan refers to the territory across the Jordan river, today the Kingdom of Jordan.

36. Despite Yiḥye's low-status origins, the new economic context provided business opportunities that would previously have been inaccessible.

37. Because descent is reckoned patrilineally, the father's family obtains custody of the children.

38. Note that local forms of dealing with violence (e.g., reconciliation ceremonies organized by respected mediators) coexist with those of the state (e.g., prison sentences dispensed by a Western judicial system). Joseph Ginat (1987) has written more extensively on the intersection of these dual systems. His approach differs from mine, however, in that he considers the politics of 'honor killings' to be "additional factors" rather than integral to their conception. Despite the fact that he must always add the political circumstances as a postscript, the core of his analysis focuses on whether the hypothetical "norm" of a public accusation effecting a killing was enforced or evaded. Further, Ginat assumes that the increasing number of Bedouin and rural Arabs working as wage laborers indicates an integration into Jewish Western-oriented society and that this will cause a breakdown of traditional norms. This modernization approach, however, neglects the conflictive context of this transformation and its consequences for local politics.

39. This analysis refers to a political conjuncture at a particular moment in history. I do not mean to imply that the Shahīns could never endorse radical nationalism; on the contrary, both relationships between families and among parties are constantly in flux.

40. For a fuller argument against understanding 'clans' as corporate groups, see Meeker (1976).

41. Similarly, for those who distrusted the PLP candidate, an old accusation that he was responsible for the death of his unmarried daughter who was mistakenly believed to have been pregnant was revitalized and offered as evidence of his poor judgment.

42. For other examples of elections riddled with accusations and counter-accusations of deception and forgery and related attempts to find the "truth," see Abner Cohen (1965: 157–158) and Khalil Nakhleh (1975: 510). For a different cultural response to a perceived disjuncture between appearance and reality, see the chapter in this volume by Kay Warren, from whom I have borrowed the term *culture of skepticism*.

43. Also, the parallels with the current internalized violence in South Africa are striking and suggest a cross-cultural comparison of nationalist struggles under occupation. Just as 'clan feuds' are manipulated in an effort to deny a Palestinian national identity, so tribal cleavages—especially between Zulu and Xhosa—are mobilized, funded, and offered as proof of the primitive state of black South Africans who are not yet "ready" to govern themselves.

BIBLIOGRAPHY

Abu-Lughod, Lila. *Veiled Sentiments: Honor and Poetry in a Bedouin Society.* Berkeley: University of California Press, 1986.

Anderson, Benedict. *Imagined Communities: Reflections on the Origin and Spread of Nationalism.* London: Verso, 1983.

Antoun, Richard. "On the Modesty of Women in Arab Muslim Villages: A Study in the Accommodation of Traditions." *American Anthropologist* 70, no. 4 (August 1968): 671–697.

Asad, Talal. "Anthropological Texts and Ideological Problems: An Analysis of Cohen on Arab Villages in Israel." *Economy and Society* 4 (August 1975): 262–285.

Benvenisti, Meron. "The Bi-National State Has Burst Out." *Hadashot,* December 25, 1987.

Bourdieu, Pierre. *Outline of a Theory of Practice.* London: Cambridge University Press, 1977.

Budeiri, Musa. *The Palestine Communist Party 1919–1948.* London: Ithaca Press, 1979.

Cohen, Abner. *Arab Border Villages in Israel.* Manchester: Manchester University Press, 1965.

Enloe, Cynthia. "Feminism, Nationalism, and Militarism: Wariness Without Paralysis?" Paper presented at the annual meeting of the American Anthropological Association. Chicago. November 21, 1991.

Flores, Alexander. "Political Influences Across the Green Line." In Alexander Scholch, ed., *Palestinians over the Green Line*. London: Ithaca Press, 1983, 186–207.

Ginat, Joseph. *Blood Disputes Among Bedouin and Rural Arabs in Israel*. Pittsburgh: University of Pittsburgh Press in cooperation with Jerusalem Institute for Israel Studies, 1987.

Hiltermann, Joost. "The Enemy Inside the *Intifada.*" *The Nation* 251, no. 7 (September 1990): 229–394.

Jiryis, Sabri. *The Arabs in Israel 1948–1966*. Beirut: Institute for Palestine Studies, 1968.

Lustick, Ian. *Arabs in the Jewish State: Israel's Control of a National Minority*. Austin: University of Texas Press, 1980.

Meeker, Michael. "Meaning and Society in the Near East: Examples from the Black Sea Turks and the Levantine Arabs." *International Journal of Middle East Studies* 7, nos. 2 and 3 (1976): 243–270 (2) and 383–422 (3).

Nakhleh, Khalil. "The Direction of Local-Level Conflict in Two Arab Villages in Israel." *American Ethnologist* 2, no. 3 (August 1975): 497–516.

Rosenfeld, Henry. "From Peasantry to Wage Labour and Residual Peasantry: The Transformation of an Arab Village." In Robert A. Manners, ed., *Process and Pattern in Culture: Essays in Honor of Julian Steward*. Chicago: Aldine, 1964, 211–234.

_____ . *They Were Felaheen*. Tel Aviv: Hakibbutz Hameuchad (Hebrew), 1964.

_____ . "Change, Barriers to Change, and Contradictions in the Arab Village Family." *American Anthropologist* 70 (August 1968): 732–752.

_____ . "The Class Situation of the Arab National Minority in Israel." *Comparative Studies in Society and History* 20, no. 3 (July 1979): 374–407.

Rosenfeld, Henry, and Majid Al-Haj. *Arab Local Government in Israel*. Boulder: Westview Press, 1990.

Rubenstein, Sondra Miller. *The Communist Movement in Palestine and Israel, 1919–1984*. Boulder: Westview Press, 1985.

Rudge, David, and Ken Schachter. "The Leaking Green Line." *Jerusalem Post Magazine*, March 4, 1988.

Scott, Joan. *Gender and the Politics of History*. New York: Columbia University Press, 1988.

Shammas, Anton. "The Morning After." *New York Review of Books* 35 (September 1988): 47–50.

Stolar, Ann. "Carnal Knowledge and Imperial Power: Gender, Race, and Morality in Colonial Asia." In Michaela diLeonardo, ed., *Gender at the Crossroads of Knowledge: Feminist Anthropology in the Postmodern Era*. Berkeley: University of California Press, 1991, 51–101.

Zureik, Elia. *The Palestinians in Israel: A Study in Internal Colonialism*. London: Routledge and Kegan Paul, 1979.

4 Religious Networks & Urban Unrest: Lessons from Iranian & Egyptian Experiences

GUILAIN DENOEUX

Although the renewed relevance of Islam to Middle Eastern politics has received much attention since the late 1970s, scholars have focused almost exclusively on two aspects of this phenomenon. One has been the political manipulation of Islamic symbols and concepts by regimes and opposition groups.[1] The other has been the presumed ideological and structural causes of Islamic movements, including the lack of legitimacy of Middle Eastern regimes, rapid modernization and the stresses and tensions it generates, the search for cultural authenticity and meaning, the "exhaustion" of the modern secular state in the Middle East, and a general disillusionment with Western-inspired ideologies, values, and ways of life.[2] Much less is known, however, about the groups through which the Islamic revival has expressed itself and the Islamic message has been transmitted. Although observers have noted repeatedly that one important manifestation of the resurgence of Islam has been the multiplication of informally organized, locally based, and loosely connected networks that are vaguely labeled "Islamic," little effort has been made to look at these networks—and in particular at their impact on political stability—from a comparative perspective. This analysis is an attempt to do so.

URBAN NETWORKS AND POLITICAL STABILITY IN THE THIRD WORLD

Three decades of research on the politics of rapid urbanization in developing countries have pointed to the vitality of informal associations in Third World cities, especially among the poor. In order to adjust to the urban environment and to promote their common interests in it, individuals often create networks based on ethnic, religious, residential, or place-of-origin ties.[3] Recent scholarship[4] has emphasized the stabilizing impact of such networks, which exert an integrative influence at several levels.

First, these networks provide avenues for genuine participation in public life in countries in which such avenues are rare and where formally organized political groups such as parties, trade unions, and youth and women's associations are usually tightly controlled by the regime and therefore lack the ability to act as effective instruments for the representation of the population's actual interests and needs. Networks also frequently fulfill other essential political functions, such as mediating disputes, allocating resources, conveying information, and providing for order and social integration.

On an economic level, circles of kin, neighbors, and friends or access to a powerful patron is a valuable source of aid and assistance. In fact, individuals often are drawn into informal groups because of these networks' ability to deliver material support in ways that are perceived as more personal and effective than is the case with many formal, official institutions explicitly designed to help the population economically. [5] In situations characterized by widespread unemployment, low wages, physical vulnerability, and material scarcity, networks provide essential channels for securing access to food, shelter, jobs, licenses and permits, medical aid, credit, and other vital necessities. Frequently, for instance, individuals will pool their resources to create informal credit associations they can use in times of emergency or in order to accumulate money for a much-needed but expensive item.

Finally, networks offer channels for socializing and for discussion among peers of common problems and aspirations. In the process, they provide for a sense of belonging, community, and collective identity—sheltering individuals against some of the most disruptive effects of rapid socioeconomic change, including alienation, anomie, normlessness, and personal disorientation.[6]

Two additional features of informal networks explain why observers have tended to see them as exerting a stabilizing influence on the politics of the Third World city. First, networks usually cut across wealth and income criteria and therefore preempt, dilute, or erode class consciousness and class loyalties among the poor. Second, networks tend to be co-opted by the central authorities following a traditional patron-client pattern.[7] Typically, community leaders and brokers lobby well-placed officials for access to goods, services, and vital amenities in exchange for which they commit themselves to delivering the political cooperation of the population they represent.[8] Thus, networks facilitate the smooth and effective articulation of local communities and the state and promote the integration of the poor into the urban political order.

In this context, the vitality of informally organized groups in Third World cities constitutes one of the main reasons scholars have been inclined to downplay the political dangers traditionally associated with rapid urbanization. Field research has shown that although rapid socioeconomic and political change does generate a potentially dangerous increase in political participation, this participation has expressed itself primarily through the multiplication of informal networks based on residential, tribal, ethnic, sectarian, or patron-client relationships (Nelson 1987: 119–120). Participation within such networks, scholars have frequently noted, takes place within— not against—the established political system. It is also more likely to lead to pragmatic bargaining with state officials rather than to a recalcitrant and boisterous call for a radical restructuring of society.[9]

On the whole, it is difficult to deny the stabilizing influence informal associations exert on urban politics in developing countries. Nevertheless, the following analysis of five kinds of religious networks—the first three in the shah's Iran and the following two in Sadat's Egypt—reveals that informally organized groups based on religious ties can be highly destabilizing at the macrolevel even while at the microlevel they fulfill the kind of integrative functions, highlighted above, that informal associations perform throughout the Third World.

The Fada'iyan-e Islam, *1945–1955*

In the late 1940s and early 1950s, Iran experienced a wave of terrorist activities perpetrated by a small group known as the *Fada'iyan-e Islam* (often translated as "the Devotees of Islam" but literally "those who sacrifice themselves for Islam," or "the martyrs of Islam"). Although we know more about the ideology of this group than about its internal structure and modes of operation, there is little doubt that from the time of its creation in 1945 by a *talabeh* (seminarian) operating under the pseudonym Navvab Safavi[10] until its banning by the government in November 1955, the Devotees of Islam never developed into an organization but instead remained an informally organized brotherhood of fanatical Shiite activists bound to one another by intensely personal ties (Kazemi 1984: 169).

> The [*Fada'iyan's*] organizational set-up . . . consisted of a series of horizontally connected cells. . . . New members were entrusted to the care of a more senior one, who was responsible for testing them and before long assigning them to specific tasks, which varied according to each member's abilities. The most common one was observation—keeping an eye on one's friends, relatives and neighbors to make sure that they did not transgress the rules of Islam. A woman who did not wear the veil would be admonished. A young man who

liked drinking beer would be encouraged to return to the right path. Evil-doers in the neighborhood would be identified and exposed, so that believers would ostracize them. Shops belonging to non-Muslims would be marked and boycotted. But above all, a new member had to attend as many religious ceremonies as possible; he had to be seen to be an exemplary Muslim (Taheri 1987: 59–60).

A central characteristic of the *Fada'iyan* was its ability to combine highly disruptive activities at the level of society as a whole with a vital integrative and supportive role with respect to its own members. To be sure, the Devotees of Islam's actions as a terrorist group have received the most attention from scholars. And we cannot deny that the *Fada'iyan,* who advocated the physical elimination of "the enemies of Islam," engaged in numerous acts of violence between 1945 and 1955. Secular politicians and writers were favorite targets of the group. In less than a decade, the *Fada'iyan* assassinated more than a dozen individuals—among them a prominent anticlerical historian,[11] two prime ministers,[12] and a former education minister and president of the Teheran University law faculty.[13] *Fada'iyan* members also engineered assassination attempts against the shah,[14] Hossein Fatemi[15] (a well-known Teheran publisher, parliamentarian, and former deputy prime minister under Mossadegh), and Prime Minister Hossein Ala.[16] Through these and similar actions, the Devotees of Islam created a climate of political terror and frightened secular intellectuals and politicians.

The *Fada'iyan,* however, was more than simply a terrorist society. To understand the social and psychological needs the group also answered, one has to remember the general sociopolitical context in which it emerged. In the late 1940s and early 1950s, Iran experienced an economic recession, considerable political turmoil, and repeated interferences of outside powers in its internal affairs. The country was in the midst of rapid socioeconomic and political change, which in turn triggered an erosion of traditional norms, values, and patterns of behavior. Prominent among those particularly affected by these developments were the illiterate or semiliterate lower echelons of the *bazaar,* the traditional commercial artery of urban Iran. These small shopkeepers, store attendants, apprentices, footboys, and peddlers have always been among those most immediately and directly hurt by economic crises; and they tend to be somewhat parochial, suspicious of the outside world, concerned with moral and cultural norms, and traditional in their interpretation of Islam. It is not surprising that they also constituted the rank and file of the *Fada'iyan,* whose ideology emphasized the need to uphold "Islamic" standards of morality and to fight the rampant "moral corruption" brought about by modernization and the excessive presence of foreigners in Iran (Ferdows 1983: 242; Kazemi 1984: 168; Taheri 1987: 58).

Thus, the *Fada'iyan*'s violence can be seen as a desperate attempt to fight the "impure" forces of modernity and of the "infidel" West, which were making rapid headway in Iran's largest urban centers[17] and were threatening to create a world in which there would be no room for the values and ways of life associated with lower- and lower-middle-class *bazaaris* (the generic term used to refer to the craftsmen, merchants, moneylenders, and shopkeepers located in the *bazaar*). As a temporary substitute for the establishment of an Islamic order in Iran, which was the *Fada'iyan*'s ultimate goal and prompted the group's violence, the Devotees of Islam also provided membership in a tightly knit community of individuals who shared the same outlook on life and the same firm belief that a return to the "Golden Age of Islam" represented the only chance for personal and collective survival. To traditional youth in the urban lower classes, who were the Devotees of Islam's primary constituency, the *Fada'iyan* ideology was attractive primarily because it was simple and was consonant with a traditional upbringing and deeply held religious values and because it most directly addressed their concerns and aspirations, which were primarily cultural and moral. At a time when many lower-class *bazaaris* felt their lives were increasingly beset by disorder and by material and psychic insecurity, the *Fada'iyan* ideology seemed to hold the promise of restoring the perceived coherence of the past.

Religious Networks, the Urban Poor, and the Iranian Revolution

Scholars of Iran in the 1970s have pointed to the existence in both the squatter settlements and the poor sections of the cities of Shiite religious associations known as *hay'ats*. Led by a lower-ranking cleric, these *hay'ats* met in members' homes, not in the mosque (Kazemi 1980a: 63; Mottahedeh 1985: 350). They were relatively small in size—typically around thirty people—and were formed on the basis of regional or ethnic origin, neighborly contacts, or place of work (Kazemi 1980a: 63; Mottahedeh 1985: 350).[18]

Only a minority of the urban poor belonged to *hay'ats,* which met on an irregular basis. Yet these networks were significant in at least two respects. First, they were the only voluntary associations independent of the government found among the urban poor in Iran prior to the revolution, and some of their members were extremely attached to them (Kazemi 1980a: 63; Mottahedeh 1985: 355–356). Second, *hay'ats* created lines of communication and feelings of solidarity and mutual understanding between clerics

(*ulama*) and the urban poor as well as among the urban poor themselves because *hay'ats* from different parts of the city were connected to one another
(Kazemi 1980a: 63).[19]

Until about 1978, the *hay'ats* of the poor remained largely irrelevant to Iranian politics. If anything, they played a stabilizing role, providing the urban
poor with a much-needed sense of community. As one young squatter in Teheran declared, "Nothing brings us together more than the love for Imam
Husayn. My personal view is that these *hay'ats* have a positive aspect in uniting us and keeping us informed about each other's affairs" (Kazemi 1980a:
63). More specifically, in a city such as Teheran, where in the mid-1970s over
50 percent of the population were migrants, *hay'ats* offered spiritual guidance
in what must have seemed a baffling environment to many recently urban-
ized Iranians—many of whom originated in small communities (Mottahedeh
1985: 348). It is significant that many of the questions typically addressed to
clerics who led the discussions in *hay'ats* were about what constituted proper
Islamic behavior, what was pure or impure, and how one could protect oneself against the new material and sexual temptations to which one was inevitably exposed in the city (Mottahedeh 1985: 350–351).

These stabilizing functions notwithstanding, there is also evidence that
when revolutionary activities gathered momentum in the late summer and
fall of 1978, militant clerics were able to use the *hay'ats* to mobilize large segments of the poor, who until then had remained politically passive (Kazemi
1980b: 259; Mottahedeh 1985: 356). Ever since the late 1960s, cassettes
containing sermons of preachers critical of the regime had been played during
many *hay'at* meetings (Mottahedeh 1985: 351) . In 1978 this phenomenon
took on a new dimension, as messages of Khomeini in Paris were transmitted
by telephone to Teheran where they were rerecorded and distributed
throughout the country, especially in the largest urban centers (Taheri 1987:
213; Zonis 1983: 592–593). Tapes containing the Ayatollah's virulent denunciations of the shah were listened to avidly in many *hay'ats,* and they
helped draw substantial segments of the poor to the demonstrations of late
1978 and early 1979 (Mottahedeh 1985: 356). Thus, by fostering group solidarity, disseminating information, and creating lines of communication between militant clerics and the poor, *hay'ats*—which acted in coordination
with the nationwide network of mosques—played a significant role in the
revolutionary process.[20]

The informal networks connecting the poor and the fundamentalist clerics
grouped around Khomeini proved even more important *after* the shah left
Iran. The Iranian monarch was overthrown by a wide coalition of social

forces that included Westernized liberals, leftists, moderate clerics, and radical clerics. One of the key elements that enabled Khomeini's followers to gain the upper hand in the postrevolutionary struggle for power was the control they rapidly established over the revolutionary committees (*komitehs*), revolutionary courts, councils (*shuras*), and other informally organized, ad hoc groups and associations that had appeared in the course of the revolution. Between 1979 and 1983, the radical *ulama* expanded and centralized this network, using it to harass their opponents and consolidate their hold over the state apparatus.[21]

Bazaar-Centered Networks and Urban Unrest in Iran, 1945–1979

Throughout the post–World War II period, the *bazaaris* remained linked to one another through membership in guilds, religious brotherhoods, gymnasiums (*zurkhanehs*), and Sufi houses of worship as well as through ties of patronage and mutual help. Specific restaurants, coffeehouses (*qahvekhanehs*), and teahouses (*chaikhanehs*) served as the informal headquarters for those in a given trade or craft (Bill 1973: 132–133; Miller 1969: 165). The main *bazaar* mosque, where merchants and guild leaders would meet for the midday and late-afternoon–early-evening congregational prayers, also offered the *bazaaris* opportunities to exchange news and rumors and discuss issues of common interest (Ashraf 1988: 543). Yet what has been referred to as "the most significant institutions for group activities in the *bazaar*" (Spooner 1971: 171) were the *hay'at-e senfis,* the religious gatherings organized by individuals who shared a common craft or trade in the *bazaar* (Thaiss 1972: 353). In the 1960s and 1970s, *hay'at-e senfis* were taking over functions that previously had been assumed by the guilds (Spooner 1971: 172; Thaiss 1971: 202).

Although similar in size to the *hay'ats* of the urban poor and recent migrants, the *hay'at-e senfis* were a much older and better-established institution that met more often, usually once a week (Mottahedeh 1985: 347; Thaiss 1971: 201, 1972: 353).[22] They played a vital role in the collective life of the *bazaaris* and also gave concrete expression to the long-standing alliance in Iran between the *bazaar* and the mosque and made the overlap of these two worlds even clearer to both insiders and outsiders.

From a political perspective, the *hay'at-e senfis* had an integrative influence in that they promoted a sense of solidarity and unity among the *bazaaris*. For instance, *hay'at-e senfi* meetings frequently became an opportunity for *bazaaris* to devise ways of helping some of their colleagues who were experiencing financial difficulty (Thaiss 1971: 202). More generally, the *hay'at-e senfis* helped overcome class cleavages by bringing together and creating lines of communication and patronage among the wealthy merchants (*tajer*), smaller shopkeepers (*kasabehs*) and craftsmen, and the mass of wage-earning apprentices and shop assistants.[23] Thus, the *hay'at-e senfis* helped counter the appeal in the *bazaar* of ideologies of structural conflict such as Marxism. They also provided an arena in which well-to-do merchants could exert some control and influence over younger, more restive, lower-class *bazaaris*. Employers in the *bazaar* were well aware of these qualities of the *hay'at-e senfis*, and they encouraged their apprentices to join such religious gatherings (Mottahedeh 1985: 347).

These integrative functions notwithstanding, the *hay'at-e senfis* and other *bazaar*-centered networks always represented a potential problem for the authorities. They were, after all, one of the essential channels through which the *bazaaris* expressed and maintained their sense of collective identity. And it is this sense of distinct identity that led the *bazaaris* to mobilize against the authorities whenever they felt threatened by the state (due to high taxation, government threats to the autonomy or physical integrity of the *bazaar*, or policies harmful to trade and domestic manufacturing) or by excessive foreign influence in the country.[24] Because of their relative fluidity and informal nature, the *hay'at-e senfis* were also much harder for political authorities to control than more formally organized groups such as the guilds (Bill 1973: 133, footnote 6).

Due to the frequency of their meetings, the large numbers of *bazaaris* they involved, and contacts across networks, these religious circles conveyed much information about government policies and the political situation in general. Writing in the late 1960s, William Green Miller (1969: 164) noted that such informal circles were "one of the most pervasive and rapid means of transmission of political information, ideas, or policies to the *bazaar*." Miller (1969: 164) estimated at the time that these networks enabled political opinions to be transmitted "within hours" from Teheran's main *bazaar* to "the mosques, caravansaries, workshops, and teahouses in the remotest corners of the South Teheran *bazaar*" and "within a day or two" to other cities of Iran or countries outside of Iran.

Furthermore, the *hay'at-e senfis* strengthened the *bazaar*'s connections with influential religious groups and personalities because they were led by clerics and, more important, because they heightened the *bazaaris'* collective identification in religious terms. They therefore provided a basis for coordination and concerted political action by the *ulama* and the *bazaaris*. It is in fact such informal ties and networks between the *bazaar* and the mosque that, from the Constitutional revolution at the turn of the century until the 1977–1979 revolution, have enabled militant *ulama* and *bazaaris* to cooperate with one another in instigating major protest movements against the authorities.

Finally, through the *hay'at-e senfis,* funds were collected to finance charitable institutions, schools, and hospitals and to provide welfare and relief services to the poor (Thaiss 1971: 202). *Hay'at-e senfis* therefore allowed the influence of the *bazaari* community to be felt far beyond the physical boundaries of the *bazaar.* They enabled the *bazaaris* to reach out to urban society at large and particularly to the urban poor. By creating a basis for patron-client relations between the *bazaaris* and the urban poor, the *hay'at-e senfis* also provided the *bazaar* with key instruments through which to mobilize large numbers of individuals in the defense of their interests.

Largely because of these features, the *hay'at-e senfis* and other *bazaar*-centered networks enabled the *bazaaris* to act as an effective political force throughout the post–World War II period. Thus, the *bazaar* played a prominent role in the unrest of the late 1940s and early 1950s, in the rise of Muhammad Mossadegh (the charismatic, nationalist politician who was a bitter foe of the shah and became Iran's prime minister between 1951 and 1953), in the urban riots of 1963, and—most significantly—during the 1977–1979 revolution.[25] Furthermore, in the course of the Iranian revolution, the *bazaaris* not only made full use of the networks already at their disposal but also created new ones. Thus, when the police and SAVAK (the much-dreaded organization in charge of internal intelligence and security) began to hire hooligans and thugs to attack, loot, and burn the shops, stores, and homes of merchants who opposed the regime, *bazaaris* organized groups of students and militant youths to protect their property. Many revolutionary committees (*komitehs*) evolved out of these groups (Ashraf and Banuazizi 1985: 15; Parsa 1989: 115–119). These *komitehs,* which the *bazaaris* often placed under the leadership of local clergy, strengthened the alliance between the *bazaar* and the mosque and provided revolutionary forces with new networks with which to reach out to the urban population at large.

Religious Networks on Egyptian University Campuses, 1970–1981

If one now leaves the shah's Iran to examine Egypt during the Sadat years (1970–1981), one can also observe the destabilizing role played by a few religious networks. In the early 1970s, small clubs and circles broadly committed to the study of Islam began to appear on most Egyptian university campuses.[26] The mid-1970s saw a dramatic increase in the number, activities, and appeal of these groups, which came to be known by the generic term *jama'at islamiyya* (Islamic groups). By 1977–1978, the *jama'at islamiyya* controlled most of the student unions and had grown into a major political force on university campuses.

Two aspects of the *jama'at islamiyya* deserve special attention: their organizational structure and their impact on political stability. On an organizational plane, the *jama'at* remained loosely organized and locally based groups. They had no list of members, no internal status and regulations, and no clearly defined program or ideology beyond a broadly defined commitment to "Islamic" causes. Nor is there any evidence that *jama'at* from various universities ever significantly coordinated their activities at the national or even regional level. What is striking is the speed with which the movement spread throughout the country's universities *despite* the absence of a formal organization and nationwide coordination. From a multiplicity of small groups of activist students operating at the local level, a national movement developed in the short span of five years—between 1973 and 1978. Only after the *jama'at* had already gained control of student unions and of the national General Confederation of Egyptian Students were the resources of formal organizations harnessed by the *jama'at* and did some form of national coordination take place among Islamicist students (Kepel 1985: 139–141). The *jama'at,* however, continued to differ in their respective views, goals, and activities and never developed into formally organized groups.

An examination of the *jama'at*'s impact on political stability shows that informal networks, which normally play an integrative and stabilizing role, can nevertheless operate as vehicles of political protest under certain circumstances. The *jama'at* were initially encouraged by the regime, which attempted to use these religious clubs to counter the influence of the Nasserites and of the Left in the student body (Kepel 1985: 133–135). More significantly, the *jama'at* played a functional role on campuses by providing students with vital goods and services; in fact, their unmatched ability to address the students' needs resulted in the *jama'at*'s success. Students who were unable to buy expensive textbooks were happy to see the *jama'at* sell photocopies at only a fraction of the books' market price. Students having difficulty taking notes in overcrowded and noisy amphitheaters were pleased to be able to buy low-priced copies of lecture notes diffused by the *jama'at*. Female students physically harassed on the public transportation system welcomed the *jama'at*'s organization of a special bus line for them. Similarly, when they requested that male and female students sit in separate rows during lectures, the *jama'at* found a receptive audience among female students, who felt their physical integrity was endangered by packed, mixed-sex lecture halls. Students who found it hard to study in noisy dormitories and who were unable to pay for expensive private tutoring eagerly joined the study groups and review sessions for examinations that the *jama'at* organized in local mosques or in places they had asked the university authorities to set aside for prayer.[27]

The most important functions of the *jama'at,* however, may have been psychological and sociological: to offer a sense of community and belonging to students who only recently had been drawn away from their traditional surroundings and families and placed in the rather impersonal, bewildering environment of a large university in Cairo or in one of the rapidly expanding provincial cities. It is significant, as several observers have noted, that the clubs out of which the *jama'at islamiyya* developed were initially known as *usar,* which literally means "families." The formation of such families shows a deliberate effort to re-create ties of intimacy and solidarity and to shelter oneself against isolation and loneliness.[28] Similarly, through their heavy emphasis on moral themes and especially on sexual mores, the *jama'at islamiyya* can be seen as providing traditionally raised youths with vehicles for the expression of their outrage at the perceived moral permissiveness prevailing on Egyptian university campuses (Davis 1984).

Although the *jama'at* supplied large segments of the student community with various mechanisms to facilitate their adjustment to university life, many also eventually became an oppositional force—both on and beyond university campuses. Bolstered by their successes in student elections and having grown into a powerful movement, the *jama'at islamiyya* became increasingly assertive. They endeavored to prevent "anti-Islamic" behavior and activities on university campuses and harassed Coptic and secularist students and faculty, frequently resorting to violence and intimidation.

> The Islamicist monolith [which the *jama'at islamiyya*] sought to impose on the universities turned those campuses on which they were the dominant force into a kind of *terra islamica* from which they banned, clubs in hand, anything that fell foul of their norms: Couples [for instance, those holding hands in public] were physically attacked for violations of upright Islamic morals; films [deemed "indecent" by the *jama'at*] could not be shown; concerts and evening dances could not be held (Kepel 1985: 151).

Some *jama'at* were not content with attempting to turn universities into "small Islamic enclaves" (Kepel 1985). After Anwar Sadat's 1977 trip to Jerusalem and the Camp David Accords in 1978, they became increasingly critical of Sadat's policies and began to spread their message beyond university premises. They agitated in favor of the application of the *shari'a* (Islamic law), criticized the regime for the peace treaty with Israel, and were even said to have instigated some of the most violent incidents of communal strife in the country's history—especially in Minia, Assiut, and Cairo (Bianchi 1989: 196–197; Kepel 1985: 156–171).

The radicalization and increased activism of some *jama'at islamiyya* after 1978 eventually forced the regime to crack down on them. Indiscriminate repression by the state, however, only turned the *jama'at* into one of the main sources of opposition to the regime (Kepel 1985: 149). It also strengthened the ties between the *jama'at* and small radical underground organizations, driving many of the former's members into the ranks of the latter.[29] Significantly, one of the factors that appears to have motivated Khalid Islambuli to kill Sadat on October 6, 1981, was the fact that a month earlier, his brother—a leader of the *jama'at islamiyya* at the University of Assiut—had been beaten by the police following his arrest during the government's crackdown on the opposition (Kepel 1985: 129–130).

The threat to the state posed by the *jama'at* should not be exaggerated. Throughout the 1970s, political activists—Islamists and others—remained a tiny minority on university campuses (Abdalla 1985: 232). Furthermore, the *jama'at*'s attempt to extend their appeal beyond university campuses met with only limited success. With the state crackdown, they found themselves politically isolated, and following Sadat's assassination, the regime found it relatively easy to destroy the *jama'at*'s infrastructure and force members underground. For at least four years, not much was heard from the *jama'at*, even in their strongholds in Upper Egypt.[30]

These limits notwithstanding, the networks formed by the campus-based *jama'at islamiyya* were responsible for much of the turbulence of the 1979–1981 period. The experience of the *jama'at* in the 1970s shows that networks that at first emerge to facilitate the adjustment of individuals to their environment, that successfully fulfill all sorts of stabilizing functions, and that for a while may even be co-opted by the state, can nevertheless—under certain conditions—escape government control, become alienated from the regime, be radicalized, and clash with authorities.

The Islamic Radical Underground in Sadat's Egypt

The official support Sadat gave the *jama'at islamiyya* in the early 1970s was part of a broader strategy that involved the manipulation of religious symbols and groups in order to bolster the regime's legitimacy. By the mid-1970s,

however, it was already clear that the Egyptian president could not fully control the forces he had unleashed only a few years earlier. Radical Islamic
groups began to confront the regime.[31] The following discussion suggests
that the success of these networks was due to their ability to offer a new sense
of security and community to young, dislocated individuals, who emerged
from their experience with modern urban society feeling betrayed and unful-
filled.

Radical Islamic groups in Egypt developed out of small cells made up of a
few individuals usually grouped around a more prominent or charismatic
leader referred to as *amir* (commander).[32] Such cells first emerged in Nasser's
prisons among Muslim Brothers[33] influenced by the militant writings of Sayyid Qutb.[34] After Sadat began to release them from jail in the early 1970s,
former members of the Muslim Brotherhood created similar cells in Egyptian
society. The informal nature of these groups, as well as the sense of brotherhood and solidarity they provided for their members, is well expressed in
some of the words used to refer to them: *usar, 'anaqid,* or *majmu'at. Usar,* as
mentioned above, means "families." *'Anaqid* literally means "clusters," or
"bunches." It comes from a root that signifies a close association or embrace
between two individuals or between individuals and a doctrine or a religion.
Majmu'at, which in this particular instance can be translated as "groups,"
comes from the same root as *jama'at,* which—as was seen earlier—conveys
the idea of community and togetherness.

These informally organized groups developed in an ad hoc, unplanned,
and largely uncoordinated fashion. To recruit new members, they relied on
friendship, kinship, and religious ties. Typically, the leaders began with close
relatives and friends (often from prison days), and these in turn enlisted relatives and trusted friends. Also important was the ability to identify potential
recruits by observing worshippers in local mosques. Discreet contacts established in mosques located in neighborhoods in which members of a given
group were already well established became one of the most frequently used
channels for bringing new members into the movement.[35] Leaders of the major groups of the 1970s knew and interacted with one another and were mu-
tually related through ties of kinship and friendship and through common regional roots (Springborg 1989: 238).

The intense personalism that sustained radical Islamic groups in their early
stages did not diminish over time, and none of these groups ever evolved into
an "organization" in the formal and technical sense of the term. Even in the
late 1970s, *Jihad* (Holy War, the group that assassinated Sadat) seems to have
been little more than a label put by observers and members alike on semiau-

tonomous and rather self-contained cells (Dekmejian 1985: 98–99). The Cairo branch of *Jihad,* Kepel (1985: 206) tells us, "was composed of five or six groups (*majmu'at*), each of which had its own *amir.* The *amirs* met weekly to work out general strategy [but] each *amir* seems to have retained some degree of autonomy."

One way to identify the forces that led to the multiplication of radical Islamic groups in Egypt in the 1970s is to look at the social basis of these groups. We know that throughout the 1970s, members of radical Islamic groups were primarily young, educated, and achievement-oriented individuals (typically, university students or recent graduates in the sciences in the twenty to twenty-five age group) with provincial backgrounds and with poor prospects of ever finding jobs commensurate with their aspirations and educations.[36] These individuals usually lived in substandard housing in the newer, poor, and overcrowded districts located on the peripheries of big cities.[37]

Against this background, a credible hypothesis—advanced by several authors—is that radical Islamic groups provide young, uprooted provincials, who have failed to find a niche in the large city to which they moved only recently, with ways to express their frustration at the system and with the social integration and sense of group membership for which they long (Davis 1984; Kepel 1985; Sivan 1985). Radical Islamic groups become a source of comfort and reassurance for individuals who might otherwise suffer from loneliness, disorientation, and sociocultural alienation and who—having been raised in traditional ways—may be shocked by the consumerism, conspicuous consumption, and perceived moral laxity prevailing in the megalopolis. At one level, therefore, the turn to radical Islam represents an individual and collective attempt to re-create a sense of community, authenticity, and identity.

There is evidence to support these hypotheses. For instance, the radical Islamic ideologies of the 1970s emphasized unity (*tawhid*), the solidarity of the *umma islamiyya* (the Islamic community of believers), and the comprehensive character (*shumul*) and integrated nature of Islam (see Davis 1984; Etienne 1987). Such ideologies appear particularly suited to individuals who are looking for "means to resist the increasing fragmentation of social life" (Davis 1984: 146). It is also significant that Islamic militants often refer to their primary organizational unit as *al-usra,* or "the family." As Eric Davis (1984: 144) suggests, "By forming cells in major urban centers and in provincial capitals, Islamic groups seek to reconstruct the corporate unity of traditional rural life. The 'Islamic family' thus provides a sense of identity and protection within what is perceived to be a hostile and capricious environment." Davis (1984:

138) also points to the revealing contrast between the primarily socioeconomic concerns of Islamic radical thought in the 1940s and 1950s and the
primarily cultural and moral concerns of the radical Islamic ideologies of the
1970s in Egypt. Membership in radical Islamic groups and the psychological
support these groups offer may also account for the fact that during their trials, many Islamic radicals impressed observers with their calm, even relative
serenity and with the inner logic of their arguments and the strength of their
convictions.

Among all the radical groups of the 1970s, Shukri Mustafa's *Takfir wa'l-
Hijra* (Excommunication and Hegira)[38] perhaps best demonstrates how radical Islamic networks can be destabilizing at the macrolevel while fulfilling vital integrative functions at the microlevel. The *Takfir wa'l-Hijra* challenged
the Egyptian state and the prevailing sociopolitical order in several respects. It
first admonished its members to separate themselves—both spiritually and
physically—from Egyptian society, which was condemned as having reverted
to a state of unbelief (*jahiliyya*). The strategy of withdrawal made it incumbent on the group's members to refuse conscription or employment in the
bureaucracy and, more generally, to deny any form of legitimacy and allegiance to the "infidel" state (Davis 1984: 155; Kepel 1985: 84; Sivan 1985:
86). More directly threatening to the authorities, however, was the group's
ideology, according to which the phase of separation from society would
eventually be followed—after the group had gained sufficient strength—by
an assault on the state as a prelude to the revolutionary transformation of society along Islamic lines. Although the *Takfir wa'l-Hijra* had a gradualist strategy, its margin for maneuver was considerably reduced after an aborted coup
by another radical Islamic group, the Islamic Liberation Organization (*al-
munazzamat al-tahrir al-islami*). Following the crackdown on the Islamic
Liberation Organization, the security forces began to arrest members of the
Takfir wa'l-Hijra. Takfir wa'l-Hijra subsequently came into open confrontation with the regime when its members kidnapped and later killed a former
minister of religious affairs.[39] In the wake of this assassination, the government ruthlessly repressed *Takfir wa'l-Hijra,* executing Shukri Mustafa and
five other leaders and imprisoning dozens of members.[40]

Although it eventually clashed with the regime, the *Takfir wa'l-Hijra* operated as a stabilizing force in the life of its members. It provided them with
membership in a much-improved society—a miniature of the perfect, genu-
inely Islamic society it aimed to establish. It was a world in which, for instance, in sharp contrast with the current situation in Egypt, marriage at an
early age was possible and housing was readily available.[41] Shukri Mustafa ar-

ranged marriages between members of the group and then provided the new couple with a place to live. He ensured the continued supply of cash needed to finance this system by sending some of the group's male members to the gulf countries. Upon their return to Egypt, these individuals were provided with a bride (if they had not left one behind) and housing, and other members of the *Takfir wa'l-Hijra* replaced them as migrant workers to Saudi Arabia and the smaller oil-rich states (Kepel 1985: 70–102).

To a large extent, the *Takfir wa'l-Hijra* enabled its members to live a communal life based on the simple and attractive ideology of a return to the Golden Age of Islam. To segments of the youth who felt excluded and trapped by contemporary Egyptian society—their dreams of upward social mobility slashed and their hopes in modernity's ability to deliver destroyed—the *Takfir wa'l-Hijra* appeared to be an attractive exit from contemporary Egyptian society and its problems. That the group provided such an escape from reality explains why the regime and many observers initially saw it—too optimistically, as it turned out—as "absorbing discontent and channeling dissent in a 'positive' way" (Sivan 1985: 87).

DOUBLE-EDGED AND RADICAL-UTOPIAN RELIGIOUS NETWORKS

From the evidence presented above, one can distinguish between two types of religious networks. The first I call "double-edged," to account for its ability to exert either a stabilizing or destabilizing influence on the political system, depending on the circumstances. The *jama'at islamiyya,* the *hay'ats,* and the *hay'at-e senfis* can be described as double-edged networks. Under normal conditions, these networks exert a stabilizing influence on the sociopolitical order in that they provide some of the social and psychological support needed to absorb tensions associated with rapid socioeconomic change. However, under conditions spelled out below, double-edged networks can also become vehicles for the mobilization of individuals into oppositional activities.

The *Fada'iyan-e Islam* in Iran and the Islamic underground in Sadat's Egypt belong to a second category of religious networks, which one might describe as "radical-utopian." Unlike double-edged networks, radical-utopian networks always have a destabilizing impact on the sociopolitical system. Yet as with their double-edged counterparts, they draw their appeal from their ability to give individuals who suffer from a lack of integration into contemporary urban society much-needed channels for membership into a tightly knit, solidaristic community. Although the radical-utopian ideologies on which these groups are based encourage and legitimize violent actions toward the outside world, they also fulfill vital functions that help individuals adjust to their surroundings.

Indeed, when looking at such groups, the observer is faced less with terrorist organizations than with secret brotherhoods of individuals brought and kept together by intensely personal ties and by an unfailing devotion to a militant, fundamentalist version of Islam. Accordingly, the overt hostility the members of such groups express toward the political system and their surrounding environment is mirrored only by the equally high degree of solidarity and sense of community they feel among themselves. Therefore, radical-utopian groups not only offer their members an opportunity to fight for the re-creation of an Islamic order, but—pending the advent of this ideal society—they also give alienated individuals a chance to experience membership in microcommunities that provide a refuge from the perceived chaos and incoherence of life.

The existence of double-edged and radical-utopian networks raises fundamental questions. For one, under what conditions do double-edged networks shift their role from system supportive to system challenging? Similarly, when one looks at radical-utopian networks such as the *Fada'iyan-e Islam* or the violent Islamic groups of the 1970s in Egypt, is one faced with phenomena that are peculiar to the Middle East? Or are these networks essentially similar to other destabilizing groups elsewhere in the Third World? The following sections pursue answers to these questions.

WHEN DOUBLE-EDGED RELIGIOUS NETWORKS BECOME DESTABILIZING

The experience of the *hay'ats* and *hay'at-e senfis* in Iran suggests that double-edged networks can be most destabilizing when the following four conditions are met.

1. The networks are controlled by a counter-elite (in Iran's instance, the *ulama* and the *bazaaris*).
2. This counter-elite has access to far-ranging resources independent of those controlled by the state.[42] (In Egypt, by contrast, another counter-elite—the leaders of the *jama'at islamiyya*—lacked the extensive social contacts and organizational and financial resources that could have enabled them to challenge the state more effectively.)

3. The counter-elite feels threatened by hostile forces and sees these forces as being directly or indirectly associated with the authorities.
4. The counter-elite benefits from a sudden weakening of the state[43] and from the state's failure to isolate the most radical elements of the opposition.[44]

The counter-elite's perception of being besieged by malevolent forces is of particular importance. Thus, in Iran the mobilization of *bazaar-* and mosque-centered networks against the shah was a primarily defensive movement. The overwhelming majority of the *ulama* and the *bazaaris* became involved in antiregime activities because they felt endangered by certain state policies and trends in Iranian society at large. For instance, one factor that greatly alarmed the *bazaaris* was the state's repeated and increasing encroachments on the *bazaar.* Throughout the 1960s and 1970s, the *bazaaris* suffered from numerous arbitrarily implemented commercial regulations and tax laws (Ashraf 1988: 555). In the early to mid-1970s, state provocations of the *bazaaris* took new dimensions. In 1975 the government disclosed plans for an eight-lane highway that would cut through the main *bazaar* in Teheran (Halliday 1979: 220). In 1975–1976, the newly created ruling *Rastakhiz* party was forced on the *bazaari* community and began to interfere in its affairs (Abrahamian 1982: 443–444).

Most consequential, however, was the so-called antiprofiteering campaign of 1975–1976, which was an attempt to blame high rates of inflation on the *bazaaris;* this resulted in hundreds of *bazaaris* being fined, jailed, or banned from their hometowns.[45] The antiprofiteering campaign generated much resentment, bitterness, and anger and was perhaps the most decisive event that served as a catalyst for the mobilization of the *bazaaris* against the regime (Ashraf 1988: 557). Against this background, the mobilization of the *bazaaris* against the shah was largely an attempt by a substantially unified community to demonstrate and reassert its power and influence in relation to a state whose policies and attitude were increasingly perceived as arbitrary and despotic.

The *ulama* also had reasons for concern. In the 1960s, the government had taken over many of their properties (during the 1963 land reform), interfered in the administration of religious institutions, and diminished the number of places in which clerics could teach and preach (Akhavi 1980: 91–143). In the early 1970s, the Pahlavi dynasty's attack on the power and social influence of the clergy reached new heights as new state-controlled agencies were assigned many of the religious and social service functions that traditionally had been the preserve of the religious institution (Akhavi 1980: 138–143). By doing so, the government was attempting to deprive the *ulama* of the last prerogatives they had managed to retain: their historic monopoly over religious symbols and their standing as the only legitimate propagators of Shiism (Akhavi 1980: 138–142).

Scholars have also pointed to specific government policies in the early 1970s that further contributed to the *ulama*'s perception of an all-out attack on the Shiite establishment: the arrest of several leading clerics and the death of at least two of them[46] at the hands of SAVAK; the regime's increasing control over mosques, shrines, and religious endowments; the destruction of religious seminaries in Mashhad in 1975 to create a green belt around the shrine; and the army's attack on the Fayziyyeh seminary in 1975 (Bill 1988: 186–190; Fischer 1980: 120–123). Michael Fischer (1980: viii, 3) summarizes the cultural stakes of the conflict when he writes that "the atmosphere in Qom in 1975 was one of siege and courageous hostility to a state perceived to be the stronger, but morally corrupt, opponent" and that "the [clerics felt] themselves engaged in a life-and-death defense of the coherence, rationality, and integrity of a culture under siege."

Both the *bazaaris* and the *ulama* resented the shah's frequently expressed contempt for them and the world they represented. In the 1970s Reza Shah repeatedly proclaimed his disdain for the *bazaaris* and their "worm-ridden shops." He denounced them as a reactionary group opposed to change and as an obstacle to the country's socioeconomic modernization. He also frequently referred to the *ulama* and the religious students as "parasites" and portrayed the clerical opposition to his reforms as the "black reaction" (Algar 1972: 247). Such public attacks were humiliating to the *ulama* and the *bazaaris* and offended their sense of self-worth and self-respect. Inevitably, they reinforced the belief by both groups that government policies were creating a world in which their role would be considerably diminished.

Such considerations make it clear that, as Said Amir Arjomand (1988) has noted, both material interests and cultural concerns played a role in the mobilization of the clergy against the shah. Yet one can only be struck by the relative importance of cultural factors in alienating the *ulama* and the *bazaaris* from the monarchy. In view of this volume's interest in the relationship between culture and conflict, this point deserves some elaboration.

Throughout the 1960s and 1970s, differences in the cultural outlook of the *bazaaris* and the elite became increasingly pronounced. Many *bazaaris*

resented what they saw as the state's growing disregard for Islamic values and
life-styles and the unwillingness of the shah to preserve the moral and cultural
fabric of Iranian society against foreign cultural penetration.

> Among the more conflict-arousing issues in this sphere were the life-styles and
> appearance of the more privileged Westernized classes, particularly the un-
> veiled and often "provocatively clad" upper-class women, and among other
> things violation of Islamic codes of behavior in public, un-Islamic or anti-Is-
> lamic ideas disseminated by the state-controlled media, non-Islamic contents
> of the curriculum in modern schools, and the increasing influence and pres-
> ence of Americans and other Westerners at all levels of the country's economic
> and social life (Ashraf 1988: 557).

Cultural grievances played an even clearer role in the mobilization of the
mosque network. An analysis of Khomeini's declarations from the early
1960s onward reveals that the Ayatollah and the small group of militant clerics who began to rally to his cause were most concerned with broad moral and
cultural themes, often inextricably mixed with the issue of excessive foreign
influence in the country (Tabari 1983).[47] What incensed Khomeini and his
followers were the "moral corruption" and "cultural decadence" generated by
the shah's policies as well as the regime's perceived subservience to the United
States and Israel.[48] Subordination to foreign interests was seen as leading to
moral decadence; reciprocally, moral laxity was said to make Iran an easy prey
for infidels.

By portraying the problems faced by Iran as moral ones and by emphasizing the link between these moral issues and foreign influence in the country,
Khomeini achieved several objectives. Most important, he was able to reach
millions of people who were particularly receptive to a political discourse
phrased in moral terms because they were experiencing the moral and existential dilemmas of traditionally raised individuals caught in the midst of a
dislocating process of rapid socioeconomic change. Similarly, by making people's personal dignity and integrity dependent on the integrity of Iran, which
was said to be best preserved by fighting Western influence in the country,
Khomeini formulated a new definition of nationalism—based on a fierce ani-
mosity toward the West—that once again could mobilize millions of until-
then largely apolitical Iranians. Personal identity crises and a desire for self-
purification could be seen as parts of a larger process of national redemption
involving the revitalization of old cultural forms. By the same token, feelings
of guilt based on an individual's own moral failings could be blamed on the
West. Finally, by defining the problems confronting Iran in moral and cul-

tural terms, Khomeini was also justifying the clergy's involvement in politics because clerics could legitimately be said to be in the best position to speak about issues of morality—especially in a country portrayed as a Muslim nation threatened by infidels.

In 1978 cultural and moral concerns also played a part in convincing the majority of the *ulama* (as opposed to the small nucleus of militant clerics grouped around Khomeini) to become involved against the shah. Initially—during the early phase of political mobilization against the monarchy throughout 1977 and in the first few months of 1978—most *ulama* remained inactive and their leaders even appealed for calm, condemning the use of violence by protesters.[49] The *ulama's* ultimate conversion from tolerance of the regime to active opposition to the shah was largely a product of the momentum of the revolution, the government's mishandling of the uprising, and the relentless pressures Khomeini and his radical followers exerted on the rest of the religious establishment to force it to adopt a more militant stance. But cultural issues, around which the *ulama's* most important fears revolved, also paved the way for the eventual emergence of the crucial antigovernment alliance between moderate and radical clerics.

First, there was the regime's increasing downplay of Iran's Islamic identity and its growing emphasis on the country's pre-Islamic roots and history.[50] More important, throughout the 1960s and 1970s, the *ulama* became horrified by what they perceived to be the growing moral "corruption" and "decadence" produced by the shah's modernization program and by increasing Western (especially U.S.) influences in the country. Drawing on a speech made after the revolution by Ayatollah Khomeini's influential son Ahmad, Ervand Abrahamian suggests that more than any other factor, it was this "moral laxity" that led the majority of the clerics to slowly join the militant lower clergy in its campaign against the shah.[51] More generally, a concern with moral corruption, roots, authenticity, and the regeneration of an indigenous culture seen as besieged by the forces of the West was the one generalized grievance against the shah shared by the *ulama,* the *bazaaris,* and the intelligentsia. This cultural critique proved crucial in bringing together the segments of Iranian society that provided the organizational backbone of the revolution (Arjomand 1988; Bayat 1980; Najmabadi 1987).

An examination of what the radical *ulama* have done since 1979 also gives some indication of their objectives and motives in overthrowing the monarchy. Clearly, the Islamic republic has put the strict enforcement of Islamic values, morality, and codes of behavior high on its list of priorities. The Islamization of Iranian society, which the clerics promoted relentlessly through the first decade of the revolution, is perhaps the most undeniable "achievement" of the new regime. It shows that for those now in control of the state, "moral purification" has been the most important goal.[52] It has also provided new modes of political control. Thus, from a language for oppositional politics, religion became a language to exert and justify the clergy's domination over Iranian society and politics. For instance, between 1979 and 1981 the fundamentalists' fight against the universities, which were strongholds of the Left and the Islamic Left, was legitimized in the name of cultural purification and the eradication of Western influences in the country (Milani 1988: 294–295). More generally, by presenting political authority in the Islamic republic as sacred and by making obedience to the new laws of the land a religious duty, radical clerics have articulated a new language that entirely redefines the basis of political legitimacy (Arjomand 1988: 181–183).

THE *HIJRA* PARADIGM, OR
THE ISLAMIC SEARCH FOR UTOPIA

Notwithstanding the fact that networks such as the Iranian *Fada'iyan* and the radical Islamic groups of the 1970s in Egypt are nominally "Islamic," how important is Islam in influencing the forms these networks assume, their modes of operation, and their impact on political stability? Is there anything in Islamic doctrine or history that facilitates the emergence of these radical-utopian groups? Or do these networks develop in reaction to worldwide forces that have little or nothing to do with Islam?

From the evidence presented above, radical-utopian Islamic networks can be seen—in part at least—as responses to forces that can be felt throughout the Third World, including rapid modernization and uneven development, the expansion of higher education, the quest for identity through the language of cultural authenticity, the resentment of foreign domination and the cancer-like spread of Western culture, the search for individual and collective empowerment, and the failure of the Third World state's modernizing ideologies and projects. However, even though such general socioeconomic and political trends have paved the way for the development of radical-utopian Islamic networks, many of the particular characteristics, forms, modes of operation, and destabilizing effects of these groups have been heavily influenced by Islam. More specifically, when one looks at groups such as the *Fada'iyan-e Islam* or the *Takfir wa'l-Hijra* and some of the more militant and violent *jama'at islamiyya* on Egyptian university campuses in Egypt in the 1970s, it is hard to avoid the impression that these groups' basic strategies and ultimate goals were modeled after those of the Prophet Muhammad himself as he was trying to build the Islamic community.

Similarities between such groups and Muhammad's original community can be observed at several levels. One is the use of kinship, friendship, and other personal ties and loyalties to bring new members into the movement. Another is the reliance on small, highly personal, and secretive cells. Both of these features closely resemble the strategy followed by Muhammad to integrate and consolidate the early Islamic community. [53] Although some may object that this is mere coincidence or similarity, others will undoubtedly see a deliberate effort to reproduce a cultural and historical pattern endowed with the greatest legitimacy of all: that of having been used by the Prophet himself and therefore of being the Islamic way as revealed by God. It is significant that in an effort to legitimize their own actions, the leaders of Islamic radical groups often make explicit references to Muhammad's dependence on small groups and personal ties.[54]

Most important is what I call "the *hijra* paradigm." *Hijra* originally refers to the flight of Muhammad and his followers from Mecca to Madina in 622. In Mecca the leading families' opposition to Muhammad's teachings greatly constrained the Prophet's activities. In the much more receptive environment of Madina, Muhammad could operate freely, which made it possible for him to expand the size of his incipient Islamic community and create a strong esprit de corps among his followers. Eventually, from this strengthened power base, the Prophet was able to defeat the Meccans. Soon afterward, he converted many Arabian tribes to Islam, which in turn provided the basis for the rapid and dramatic expansion of the new religion beyond Arabia.

Because Muslims are fully aware of the contribution of *hijra* to the triumph and expansion of Islam, there is much room for political entrepreneurs to admonish the faithful to practice *hijra* themselves—that is, to withdraw from a world denounced as corrupt and to find refuge in microcommunities patterned after Muhammad's at the time of his *hijra*. The *Takfir wa'l-Hijra* (the name is revealing), the *Fada'iyan,* and the more radical *jama'at islamiyya* represent—to some extent—contemporary manifestations of this phenomenon.[55] Furthermore, it is Islam that, in part at least, gives these small groups their janus-faced character of fulfilling stabilizing and integrative functions at the microlevel and destabilizing functions at the macrolevel. At the microlevel, these groups give their members an escape from contemporary society, into which these individuals have difficulty fitting, and membership in a solidaristic community that defines their needs for authenticity, moral purity, and brotherhood. At the same time, however, the explicitly stated objective of many of these networks is—following the precedent created by Muhammad's conquest of Mecca—to regroup the faithful, resocialize them, indoctrinate them, and enable them eventually to move against the state, defeat it, and reestablish a true Islamic society.

Islamic networks in this context fulfill both short-term and long-term functions. In the short term, they enable individuals to escape the vices of societies that are seen as having reverted to unbelief and to build small Islamic enclaves in the midst or on the fringes of these corrupted societies. In the long term, they constitute the road toward the building of a much larger Islamic utopia. They are at once arenas of communal life for their members and centers of opposition to the authorities. By the same token, radical Islamic groups are simultaneously past- and future-oriented. They are past-oriented because they draw much of their inspiration from the state of the Islamic community during the Golden Age of Islam, the period of Muhammad and the first four Caliphs for the Sunnis and of Muhammad and Ali for the Shiites. They are also future-oriented because their objective is less to turn the clock back to the seventh century than to use the image of the early Islamic community as a blueprint to build an Islamic utopia in the late twentieth century. The countersociety they build is not only the vanguard of dedicated Muslims that will overthrow the present corrupt order; it is also a model for the society of the future (Sivan 1985: 85).

IMPLICATIONS

The ability of informal networks to provide powerful avenues for political dissent is clearly not limited to the Middle East or to Arab-Muslim cultures. In fact, in the yet-predominantly authoritarian political contexts of most Third World countries, where co-opted or repressed formal organizations do not constitute an option to express dissatisfaction with the regime, resistance to the state is likely to express itself through informally organized and nominally apolitical associations. In this context, scholars might wish to reassess the prevailing consensus concerning the stabilizing role informal networks play among the urban poor. As this analysis has demonstrated, groups that reduce individual and social stress by providing much-needed avenues for membership in new communities at a time of dislocating socioeconomic change can also operate as highly effective structures for political mobilization against a regime. More attention should be paid to the cross-national study of those conditions under which double-edged networks can and have become destabilizing.

Similarly, at a time when there is much talk about the reassertion of civil society in relation to the state in Eastern Europe, Latin America, the Middle East, Africa, and Asia, and when it is clear that informal associations are often a primary vehicle of this new grass-roots political dynamism, scholars need to go beyond the analysis of informal networks among the urban poor and examine the role these networks play in the population at large.

NOTES

I express my gratitude to the MacArthur Foundation and the Sternberg Fund for financing part of the research on which this analysis is based. I would also like to thank John Waterbury, Samir Khalaf, Henry Bienen, and Kay Warren for their very helpful comments on earlier drafts of this chapter.

1. See, for instance, Fischer (1980) on the "Kerbala paradigm," Ansari (1986) on Sadat's use of religion as a legitimizing device, and Antoun and Hegland (1987) for a few case studies.

2. Consult, for example, Hudson (1980), Dekmejian (1980, 1985), Dessouki (1982), Ayubi (1982–1983), and Sivan (1985).

3. For the purposes of this chapter, the term "networks" refers to informally organized groups of individuals linked to one another by noncontractual and highly personal bonds and loyalties.

4. See, inter alia, Cornelius (1975) on Mexico, Perlman (1976) on Rio, Karpat (1976) on Turkey, Dietz and Moore (1979) on Peru, and Nelson (1979) and Bienen (1984) for two comprehensive reviews and analyses of the literature.

5. Networks based on "primordial" ties and loyalties can also serve as avenues for the economic promotion of a given ethnic or religious group. Abner Cohen, for instance, showed how the Hausa of Nigeria were able to capitalize on such networks to dominate the long-distance trade between the savanna and the forest belt (Cohen 1969, 1974). Cohen also notes that the mobilization of ethnic ties and solidarities helps explain the economic success of Lebanese and Syrian communities in West Africa and of Chinese communities in parts of the Far East and of Southeast Asia (1969: 191). In a similar vein, John Waterbury (1972) has documented how the Swasa of Morocco were able to use tribal networks to gain control over much of the retail trade in Morocco's northern cities, especially Casablanca, in the relatively short span of twenty-five years (1920–1945).

6. See, for instance, Karpat (1976: 231–232) on the *Gecekondu* in Turkey.

7. Patron-client relations "represent a special kind of personal exchange, one where two individuals of different socioeconomic status enter into a relationship in which the individual of higher status uses his influence and resources to provide protection and benefits for the person of lower status, the latter reciprocating by offering his personal services, loyalty, and general support" (Rassam 1977: 158; see also Scott 1972: 92).

8. See, for instance, Cornelius (1975, 1977) on the *cacique* in Mexico.

9. See, for instance, Bienen (1984: especially 669), Nelson (1979), and Huntington (1968: 280).

10. Navvab Safavi's real name was Sayyid Mojtaba Mir-Lowhi. The pseudonym refers to the Safavid dynasty, which made Shiism the state religion of Iran in the early sixteenth century.

11. Ahmad Kasravi (in March 1946).

12. Abdul-Hossein Hazhir (in November 1949) and Haj-Ali Razmara (in March 1951).

13. Hamid Zangeneh (in March 1951).

14. In February 1949.

15. In February 1952.

16. In November 1955.

17. The membership of the *Fada'iyan* was overwhelmingly urban and was concentrated in the largest cities, especially Teheran and Mashhad (Kazemi 1984: 168).

18. For a brief description of a typical meeting of a *hay'at* among the urban poor, see Mottahedeh (1985: 350–351).

19. In several respects the *hay'ats* resemble the better-known Latin American grassroots activist Catholic groups called *comunidades eclesiales de base*—that is, "Christian base communities." Like the *hay'ats,* the Christian base communities developed from the late 1960s onward largely as a result of two trends. The first was the emergence of a new generation of militant priests and lay Catholics who tried to make religion more relevant to the concerns and aspirations of the poor in order to rejuvenate the church and reverse the trend toward its loss of influence. The second trend was the increasing demand for religion among members of the lower classes as poor people and clerical and lay activists turned to religion to find guidance in confronting their problems.

There are at least three additional similarities between Christian base communities and Iranian *hay'ats*. First, various Christian base communities are indirectly linked to one another through their common relationship to an established church endowed with considerable material resources and symbolic power. Second, Christian base communities originally developed independently of the religious hierarchy, which was very reluctant to confront the authorities. Finally, as in the case of the Iranian *hay'ats,* whose main activities were centered around the reading and discussion of the Qur'an and the Shiite traditions, exposure to the Bible and commenting on its teachings represent the core of the activities of Christian base communities (see Levine 1986a: 10). One important difference between *hay'ats* and Christian base communities, however, is that whereas the former are an exclusively urban phenomenon, the latter are by no means restricted to the cities (on Nicaragua, see Dodson 1986; on Brazil, see Bruneau 1986).

20. Here again, one should note some general similarities between *hay'ats* and Christian base communities. As with the *hay'ats,* the Christian base communities were

not created originally for political purposes. They emerged to provide arenas for sociability and mutual support and to foster a sense of community. Over time, however, Christian base communities have often developed into groups that have challenged the authorities—especially in Nicaragua, Brazil, Chile, Guatemala, and El Salvador. (For evidence and an analysis of the reasons that led Christian base communities to clash with the state, see Levine [1986a: 10–15, 1986b: 825–828] and Bruneau [1986: 110].) Thus, for instance, Christian base communities played an instrumental role in mobilizing thousands of Nicaraguans in the Sandinist revolution. In the late 1960s, sporadic clashes began to take place between the authorities and the militant clergy and activist youth working at the local level through Christian base communities. This conflict culminated in the late 1970s, when clerical and lay activists involved in Christian base communities moved into open and direct support of the Sandinist Front of National Liberation (FSLN). The support of such individuals and of Christian base communities, Michael Dodson (1986: 86, 93) argues, "was clearly a valuable resource to the FSLN, which found the work of organizing people in the insurrection [against Somoza] to be much easier in the areas where [Christian base communities] were firmly rooted. These institutions of religious inspiration were, in short, effective vehicles of grass-roots political action in the revolutionary setting of the popular insurrection. . . . Indeed the [Christian base communities] provided intelligence, communication links, food, safe houses, medical aid, and combatants."

21. See Bakhash (1990) for details.

22. For a description of a typical meeting of a *hay'at-e senfi,* see Thaiss (1972: 353–356).

23. On the socioeconomic stratification of the Iranian *bazaar,* see Mobasser (1985), Miller (1969), and Ashraf (1983).

24. The *bazaar*'s sense of distinct collective identity has been all the more consequential for Iranian politics because except for the clergy, other strata and classes in Iranian society have failed to develop a sense of group solidarity. See, for instance, Zonis (1971) on the lack of cooperation and widespread distrust among members of the political elite, and Arjomand (1988: 108–114) on how the shah's policies were able to keep the new middle class divided, atomized, and therefore incapable of acting as "a class for itself."

25. See, for instance, Ashraf (1988) and Parsa (1989: 91–125). The role of the *bazaar* in the 1977–1979 revolution has been well explored by scholars. Suffice it to mention that the *bazaars* of Iran's major cities repeatedly closed down in support of the revolutionary forces. (They did so at first on a local basis but, beginning in the summer of 1978, also sometimes on a coordinated, countrywide basis; see Ashraf 1988: 558.) The *bazaar* also organized numerous demonstrations. According to Ashraf and Banuazizi (1985: 25), approximately two-thirds of the demonstrations that occurred during the revolution were arranged by the *bazaar*-mosque alliance. In addition, wealthy *bazaaris* financed revolutionary groups and activities, established funds to pay the salaries of

striking workers and professionals, and provided financial help for the families of the "martyrs" of the revolution.

26. On the genesis of these groups, see Kepel (1985: 129–141), Abdalla (1985: 226), and Bianchi (1989: 193–194).

27. On these and other services provided by the *jama'at,* see Kepel (1985: 142–146), El Guindi (1981), and Bianchi (1989: 194–195).

28. For hypotheses along these lines, see Davis (1984).

29. This is particularly clear in the case of the *Jihad* group in Middle Egypt. See Kepel (1985: 205–206).

30. For an overview of the activities of the *jama'at* under Mubarak, see Springborg (1989: 215–245) and Bianchi (1989: 197–199).

31. The genesis and activities of these groups have been well documented. See, inter alia, Ibrahim (1982), Kepel (1985), Sivan (1985), and Dekmejian (1985: Chapter 6). For the more recent period, see Springborg (1989: 215–245) and Bianchi (1989: 199–204).

32. *Amir* often has a religious connotation, as in *amir al-mu'minin,* "commander of the faithful."

33. The Muslim Brotherhood, created in 1928, became Egypt's first truly mass-based movement and the major political force in the country during the late 1940s. It was outlawed in 1954 after the new regime blamed it for a failed attempt on Nasser's life. Thereafter, it went underground, where it managed to survive despite successive crackdowns by the state.

34. A Muslim thinker executed in Cairo in 1966, whose writings have served as a source of inspiration for the current generation of Islamic radicals throughout the Sunni world.

35. See Ibrahim (1982: 128), Dekmejian (1985: 95), Ansari (1986: 216–218), and Kepel (1985: 206).

36. See the studies of Ansari (1986), Davis (1984), Ibrahim (1982), and Kepel (1985).

37. On the *Jihad* group in particular, see Kepel (1985: 217–218) and Ansari (1986: 221).

38. *Takfir wa'l-Hijra* is a name that was given to the group by outside observers. The group's real name was *jama'at al-muslimin* (the Society of Muslims).

39. Dr. Husain al-Dhahabi, one of Egypt's top *ulama* at the time.

40. For details, see Kepel (1985: 91–102), Ibrahim (1982: 134–135), and Dekmejian (1985: 96).

41. In contemporary Egypt, young people often have to postpone marriage because they do not have the money to rent a place to start their household.

42. In fact, in Iran the *bazaar* and the mosque were the only two centers of power that had managed to retain some form of autonomy from the state. They also combined this autonomy with a control over considerable financial, organizational, and symbolic resources.

43. The shah's cancer and Jimmy Carter's pressures on him to liberalize his regime created confusion, indecisiveness, and lack of resolve at the highest levels of the Iranian government.

44. Even as late as mid-1978, the majority of the senior Shiite clerics favored an accommodation with the regime. The shah, however, proved unable to capitalize on political differences among the *ulama* to split the opposition (Arjomand 1988: 192; Bakhash 1984). In Egypt as well, Sadat failed to differentiate, both in his actions and in his public declarations, between the moderate and radical wings of the Islamic movement. This strategy cost him dearly because instead of isolating the radicals, it often drove the moderate factions into the arms of the extremists. Mubarak appears to have learned from Sadat's mistake, and throughout his first decade in office, he has proven skillful at playing the different segments of the political opposition against one another.

45. See Taheri (1978: 98–101), Halliday (1979: 220), Abrahamian (1982: 498), Ashraf (1988: 557), and Parsa (1989: 103–105).

46. Ayatollahs Sa'idi and Ghoffari.

47. For example, in a particularly important speech delivered only a few days after his triumphant return to Teheran, Khomeini summarized the damage caused by the shah's policies in the following terms: "That man [the shah] destroyed all our human resources. In accordance with the mission he was given as the servant of foreign powers, he established centers of vice and made radio and television subservient to immoral purposes. Centers of vice operated with complete freedom under his rule. As a result, there are now more liquor stores in Teheran than there are bookstores. Every conceivable form of vice was encouraged" (Algar 1981: 257–258).

48. Khomeini thought this subservience was so pronounced that it implied the shah's complicity in a foreign plot presided over by the U.S. and Israeli governments, the Jews, and the Bahais (the latter acting in Iran as agents of the Jews and of Israel). More important, perhaps, Khomeini saw this conspiracy as representing a lethal threat to the independence and cultural identity of Iran (Bakhash 1990: 24–30).

49. See Bakhash (1984: 178–181) and Parsa (1989: 201–205).

50. Manifestations of these trends included the 1971 Persepolis celebration and the replacement of the Islamic calendar with an imperial one.

51. "According to Ahmad Khomeini, what . . . led [the majority of] clerics to break their silence was not the realization that the shah was destroying the country and selling Iran to Western imperialism, but rather the shock of seeing 'moral decadence' flaunted in the streets and the double shock of finding that the authorities were unwilling, if not incapable, of cleaning up the 'social filth.' Having no channels through which they could communicate [their] grievances to the political system, they reluctantly joined the antiregime clergy to mount the final assault against the shah" (Abrahamian 1980: 26). See also Parsa (1989: 204) on the heavy cultural and moral content of many of the demands put forward by the moderate senior clerics throughout 1978.

52. For a description of some of the specific government policies and decisions aimed at the Islamization of Iranian society, see Milani (1988: 308–309).

53. See Bill and Springborg (1990: 139–151) on "the politics of a Prophet."

54. See, for instance, Taheri (1987) on Navvab Safavi, the *Fada'iyan-e Islam*'s founder, and Sivan (1985: 86).

55. For instance, the summer camps the *jama'at islamiyya* organized in the early 1970s were "micro-cosmic experiments in Islamicist utopia, past and future . . . [they] were meant to be a model of the future Islamic society that the young Islamicists intended to build on the ruins of *jahiliyya* ['the corrupt society']" (Kepel 1985: 139).

BIBLIOGRAPHY

Abdalla, Ahmed. *The Student Movement and National Politics in Egypt, 1923–1973.* London: Al Saqi Books, 1985.

Abrahamian, Ervand. "Structural Causes of the Iranian Revolution." *Merip Reports* 87 (May 1980): 21–26.

_____ . *Iran Between Two Revolutions.* Princeton: Princeton University Press, 1982.

Akhavi, Shahrough. *Religion and Politics in Contemporary Iran: Clergy-State Relations in the Pahlavi Period.* Albany: State University of New York Press, 1980.

Algar, Hamid. "The Oppositional Role of the Ulama in Twentieth-Century Iran." In Nikki R. Keddie, ed., *Scholars, Saints, and Sufis: Muslim Religious Institutions Since 1500.* Berkeley: University of California Press, 1972, 231–255.

_____ . *Islam and Revolution: Writings and Declarations of Imam Khomeini.* Berkeley: Mizan Press, 1981.

Ansari, Hamied. *Egypt: The Stalled Society.* Albany: State University of New York Press, 1986.

Antoun, Richard, and Mary Hegland, eds. *Religious Resurgence: Contemporary Cases in Islam, Christianity, and Judaism.* Syracuse: Syracuse University Press, 1987.

Arjomand, Said Amir. *The Turban for the Crown: The Islamic Revolution in Iran.* New York: Oxford University Press, 1988.

Ashraf, Ahmad. "Bazaar and Mosque in Iran's Revolution." *Merip Reports* 113 (March-April 1983): 16–18.

_____ . "Bazaar-Mosque Alliance: The Social Basis of Revolts and Revolutions." *Politics, Culture, and Society* 1, no. 4 (1988): 538–567.

Ashraf, Ahmad, and Ali Banuazizi. "The State, Classes, and Modes of Mobilization in the Iranian Revolution." *State, Culture, and Society* 1, no. 3 (1985): 3–40.

Ayubi, Nazih N. M. "The Politics of Militant Islamic Movements in the Middle East." *Journal of International Affairs* 36, no. 2 (Fall-Winter 1982–1983): 271–283.

Bakhash, Shaul. "Sermons, Revolutionary Pamphleteering, and Mobilization: Iran, 1978." In Said Amir Arjomand, ed., *From Nationalism to Revolutionary Islam.* Albany: State University of New York Press, 1984, 177–194.

_____ . *The Reign of the Ayatollahs: Iran and the Islamic Revolution.* Rev. ed. New York: Basic Books, 1990.

Bayat, Mangol. "Islam in Pahlavi and Post-Pahlavi Iran: A Cultural Revolution?" In John L. Esposito, ed., *Islam and Development: Religion and Sociopolitical Change.* Syracuse: Syracuse University Press, 1980, 87–106.

Bianchi, Robert. *Unruly Corporatism: Associational Life in Twentieth-Century Egypt.* New York: Oxford University Press, 1989.

Bienen, Henry. "Urbanization and Third World Stability." *World Development* 12, no. 7 (1984): 661–691.

Bill, James A. "The Plasticity of Informal Politics: The Case of Iran." *Middle East Journal* 27, no. 2 (1973): 131–151.

_____ . *The Eagle and the Lion: The Tragedy of American-Iranian Relations.* New Haven: Yale University Press, 1988.

Bill, James A., and Robert Springborg. *Politics in the Middle East.* Glenview: Scott, Foresman, 1990.

Bruneau, Thomas C. "Brazil: The Catholic Church and Basic Christian Communities." In Daniel H. Levine, ed., *Religion and Political Conflict in Latin America.* Chapel Hill: University of North Carolina Press, 1986, 106–123.

Cohen, Abner. *Custom and Politics in Urban Africa: A Study of Hausa Migrants in Yoruba Towns.* Berkeley: University of California Press, 1969.

Cornelius, Wayne. *Politics and the Migrant Poor in Mexico City.* Stanford: Stanford University Press, 1975.

_____ . "Leaders and Official Patrons in Urban Mexico." In Steffen W. Schmidt, James C. Scott, Carl Lundé, and Laura Guasti, eds., *Friends, Followers, and Factions: A Reader in Political Clientelism.* Berkeley: University of California Press, 1977, 337–352.

Davis, Eric. "Ideology, Social Class, and Islamic Radicalism in Modern Egypt." In Said Amir Arjomand, ed., *From Nationalism to Revolutionary Islam.* Albany: State University of New York Press, 1984, 134–157.

Dekmejian, R. Hrair. "The Anatomy of Islamic Revival: Legitimacy Crisis, Ethnic Conflict, and the Search for Islamic Alternatives." *Middle East Journal* 34, no. 1 (1980): 1–12.

_____ . *Islam in Revolution.* Syracuse: Syracuse University Press, 1985.

Dietz, Henry, and Richard J. Moore. "Political Participation in a Non-Electoral Setting: The Urban Poor in Lima, Peru." (Monograph.) Athens: Center for International Studies, Ohio University, 1979.

Dodson, Michael. "Nicaragua: The Struggle for the Church." In Daniel H. Levine, ed., *Religion and Political Conflict in Latin America.* Chapel Hill: University of North Carolina Press, 1986, 79–105.

El Guindi, Fadwa. "Veiling Infitah with Muslim Ethic: Egypt's Contemporary Islamic Movement." *Social Problems* 28, no. 4 (1981): 465–485.

Etienne, Bruno. *L'Islamisme Radical.* Paris: Hachette, 1987.

Ferdows, Amir. "Khomeini and Fadayan's Society and Politics." *International Journal of Middle East Studies* 15 (1983): 241–257.

Fischer, Michael M. J. *Iran: From Religious Dispute to Revolution.* Cambridge: Harvard University Press, 1980.

Halliday, Fred. *Iran: Dictatorship and Development.* New York: Penguin Books, 1979.

Hudson, Michael. "Islam and Political Development." In John L. Esposito, ed., *Islam and Development: Religion and Sociopolitical Change.* Syracuse: Syracuse University Press, 1980, 1–24.

Huntington, Samuel P. *Political Order in Changing Societies.* New Haven and London: Yale University Press, 1968.

Ibrahim, Saad Eddin. "Islamic Militancy as a Social Movement: The Case of Two Groups in Egypt." In Ali E. Hillal Dessouki, ed., *Islamic Resurgence in the Arab World.* New York: Praeger, 1982, 117–137.

Karpat, Kemal H. *The Gecekondu: Rural Migration and Urbanization.* Cambridge: Cambridge University Press, 1976.

Kazemi, Farhad. *Poverty and Revolution in Iran: The Migrant Poor, Urban Marginality, and Politics.* New York: New York University Press, 1980a.

_____ . "Urban Migrants and the Revolution." *Iranian Studies* 13, nos. 1–4 (1980b): 257–277.

_____ . "The *Fada'iyan-e Islam:* Fanaticism, Politics, and Terror." In Said Amir Arjomand, ed., *From Nationalism to Revolutionary Islam.* Albany: State University of New York Press, 1984, 158–176.

Kepel, Gilles. *The Prophet and Pharaoh: Muslim Extremism in Egypt.* London: Al Saqi Books, 1985.

Levine, Daniel H. "Religion, the Poor, and Politics in Latin America Today." In Daniel H. Levine, ed., *Religion and Political Conflict in Latin America.* Chapel Hill: University of North Carolina Press, 1986a, 3–23.

_____ . "Is Religion Being Politicized? And Other Pressing Questions Latin America Poses." *Political Studies* 19, no. 4 (1986b): 825–831.

Milani, Mohsen M. *The Making of Iran's Islamic Revolution: From Monarchy to Islamic Republic.* Boulder: Westview Press, 1988.

Miller, William Green. "Political Organization in Iran: From Dowreh to Political Party (Part One)." *Middle East Journal* 23, no. 2 (1969): 159–167.

Mobasser, Soussan. "Le Bazaar de Téhéran." *Economie et Humanisme* 286 (1985): 49–61.

Mottahedeh, Roy. *The Mantle of the Prophet: Religion and Politics in Iran.* New York: Simon and Schuster, 1985.

Najmabadi, Afsaneh. "Iran's Turn to Islam: From Modernism to a Moral Order." *Middle East Journal* 41, no. 2 (1987): 202–217.

Nelson, Joan. *Access to Power: Politics and the Urban Poor in Developing Nations.* Princeton: Princeton University Press, 1979.

_____ . "Political Participation." In Myron Weiner and Samuel P. Huntington, eds., *Understanding Political Development*. Boston: Little, Brown, 1987, 103–159.

Parsa, Misagh. *Social Origins of the Iranian Revolution*. New Brunswick: Rutgers University Press, 1989.

Perlman, Janice E. *The Myth of Marginality: Urban Poverty and Politics in Rio de Janeiro*. Berkeley: University of California Press, 1976.

Rassam, Amal. "Al-Taba'iyya: Power, Patronage, and Marginal Groups in Northern Iraq." In E. Gellner and J. Waterbury, eds., *Patrons and Clients in Mediterranean Societies*. London: Duckworth, 1977, 157–166.

Scott, James C. "Patron-Client Politics and Political Change in Southeast Asia." *American Political Science Review* 66, no. 1 (1972): 91–113.

Sivan, Emmanuel. *Radical Islam: Medieval Theology and Modern Politics*. New Haven: Yale University Press, 1985.

Spooner, Brian. "Religion and Society Today: An Anthropological Perspective." In E. Yarshater, ed., *Iran Faces the Seventies*. New York: Praeger, 1971, 166–188.

Springborg, Robert. *Mubarak's Egypt: Fragmentation of the Political Order*. Boulder: Westview Press, 1989.

Tabari, Azar. "The Role of the Clergy in Modern Iranian Politics." In Nikki R. Keddie, ed., *Religion and Politics in Iran: Shiism from Quietism to Revolution*. New Haven: Yale University Press, 1983, 47–72.

Taheri, Amir. "The Bazaar." *Kayhan International*, October 2, 1978.

_____ . *Holy Terror: The Inside Story of Islamic Terrorism*. London: Hutchinson, 1987.

Thaiss, Gustav. "Religion and Social Change in Iran: The Bazaar as a Case Study." In E. Yarshater, ed., *Iran Faces the Seventies*. New York: Praeger, 1971, 189–216.

_____ . "Religious Symbolism and Social Change: The Drama of Husain." In Nikki R. Keddie, ed., *Scholars, Saints, and Sufis: Muslim Religious Institutions Since 1500*. Berkeley: University of California Press, 1972, 349–366.

Waterbury, John. "Tribalism, Trade, and Politics: The Transformation of the Swasa of Morocco." In Ernest Gellner and Charles Micaud, eds., *Arabs and Berbers: Ethnicity and Nation-Building in North Africa*. London: Duckworth, 1972, 231–257.

Zonis, Marvin. *The Political Elite of Iran*. Princeton: Princeton University Press, 1971.

_____ . "Iran: A Theory of Revolution from Accounts of the Revolution." *World Politics* 35 (July 1983): 586–606.

5 Contested Images & Implications of South African Nationhood

ANTHONY W. MARX

Groups have often imposed their control of a state through violent means legitimized by claims of representing a nation. Once established, such national rule is often reinforced through cultural forms of violence, including the projection of the dominant national culture and the denigration of subordinated cultures. Oppressed and politically excluded groups frequently respond through confrontation, not only with their own physical violence but also by contesting the dominant images of the nation. Alternate forms of nationalism then develop out of experience and as a basis for understanding future experience—for instance, by giving meaning to violence suffered and perpetrated. Thus, conceptions of nationhood may be central to many of the violent confrontations described in this volume.

Conceptions of nationhood are part of the terrain of violent struggle, broadly defined to include contested justifications for physical violence. This contestation is part of what Antonio Gramsci (1971: 6, 238) called the "war of position" in which a state's efforts to project a dominant national identity as fixed are confronted by opposing groups' "organic" conceptions. This process gives rise to an array of historically specific forms of national identity by which people define themselves. These conceptions may then shape shifting repertoires of collective action. Just as ruling elites differ and redefine their own senses of nationalism to meet strategic needs, so competing images of nationhood can emerge from below and change over time. Nationhood is clearly a fluid concept despite efforts of various groups to project their national identity as ascriptive.

Claims to self-determination are often expressed in contested images of nationhood, as is the case in many of the confrontations discussed in this volume. This process is central to the unfolding events in South Africa, where exclusive claims of Afrikaner, African, and other forms of ethnic nationalism have been contested by the African National Congress's assertion of a single nation united by opposition to apartheid. To assess these conflicting claims, it is useful to begin with a discussion of relevant theoretical definitions of nations in general.

Much of the social science literature on nations implicitly adopts an ascriptive definition of this term, attesting to the attraction of formalizing otherwise-amorphous concepts to fixed terms of reference. Much as class has often been defined according to economic position and race according to physical characteristics, a nation has similarly been defined by objective characteristics. As discussed in many of the contributions to this volume, such apparently ascriptive formulations ignore the fact that such categories are instead socially constructed. It is no doubt revealing that the quintessential ascriptive definition of a nation was formulated by Joseph Stalin as "an historically evolved, stable community arising on the basis of a common language, territory, economic life, and psychological makeup manifested in a community of culture" (Davis 1978: 71). Stalin followed Lenin in asserting the right of self-determination for all nations so defined, ironically providing a justification for the nationalist claims that have pulled the Soviet Union apart.

Despite the attractions of such a fixed definition of nations, the historical process of evolution to which Stalin referred subverts his formulation. What appears as a stable nation one day may not have been so in the past and may not remain so in the future; and what appears as a distinct nation has often later divided into subunits, each claiming its own distinct nationhood. At any given point in time, the purported nation-defining characteristics of a common language, territory, economy, and culture often do not fully overlap; and no one of these characteristics by itself is definitive of a nation (Connor 1987). As Max Weber (1946: 172–176) understood, a nation is "not identical with . . . the membership of a given polity . . . [or] with a community speaking the same language. . . . The idea of the nation is apt to include notions of common descent and of an essential, though frequently indefinite, homogeneity." Nation remains an "ambiguous term" expressing a "sentiment of solidarity in the face of other groups"; it evokes a "common political destiny [that] would adequately manifest itself in a state of its own," although its boundaries and goals are developed historically and may vary.

The problem of formulating an abstract definition of what makes up a nation reflects the complex historical process from which the concept of a nation emerged. Nations did not always have the same level of salience. If they had, for instance, Great Britain would not have placed a German on its throne in 1714 (Rothschild 1981: 13). Nationhood first emerged in Europe during the period of state formation in the sixteenth century and was further consolidated during the industrialization in the nineteenth century. According to Benedict Anderson (1983: 41–49), the idea of a nation as an "imagined community" extending beyond the reach of direct personal interaction could only develop with the emergence of vernacular language and mass communication. Due particularly to the spread of newspapers, large groups of people came to perceive themselves as existing "simultaneously"—sharing ideas and information at the same time, for instance, within the extended boundaries of the readership of periodicals.

For the majority of the world beyond Europe, the idea of nationhood emerged not only out of the spread of vernacular mass communication but also out of these countries' history of being dominated, colonized, and exploited by Europe. In response to the experience of oppression, people forged the idea of their own right to self-determination. Nationalist movements emerged that called for united protest against foreign rule. Such nationalism became the basis for, first—in Gramsci's terms—a war of position, spreading an independent identity counterposed to colonial hegemony; it later became the basis for a war of maneuver in the fight for liberation. After nationalists came to power, as in most of Africa during the 1960s, the new ruling elites used the requirements of national development to demand continued unity and to justify subordination of divergent class interests. Nationalism was used in this way to justify the progressive goal of independence and later the conservative goal of regime consolidation.

The key to the concept of a nation is the perception and projection of commonality, which despite its problematic and varying nature is more central to the concept than any objectively shared attributes. Nations are social constructs of belief, the subjective element Stalin's definition omits. Karl Marx's analysis (1977: 317–318) that classes may exist objectively *in* themselves but can only become a political force if they are conscious and organized to act *for* themselves can also be applied to various concepts of nations within a political system. Commonalities of language or culture may exist, but only if people believe they are a nation can a nation be said to exist and act for itself as such. Historians have demonstrated that varying culturally informed conceptions of class can exist within the same economic system, and again the same argument can be applied to nations.

The definition of a nation thus remains subjective or, in social science terms, situational or cultural, although its link to political aspirations of self-determination provides an analytic distinction from other collectivities. Classes are mobilized to seek interests defined as economic, whereas races are mobilized to project or resist discrimination linked to perceptions of physical differences. Nations seek states, although the two do not necessarily coincide—especially when plural visions coexist. A nation is the collective aspiration, whereas the state is the legal institutionalized fulfillment of one version of this goal. If the state is the body, the nation is the soul or, in plural systems, the souls. And the soul is always difficult to define because it is subject to conflicting temptations and ideals.

COMPETING NATIONAL IMAGES IN SOUTH AFRICA

South Africa has long attracted peoples of various origins, languages, and cultures into its vast territory at the tip of the southern African subcontinent. Indigenous peoples, enjoying rich pastoral land and abundant game, expanded their settlements throughout the region long before the first whites arrived. In the late seventeenth century, the Dutch established a station in Cape Town to service their trade route to the East. During the subsequent two centuries, the settler population grew—attracted by fertile land, the opportunity to establish a new social order, and colonial interests. By the early eighteenth century, the English had taken control of the strategically located cape, provoking groups of Dutch descendants—called Afrikaners—to set off to the north in order to avoid British rule. The discovery of diamonds and gold in the Transvaal region during the late nineteenth century exacerbated the growing conflict for control of the land. British forces suffered significant setbacks but eventually succeeded in defeating the Zulus in Natal, other indigenous groups, and finally the Afrikaners with whom they fought during the Boer War at the turn of this century (Davenport 1977; Thompson 1990).

Given the intense conflict for political control among the different peoples who came to live in South Africa, it is not surprising that cultural differences generated distinct claims of national rights to self-determination. Such claims developed historically—particularly among the indigenous peoples and the Afrikaners, who did not share British loyalties to a distant state. It was the Afrikaners, well versed in the European political traditions, who first enunciated their aspirations in explicitly national terms.

Afrikaner nationalism was forged in the crucible of the Boer War. During this conflict, one out of every six Afrikaners lost his or her life, including women and children who died of starvation in British concentration camps. This searing collective experience and the British domination that followed fanned the growing flames of Afrikaner nationalism. In 1918 elites of Dutch descent formed a secret society, the Broederbond, to coordinate efforts at spreading the imagery of Afrikaner culture and ensuring the use of the Afrikaans language. The Broederbond included a particularly large contingent of teachers—strategically placed to indoctrinate the youth—and clergymen from the Dutch Reformed church (Harrison 1981: 26, 84–102). In 1938 this group further encouraged Afrikaner nationalism by staging elaborate celebrations of the one hundredth anniversary of "the Great Trek" of Afrikaners north from the cape, contributing to a rising "mythology of apartheid" reinforced by manipulation of religious imagery (Thompson 1985). Ten years later—in 1948—the Afrikaners' National party channeled the sentiment of nationalism into an electoral victory. Apartheid restrictions on political and social rights differentiated by official categories of race were formally established to preserve Afrikaner culture and political power against the threat posed by the African majority.

Although Afrikaner nationalism was projected as being based on ascriptive traits such as common ancestry, culture, and language, these images were purposefully manipulated by an elite seeking political power. The history of the Afrikaners as a "chosen" and oppressed people was mythologized. By projecting an innate ethnic bond as the basis for an economic and political redistribution, the Afrikaners managed to reverse their political misfortunes. They directed much of the resources from cheap black labor, the country's natural wealth, and unprecedented industrial growth during the 1950s and 1960s to the reinforcement of an Afrikaner-dominated national order. Through its control of the state, the National party's Afrikaner elite—which gained state power—was able to use educational policy, control of the state media, patronage, and coercion to reinforce cultural distinctions and its own rule (Uys 1989). Particularly since the mid-1980s, the Conservative party and other right-wing Afrikaner groups have mobilized against reforms of this rule without the advantage of direct control over state resources.

The rise of Afrikaner identity brought the imagery of nationhood into the center of South African politics, establishing a conceptual terrain other groups sought to contest. Prominent among these alternatives was the imagery of an inclusive South African nationalism that was developed by the African National Congress (ANC), which was an opponent of minority rule. Founded in 1912 by a coalition of black middle-class and traditional elites, the ANC began as a relatively nonmilitant group pressing for a modicum of black political rights (Lodge 1983). By 1952, according to the Congress's then-president Chief Albert Luthuli, thirty years had been spent "knocking in vain, patiently, moderately, and modestly at a closed and barred door" (Mandela 1965: 165).

The emergence in the 1940s of a new generation of ANC activists, organized as the ANC Youth League, led to a shift of the ANC as a whole away from its history of elite protest toward more confrontational mass mobilization. During the 1950s, the ANC joined with white, "coloured" (the state's category for people of "mixed race"), and "Indian" groups to form a congress alliance that was able to mobilize even broader opposition to the minority regime (Gerhart 1978: 105–123).

The alternative nationalism of the ANC and its allies was formalized in the Freedom Charter, which was unveiled at a Congress of the People in 1955. The charter, adherents of which are identified as Charterists, proclaims that "South Africa belongs to all who live in it, black and white" (Suttner and Cronin 1986: 262). Although the charter goes on to advocate the "equal rights . . . for all national groups . . . to use their own language and to develop their own folk culture and customs," the central imagery of the charter remains a single, South African, democratic nation. Responding to subsequent criticism from radical intellectuals, most notably Neville Alexander (alias "No Sizwe"), more recently the ANC has downplayed any rhetorical reference to separate national or racial groups, focusing instead on its claim to represent all South Africans (Alexander 1985; No Sizwe 1976). Ascriptive definitions of nationhood were at least rhetorically rejected and were replaced by references to a Weberian collective sentiment, as enunciated by the ANC leadership: "The nation then is not defined by skin color or racial designation, its parameters are set by individual acts of voluntary adherence . . . by a commitment to the country, its people, and its future" (Diepen 1988: 10). Only "committed racists" were excluded by their own beliefs from this image of a unified "nonracial" South African nation, effectively labeling themselves "foreigners" by their own beliefs (Diepen 1988: 10, 118).

The ANC's efforts to project an inclusive nationalism did not win over white racists; it also antagonized more militant blacks. Within the ranks of the ANC Youth League—together with Nelson Mandela, Walter Sisulu, and others who became the next generation of ANC leaders—was another group that continued to be inspired by the separatist rhetoric of a founder of the league, Anton Lembede (Gerhart 1978: 45–82). This group became increasingly disaffected by the ANC's efforts to cooperate with whites, coloreds, and Indians in a congress alliance and as enunciated by the Freedom Charter. Under the subsequent leadership of Robert Sobukwe, this group broke away from the ANC in 1959 to found the Pan Africanist Congress (PAC).

These Africanists propounded yet another form of nationalism, claiming the right to self-determination of Africans alone. According to analyst Gail Gerhart, this African nationalism was more "orthodox" than that of the ANC and was defined according to the ascriptive commonality of the indigenous peoples and their right to the land (Gerhart 1978: 129). All who accepted the primacy of African nationalism were officially invited to join the PAC, acknowledging the subjective element of such a collective identity, although the organization remained open effectively to only black Africans.

The state's 1960 banning of both the ANC and the PAC, a move that was intended to curtail growing mass protests, left unresolved the debate within the opposition between competing images of an inclusive South African nationalism and an exclusive Africanism. Continued state repression funded through economic growth during the subsequent fifteen years enabled the National party to solidify its hold on power. Having consolidated Afrikaner nationalism and having at least temporarily disrupted the emerging opposition, the ruling elite began to institutionalize a set of African national identities by which it hoped to divide future potential resistance to minority rule. Under the 1961–1966 leadership of Prime Minister Hendrick Verwoerd, the state began to set in place its plan of "separate development." Africans were officially divided into nine major tribal groups, with each given its own "homeland"—all of which together eventually made up roughly 13 percent of South Africa's territory. By 1985, 3.5 million Africans had been forcibly relocated.[1] By granting a limited form of autonomy to these homelands, the South African government hoped to deflect demands of common political rights for all South Africans into the development of separate national aspirations. However, the homelands remained too impoverished, overpopulated, and dependent on South African funding and migratory labor in the white areas to succeed at redirecting the political aspirations of the majority.

Kwazulu—the territory in Natal designated for South Africa's largest ethnic grouping, the Zulus—was the only homeland in which a distinct form of nationalism did develop. The chief minister of Kwazulu, Gatsha Buthelezi, shrewdly used his control of local patronage, the police force, and other administrative apparatuses funded directly by the South African state to solidify his popular appeal. In 1975 Buthelezi established Inkatha, a "cultural organization" that manipulated traditional Zulu imagery of a warrior chieftaincy to mobilize ethnic nationalism (Brewer 1986, 1989). Buthelezi's condemnation of both the ANC's guerrilla activities and the socialist rhetoric of its allies brought Inkatha additional support from white South Africans and international business (Brewer 1986: 374–379). But these same positions alienated increasingly militant blacks who were inspired by the ANC attacks and favored some form of economic redistribution. As popular black support shifted accordingly away from Inkatha in the mid-1980s, Buthelezi's operatives turned increasingly to the use of violence to assert his will (Orkin 1986:

37–44). Thousands died in violent clashes between Inkatha and supporters of the ANC-aligned United Democratic Front (UDF). This conflict was concentrated first in Natal and by 1990 had spread into the Transvaal. Although this strategy of coercion won Buthelezi a place in the negotiations of the early 1990s, Inkatha and emergent Zulu nationalism remain dependent on state support. As such, Inkatha can be described as largely a sideshow, albeit a violent and disruptive one, to the ongoing development of mainstream opposition to minority rule.

During the 1970s, the focus of South African opposition shifted from the then-exiled ANC and PAC to the internal development of the Black Consciousness (BC) movement founded by Steven Biko. Emerging first among students, BC largely abandoned the nationalist rhetoric of its predecessors, stressing instead the racial identity of blacks. The state's official definitions of racial categories were challenged by BC, which redefined black to include the coloured and Indian populations who also suffered from official discrimination. Whites were excluded from the movement in order to encourage black self-reliance and assertiveness, by which the BC movement hoped to inspire a revitalization of internal opposition. The Soweto uprising of 1976, although not directly orchestrated by BC, attested to the psychological impact of the movement. During this period, a black working-class movement was reconstituted by newly established unions, as I have described elsewhere (Marx 1989). Gender issues also gained greater salience, as indicated by the later resurgence of the Federation of South African Women. However, both the union and women's movements remained subordinate to the more popular efforts of BC and later the UDF, with only the latter explicitly employing nationalist rhetoric (Marx 1991).

Given the heterogeneity of the South African population, this array of political movements is not surprising. That various movements developed distinct forms of nationalism or ideologies based on other forms of identity, such as race and class, reflects the diversity of collective sentiments possible in South Africa. Each of these movements, black and white, was constructed with reference to particular essentialized characteristics, but how these were interpreted and defined was central to the political process of group formation. Afrikaner nationalism, the ANC's inclusive South African nationalism, the PAC's exclusive African nationalism, and Inkatha's Zulu nationalism all expressed aspirations of self-determination of distinct forms. Whereas the Afrikaners and Inkatha claimed the rights of distinctive cultural identity, Africanists claimed indigenous rights to the land and the ANC claimed the political rights of all South Africans to democratic participation. No single fixed definition of nationalism could account for such diversity or for the development of nonnationalist sentiments; nor could it account for the resurgence of Charterist nationalism in the years since the late 1970s.

RESURGENCE OF CHARTERIST NATIONALISM

The decade of the 1980s saw the emergence of unprecedented levels of mass mobilization and political conflict in South Africa. This heightening of the conflict for power emerged from a complex interplay of popular movements, ideologies, grass-roots organizations, state repression, and economic and international changes. Activist elites played a vital role in these developments, although much of the opposition leadership was jailed or in exile during this period. The resulting conflict cannot be dismissed as simply chaotic because an underlying order to opposition efforts was evident, as suggested in the following analysis. However, in the late 1970s the direction of such ongoing opposition remained to be determined, emerging out of a combination of deliberations among activists and their responses to changing conditions.

With the banning of the BC movement in September 1977, just over a year after the Soweto uprising, the political stage of the opposition was again open for appropriation. Many activists felt the Black Consciousness psychological focus on reshaping racial identity in order to heighten mass assertiveness had exhausted its usefulness. As described by Azchar Bhaum, a student leader, these activists concluded that in the 1970s, BC had succeeded in inspiring a "psychological reawakening" despite some limitations, providing "a foundation" on which further opposition could be built.[2] Unionist Khetsi Lehoko, for example, recalls a growing sense that BC was "all talk and no action . . . unable to answer day-to-day problems in the community and workplace. It couldn't be translated into practice, and we needed a theory that presented a program for action."[3]

Although many people appreciated the achievements of BC, many were ready for a less idealistic approach to opposition—concluding that they needed "physical liberation" first, then "[we can] propagate correct ideas" (Ngwenya 1976: 56). There was also a growing sense that BC's focus on race and exclusion of whites presented a self-imposed limitation on the greater incorporation of both class analysis, which was growing in popularity among activists, and sympathetic whites. BC's image of black unity was also contradicted by the rising number of blacks working for the state, particularly in the homeland governments. These criticisms built on earlier debates within the BC movement that had been sidetracked by the 1976 uprising. BC loyalists, having reconstituted themselves as the Azanian Peoples Organization (AZAPO) in 1977–1978, sought to retain the leadership of the opposition. AZAPO adherents argued that their continued focus on race could be adjusted to new conditions, but other activists remained skeptical.

These debates about the future direction of the opposition were concentrated at first among activist elites, who were grouped together in prison after the 1976 Soweto uprising. More than eighty such activists were detained together in the group cells of Modderbee Prison outside Johannesburg, where intensive discussions led the majority to abandon the BC framework. A similar process occurred among those activists convicted of political crimes and sent to Robben Island, where Nelson Mandela and other older ANC leaders helped to influence a shift away from BC toward the ANC's Charterism. In the following years, many of these former BC activists and "graduates" of the "university" of Robben Island became leaders of a resurgent nationalist movement.

Activists in prison and others remaining at liberty during this period were further influenced by the rising guerrilla activity of the ANC. In the years following 1976, many students had decided to seek military training outside the country, with an estimated 250 fleeing South Africa each month during 1978 (Davis 1987: 57; Kane-Berman 1978: 144–145). According to activist Vincent Mogane, "Many students who left were still young and unclear; not yet fully panel beaten," or ideologically developed.[4] These students often lacked a strong preference between the ANC and the PAC, but they found that only the former was able to accommodate them and to provide training whereas the latter exile group remained small and divided. The ANC had carefully built up international financial support since 1960 and had capitalized on the independence of Mozambique and Angola in 1975, and later of Zimbabwe in 1980, to establish training bases that could accommodate the influx of students. By 1977 many of these students had already surreptitiously returned to South Africa, launching a wave of guerrilla attacks (Davis 1987: 28, 57; Lodge 1983: 340). As ANC official Joe Slovo acknowledged, this "revolutionary practice and not just revolutionary theory" won the ANC considerable support among a populace eager to see the state's repression directly challenged (Slovo 1983: 10).

The ANC's popularity was bolstered in the late 1970s, not only by increased guerrilla activity but also by growing informal and media discussions of the history and symbols of the exiled group. The Freedom Charter, which had been allowed to drift into relative obscurity, was reprinted and widely circulated. Prisoners returning from Robben Island added new stories that contributed to the mythological status of Nelson Mandela, Walter Sisulu, and the other ANC elder statesmen. Family and other informal networks further contributed to the rising popularity of the ANC, for instance, with Walter Sisulu's wife Albertina explaining that "I had to sit Zwelakhe [one of their sons who had been active in BC] down at the kitchen table and teach him about history and about his family."[5] By 1980 a poll of black students found that allegiance to the exiled ANC had risen to 49 percent from 22 percent two years earlier, whereas loyalty to BC had fallen from 54 to 35 percent during the same period (Orkin 1989: 454).

The transition from BC to Charterist nationalism cannot be fully accounted for by reference only to the external activities of the ANC or abstract deliberations concentrated among activist elites. At the same time these processes were under way, more pervasive changes in economic conditions and state policy were emerging that would help further channel popular activities and aspirations in directions consistent with Charterism.

From 1979 through 1981, the South African economy recovered briefly from the oil shocks of the 1970s, with the annual gross domestic product rising by an average of 4.5 percent during each of these years (Republic of South Africa 1989a: table 21.9). Eager to restore domestic stability and investor confidence, the South African state directed a portion of its increasing resources toward the black community while relaxing some of its security measures. In 1979, for instance, black unions were legalized and some restrictions on black urbanization were lifted. As one student group described it, the regime of P. W. Botha set out to use "reform to buy off certain sectors of the population by granting limited political and economic concessions while ensuring that ultimate power rests with itself" (Student Committee Against the New Constitution 1983).

The state's material and legal reforms had the perhaps unintended consequence of encouraging the formation of local organizations eager to capitalize on the possibility of material concessions. By the early 1980s, local civic associations were forming in townships throughout South Africa. As described by Popo Molefe, future national secretary of the UDF, this local mobilization signaled "the emergence of first level grass-roots organizations which have the ability to address that which is essential, real, and vital to them. And on that basis [we could] teach them the skills of organization and democracy, to give them the confidence that through their united mass action they can intervene and change their lives on no matter how small a scale" (National Union of South African Students 1983: 28–29).

These local organizations did not focus on changing ideas about racial identity, as the more elitist student-based BC movement had done, but instead actively sought improved living conditions and services. Their pragmatic emphasis on strategic advances over ideological refinement was consistent with the Charterist tradition of the ANC, which had similarly focused on mass mobilization in contrast to the more militant ideological concerns of the PAC. In addition, according to Cassim Saloojee, later the treasurer of the UDF, these local civic associations and service organizations "had to reach out to all who could help, including white professionals with experience and training no blacks had."[6] As a result, the grass-roots movement reinforced the growing commitment to the Charterist tradition of nonracialism and the shift away from BC's exclusivity, although local organizations remained effectively segregated according to distinct residential areas and interests. It was unavoidable, according to Albertina Sisulu, that organizers worked most effectively "where you know best."[7] Over time these local political centers shifted more explicitly toward Charterism, sharing the pragmatic belief enunciated by Lenin that "the struggle for reforms is but a means of marshalling the forces" for more fundamental change (Wolfe 1948: 120).

Local activists shared the pragmatism of the Charterist tradition but might not have emerged into a fully fledged nationalist movement if state policies in the early 1980s had not created the impetus for unifying their disparate activities. In May 1982, P. W. Botha's government proposed a new tri-cameral parliament that would have provided limited political representation for the coloured and Indian populations but not for the African majority. This proposal legally required a white referendum and subsequent elections among coloureds and Indians, but it also galvanized the local organizations around a unifying national issue. According to Ismail Mohamed, later a vice president of the UDF in the Transvaal, "the tri-cameral parliament proposals were a blessing. They gave us the opportunity to politic since the state wanted a broader base."[8] In early 1983, a national forum was founded by a coalition of Charterists, BC loyalists, and socialists such as Neville Alexander to coordinate opposition to the proposed constitution. On August 20, 1983, the Charterists set out on their own for the same purpose, launching the United Democratic Front as a coalition initially of more than six hundred locally based groups.

With the formation of the UDF, the emergent grass-roots organizations began to solidify into a national movement. Local groups, realizing that their material grievances would not be fully met without a change in the broader political dispensation, joined together for what was described as a national democratic struggle focused initially on resistance to the new constitution. Aspirations for a united democratic South Africa linked these groups, with images of nationhood used as a metaphor for their unity. The front's leadership was careful to reinforce this imagery and to avoid any formal positions that might antagonize potential adherents. At its launch, Reverend Frank Chikane described the UDF as "standing for unity in action, accepting the fact that all organizations coming together have . . . differences . . . of class, differences of ideology, differences of intent, but all of them agree that they reject the reform proposals" (United Democratic Front 1983: 3).

Linked by common opposition to the new constitution if not by a more positive agenda, the UDF incorporated individual leaders and groups with a diversity of views. In order to encourage affiliation by non-Charterists, the front did not formally endorse the Freedom Charter, although prominent officials nonetheless proclaimed that "the ideas of the Freedom Charter will be pursued by the UDF" as a guiding and unifying manifesto (United Democratic Front 1983: 32). Radical unionists described the UDF as socialist, whereas more moderate leaders countered that economic policies would be worked out later depending on the future "strength of the working class itself in the class alliance that we call a people's democracy" (Suttner and Cronin 1986: 213; United Democratic Front 1983: 20). UDF-affiliated youth called for direct confrontation with the state, whereas leaders warned that "the system has many ways of provoking people into rash actions and that is one thing you must guard against" (United Democratic Front 1983: 15).

This diversity of views is indicative of the broad coalition represented by the UDF. Affiliates ranged from militant youth groups to pragmatic civic associations and liberal white organizations. Many front officials were more moderate than affiliate members, with one analyst noting that the UDF leadership was notable for being "heavily middle class" (Lodge 1987: 2). The ability of the front to avoid debilitating divisions despite these differences can be explained in part as a result of the organization's loose structure. The leadership was never held directly accountable to the membership of affiliated organizations, which allowed potentially contentious issues to remain unresolved. Indeed, many among the rank and file were happy to let the leadership make complicated decisions for them. As described by unionist and UDF activist Gatsby Mazrui, "The grass-roots, without education and politicization, don't put demands. . . . Unfortunately, this means intellectuals tend to lead. The onus is on that level to take the initiative. It sounds undemocratic, but our situation is not a normal one."[9]

The UDF's ability to incorporate seemingly contradictory views was also indicative of its basic nature as a national movement. The underlying purpose of the front was to forge strategic unity, not to propound specific policies. As described by activist Aubrey Mokoena, all groups and tendencies were "invited to come under the big umbrella of the UDF" so that all would benefit from the advantages of united action.[10] Ideological cohesion was not seen as a necessity to achieve this end because all potential disagreements were purposefully postponed for discussion only after democracy had been achieved. The UDF sought to incorporate the broadest possible array of followers, on occasion even pressuring affiliation by reluctant groups. As described by former Robben Island prisoner Fikile Bam, "The UDF was not trying to win minds, just support, and [was] willing to use bullying and intimidation" to achieve this goal.[11]

The UDF's lack of ideological cohesion was severely criticized by more dogmatic activists such as BC loyalist Lybon Mabasa, who argued that "unity is good, but not at all costs" (Mabasa 1984: 6). But the practical benefits of the UDF's loose coalition were undeniable. With its efforts to constrain more militant adherents and by avoiding any clear commitments to socialism, the front was able to win the support of more moderate groups including middle-class blacks, liberal whites, businessmen, and international donors. These groups contributed significant resources to the front, which by 1987 had a budget of over R2 million and a professional staff of more than eighty.[12] According to UDF national treasurers Cassim Saloojee and Azhar Cachalia, more than R200 million was contributed each year to organizations formally affiliated with or linked to the front.[13] These funds were used to further spread the UDF's message of unity—emblazoned on posters, tee-shirts, and pamphlets and proclaimed in mass rallies, at concerts, and in newspaper advertisements. The front also used its funds to provide services to local groups, many of which later affiliated themselves with the UDF more for pragmatic advantage than as an expression of ideological affinity. As one squatter in Katlehong admitted in explaining his adherence to the UDF, "If they didn't have money, that would be a big problem."[14]

The Charterists shrewdly used the opportunities of the late 1970s and early 1980s to consolidate a nationalist movement, which was formally united as the UDF by 1983. Economic recovery and state reforms had encouraged the formation of locally based groups seeking material redress for their grievances. As the ANC had used armed attacks and publicity to regain its popularity, activist elites had found that the Congress's charter expressed their own pragmatic concerns. The state's constitutional proposals had provided a rationale for a front linking these activists and local groups, with the UDF carefully positioning itself to be as far-reaching and financially strong as possible.

With these developments, the UDF was well positioned to lead the South African opposition through the tumultuous years of the mid-1980s. By 1982 the South African economy was beginning to suffer from the effects of a world recession; this was exacerbated after 1985 by the impact of capital flight and formal international sanctions. Among black South Africans, unemployment and food costs soared, and overcrowding in urban housing and schools reached unprecedented levels (Gelb 1987: 42; Murray 1987: 354, 361; Planact 1990: 21–33). As the raised expectations of the post-1976 era increasingly went unmet or were reversed, popular resentment grew (Orkin 1986: 34; Schlemmer 1984).

In 1984 these pressures finally exploded, first with the spread of rent boycotts in the Vaal townships south of Johannesburg. Within a year, most of South Africa's townships—which were already organized into civic associations and related structures—initiated similar rent boycotts, consumer boycotts of white shops, and worker stay-aways. These actions were designed to put direct pressure on employers, shopkeepers, and local authorities who might influence the state. Even nonurban areas joined in protest despite the greater vulnerability of rural people to harsh police attacks. Widespread popular unrest—more pervasive and better organized than the 1976 uprising— had begun.

The Charterist organizations both inside and outside the country quickly endorsed the rising protests, providing at least the appearance of coordination for a largely locally based initiative. In January 1985 the ANC in exile issued a radio statement embracing the peoples' efforts to "render South Africa ungovernable" while at the same time almost doubling the number of guerrilla attacks launched within the country.[15] The UDF similarly embraced the protests, delicately seeking a balance between claiming credit for political advantage and distancing itself from particular incidents in order to avoid legal prosecution or conviction. Fanned in part by such encouragement, by mid-1985 unrest had left almost 900 dead. This number included the first victims of "necklacing," a form of immolation often reserved for blacks working with the state—much as collaborators met with violence in the other conflicts discussed in this collection. By the end of 1986, at least 350 had been killed by this gruesome method.[16]

Faced with this rising tide of unrest, the South African state soon dropped all pretense of continued reform. On July 21, 1985, a state of emergency was declared in 36 of the country's 266 magisterial districts. When this partial measure failed to halt the violence, a countrywide state of emergency was declared on June 12, 1986—four days before the tenth anniversary of the 1976 uprising. By early 1987 more than 26,000 people had been detained, almost 80 percent of whom were described as adherents of the UDF.[17]

Having developed in part out of the experience of repression in 1976–1977, the Charterist movement was well designed to initially withstand the states of emergency that began in 1985. Indeed, the real strengths of the movement became clearer during this period. Based on local organizations, the UDF was much better able to persevere in the face of state repression than the more centralized and elite BC movement had been. Street committees were formed to coordinate local protests, often also establishing "people's courts" that sought, for instance, to discipline youths who took advantage of the unrest to commit crimes. The state found it difficult at first to disrupt these activities; on occasion police resigned themselves to referring cases to informal local authorities in locations in which the state had clearly lost control.

With the spread of unrest, the demands associated with such protests no longer focused on local issues but called for the unbanning of the ANC, the release of Nelson Mandela, and an end to apartheid. As described at the time by Zwelakhe Sisulu, by 1986 "the masses linked up local issues with the question of political power. A set of national demands emerged which transcended specific issues or regional differences."[18] In this way, state repression helped to transform more fully the local protests of the early 1980s into a truly national movement.

The UDF sought to take full advantage of the growing national fervor by asserting its political dominance. In August 1987 the front formally adopted the Freedom Charter as a "comprehensive political program." This move indicated the UDF leadership's confidence that "the Front, through its correct line, has become the only viable home for those in the legal opposition movement who stand for political change" (United Democratic Front 1987: 1, 9). Not surprisingly, those groups that had remained outside the UDF resisted such assertions of the front's sole legitimacy. Violent conflict had already broken out between adherents of the UDF and the BC loyalists of AZAPO in the eastern Cape in 1985. By 1987 battles between the UDF and Inkatha emerged in Natal. Despite these conflicts, the UDF remained confident of its preeminence, encouraging the premature popular belief that the state's inability to restore order presaged an imminent transfer of power.

The exaggerated optimism of 1987 was quickly replaced by an equally exaggerated popular pessimism in 1988. Exhausted by continued battles with police and dislocated by large-scale detentions, mass resistance eventually began to wane. Even the street committees, with the exception of some in Soweto, were eventually disrupted by police harassment. In February 1988 the state effectively banned the UDF and related organizations. Popular disillusionment spread quickly with, for instance, squatters in Thokoza concluding in 1988 that "we will never see change in our lifetime. The UDF tried and failed."[19] Defeatism even spread into the UDF leadership with, for instance, Soweto activist Sebolelo Mohajane concluding that "the government has won. . . . Repression has worked."[20]

With this downturn in its fortunes, the previous strengths of the UDF turned into vulnerabilities. The loose structure and lack of ideological cohesion that had allowed for the front's rapid growth now left its adherents without clear principles by which a more decentralized struggle could be maintained. With few formal links between communities and the national leadership, the state's crackdown prevented UDF officials from using publicity to communicate with their followers. Divisions grew within the ranks, especially as funding of local initiatives was restricted and as the leadership became increasingly disconnected from the populace once mass meetings were banned. People increasingly criticized UDF officials for acting without consultation and for continuing to enjoy the privileges of their international connections as conditions for the rank and file deteriorated. The front seemed to some observers to be on the verge of collapse (Mufson 1987).

In a sense, the Charterist movement was saved from destruction only by the rapid pace of events in the late 1980s. For the last two years of the decade, the burgeoning union movement was able to fill the organizational void left by the effective banning of the UDF. The unions' strong organizational links between workers and officials together with their economic leverage exercised through massive strikes became the focus of popular energies and kept the pressure on the state (Marx 1989). The state was further weakened by recession, increased international economic sanctions, and capital flight as well as by the strains of a prolonged war in Namibia and Angola. By 1989 the newly elected F. W. deKlerk government had decided on a new policy direction of initiating a process of negotiations. In 1990 Nelson Mandela and other prisoners were released, and the ANC and PAC were unbanned. With the legalization of the older nationalist movements, the prospects for a settlement grew, although these were marred by the disruptive activities of Inkatha Zulu nationalism and growing right-wing Afrikaner nationalism.

CHARTERIST NATIONALISM IN PERSPECTIVE

The overview I have presented clearly demonstrates that no single form of national identity has united all South Africans at any one time. In just the last half of this century, South Africans have expressed shifting forms of Afrikaner, Charterist, Africanist, and Zulu nationalism. Groups have also formed around a primary focus on racial identity—as in the case of the Black Consciousness movement—and class identity—as in the case of the union movement. Each of these movements has expressed collective interests ranging from insistence on a cultural tradition or an end to discrimination to pursuit of material advancement.

For the majority of South Africans, collective action has long been focused pragmatically on alleviating deprivation—such as the procurement of a minimum of food, including the staple corn meal. As one Soweto resident explained figuratively, "Mealie meal is politics here. We have no other politics."[21] But even this common basic concern has been channeled at different times into rhetoric and collective action focused on varying national, racial, or class aspirations.

Although South Africans have continued to express a diversity of collective identities, during much of the 1980s popular opposition was dominated largely by the nationalist movement of the Charterists. In part, the development of this and other movements can be traced to the influence of economic conditions. Industrial growth since World War II brought large numbers of South Africans together into urban areas and large work places where it was easier for people to organize around material demands. This growth also created a small but relatively well-educated black middle class, which provided essential political leadership for the Charterist movement. During the 1980s economic growth faltered, with the country's average per-capita gross domestic product falling dramatically by 2.1 percent between 1981 and 1986 (Republic of South Africa 1989b: 485). This economic decline contributed to a rising mass militancy, providing the Charterists with a broader and energetic constituency (Hower 1985).

State policies also contributed to the development of the Charterist movement. Reforms in the late 1970s and early 1980s provided the opportunity and incentive for local organization. In 1983 these organizations joined together in the UDF to protest the state's proposed new constitution. By the mid-1980s heightened state repression further unified the opposition because as former unionist Eddie Zwane argued, "the harder [the state] tries, the better they make things for us. They organize for us."[22] Despite this optimistic interpretation, repression also exacted tremendous hardships and eventually helped to disrupt the coordination of the national movement.

Although economic changes and state policies were surely influential, they alone cannot account for the rise of Charterism. This development was also the result of a particular convergence of views and interests between elites and the rank and file. Activist leaders, particularly those brought together in prison cells in the aftermath of the 1976 uprising, engaged in lengthy discussions about the future direction of the opposition. The majority of these elites concluded that the relatively idealistic approach of BC had to be replaced by a more pragmatic focus on mass mobilization. At the same time, local groups forming to take advantage of state reforms began to engage in the sort of mobilization envisioned by the leadership. Both the elites and the local populace were impressed by the renewed guerrilla activities of the ANC and by the relatively pragmatic demands of the ANC's Freedom Charter.

The Charterist movement grew out of this coincidence of elite deliberations and mass action, although the impetus of the movement shifted between more privileged leaders and the masses. According to longtime activist Tom Manthata, "If there are no issues, people are led by the middle class. But if there is general dissatisfaction, then leaders are forced to follow the masses."[23] For instance, popular dissatisfaction during the economic decline and repression of the mid-1980s fueled mass unrest, which the UDF leadership sought to both embrace and contain. At first this development generated considerable optimism, which was later replaced by equally exaggerated defeatism once repression became more effective.

This description of the factors that contributed to the development of Charterism in the 1980s suggests the form of this nationalist movement. The UDF was built through local organization expressing material needs, on to which the leadership grafted a political agenda its followers found consistent with local demands. Achieving considerable organizational success, this agenda solidified into political allegiance that became increasingly insistent on its own dominance, seeking to but never fully succeeding at eclipsing other opposition groups.

Both the strength and the weakness of the Charterists can be traced to their fundamental objective of uniting all resistance within a single national movement. In an effort to be as inclusive as possible, the UDF sought to incorporate a wide spectrum of constituencies, ranging from militant youth to more moderate leaders and liberal allies. To achieve this goal, the UDF remained relatively vague on its specific policies, purposefully avoiding or postponing making decisions on potentially contentious issues. Aspiring to represent a diverse nation, the front saw no alternative to this pragmatic strategy, which had the immediate benefit of attracting a large following and substantial resources. The disadvantage of this strategy only became evident once the momentum of mass protest had faltered, when incipient internal divisions threatened to debilitate the movement before the initiation of negotiations between the ANC and the state.

CONCLUSION

This brief overview demonstrates the variety of historically specific forms of national identity that have emerged in recent South African history. The modern idea that nations deserve self-determination has inspired groups to define themselves accordingly. The Afrikaners gained, justified, and consolidated state rule through the violent projection of nationalism. Other groups have emerged out of the experience of domination with their own images of nationhood. Most notably, the Charterists found images of nationhood to be an effective tool for broad mobilization. The fundamental nationalist precept of inclusive pragmatism fit with popular aspirations. At the same time, this nationalism was just as fundamentally inconclusive, purposefully avoiding contentious issues that were postponed for discussion after self-determination had been achieved.

Only the future will tell whether South African nationalist unity will withstand the discussions of specific political, social, and economic policy that will become more pressing as the immediate goal of self-determination comes closer to fulfillment. Should the Charterists gain further political power in the years ahead, as seems likely, their nationalist calls for unity may shift from having a progressive to a more conservative implication. As was the experience in much of postindependence Africa, demands of unity may then be used by elites to counter the more militant and self-interested demands of various constituencies, including those of the unions and of youth. The comparatively high degree of organization achieved by such militants during the long struggle against South African minority rule may yet lead to conflict between these groups and nationalist elites. Having purposefully avoided resolving potential disputes in advance, the South African nationalist movement has implicitly accepted the risk of such subsequent disunity for the more immediate advantage of uniting antiapartheid forces.

NOTES

1. *The Star,* May 16, 1984.
2. Interview with Azchar Bhaum, April 1988.
3. Interview with Khetsi Lehoko, March 1988.
4. Interview with Vincent Mogane, March 1988.
5. Interview with Albertina Sisulu, June 1988.
6. Interview with Cassim Saloojee, February 1988.
7. Interview with Albertina Sisulu, June 1988.
8. Interview with Ismail Mohamed, March 1988.
9. Interview with Gatsby Mazrui, March 1988.
10. Interview with Aubrey Mokoena, February 1988.
11. Interview with Fikile Bam, July 1986.
12. *The Star,* May 7, 1987.
13. Interviews with Cassim Saloojee and Azhar Cachalia, February and June 1988.
14. Interview with Katlehong squatter, April 1988.
15. Tambo 1985; *Weekly Mail,* March 11, 1988.
16. Hower 1985; *The Star,* September 9, 1985 and March 1, 1986.
17. *Africa Confidential,* January 28, 1987: 5.
18. Interview with Zwelakhe Sisulu, August 1986.
19. Interview with Thokoza squatters, April 1988.
20. Interview with Sebolelo Mohajane, January 1988.
21. Interview with Soweto resident, April 1988.
22. Interview with Eddie Zwane, May 1988.
23. Interview with Tom Manthata, March 1988.

BIBLIOGRAPHY

Alexander, Neville. *Sow the Wind.* Johannesburg: Skotaville, 1985.
Anderson, Benedict. *Imagined Communities: Reflections on the Origin and Spread of Nationalism.* London: Verso, 1983.
Brewer, John D. *After Soweto: An Unfinished Journey.* Oxford: Clarendon Press, 1986.
_____ . "From Ancient Rome to Kwazulu: Inkatha in South African Politics." In Shaun Johnson, ed., *South Africa: No Turning Back.* Bloomington: Indiana University Press, 1989, 353–374.
Connor, Walker. "Ethnonationalism." In Myron Weiner and Samuel P. Huntington, eds., *Understanding Political Development.* Boston: Little Brown, 1987, 196–220.

Davenport, T.R.H. *South Africa: A Modern History.* London: Macmillan, 1977.

Davis, Horace B. *Toward a Marxist Theory of Nationalism.* New York: Monthly Review Press, 1978.

Davis, Stephen M. *Apartheid's Rebels: Inside South Africa's Hidden War.* New Haven: Yale University Press, 1987.

Diepen, Maria van, ed. *The National Question in South Africa.* London: Zed, 1988.

Gelb, Steve. "Making Sense of the Crisis." *Transformation* 5 (1987): 33–50.

Gerhart, Gail. *Black Power in South Africa: The Evolution of an Ideology.* Berkeley and Los Angeles: University of California Press, 1978.

Gramsci, Antonio. *Selections from the Prison Notebooks of Antonio Gramsci,* Quintin Hoare and Geoffrey Nowell-Smith, eds. New York: International Publishers, 1971.

Harrison, David. *The White Tribe of Africa.* Berkeley and Los Angeles: University of California Press, 1981.

Hower, George. "Cycles of Civil Unrest 76/84." *Political Monitor* 3 (Winter 1985): 1.

Kane-Berman, John. *Soweto: Black Revolt, White Reaction.* Johannesburg: Ravan Press, 1978.

Karis, Thomas, Gwendolen Carter, and Gail Gerhart. *From Protest to Challenge: A Documentary History of African Politics in South Africa 1882–1964,* 4 vols. Stanford: Hoover Institution Press, 1972–1977.

Lodge, Tom. *Black Politics in South Africa Since 1945.* Johannesburg: Ravan Press, 1983.

_____ . "The United Democratic Front: Leadership and Ideology." Photocopy of manuscript. Johannesburg: University of the Witwatersrand African Studies Institute, 1987.

Mabasa, Lybon. "Address to the AZAPO Fourth Congress." Photocopy of speech. 1984.

Mandela, Nelson. *No Easy Walk to Freedom.* London: Heinemann, 1965.

Marx, Anthony W. "South African Black Trade Unions as an Emerging Working Class Movement." *Journal of Modern African Studies* 27 (September 1989): 383–400.

_____ . "Race, Nation, and Class-Based Ideologies of Recent Opposition in South Africa." *Comparative Politics* 23 (April 1991): 313–327.

_____ . *Lessons of Struggle: South African Internal Opposition Movements, 1960–1990.* New York: Oxford University Press, 1992.

Marx, Karl. *Selected Writings,* edited by David McLellan. Oxford: Oxford University Press, 1977.

Mufson, Steven. "The Fall of the Front." *New Republic,* March 23, 1987: 17–19.

Murray, Martin. *South Africa: Time of Agony, Time of Destiny.* London: Verso, 1987.

National Union of South African Students, eds. *Beyond Reform: The Challenge of Change.* Cape Town: University of Cape Town, 1983.

Ngwenya, Joe. "A Further Contribution on the National Question." *African Communist* 67 (Fourth Quarter 1976): 48–59.

No Sizwe (Neville Alexander). *One Azania, One Nation: The National Question in South Africa.* London: Zed, 1976.

Orkin, Mark. *Disinvestment: The Struggle and the Future.* Johannesburg: Ravan Press, 1986.

_____ . "Of Sacrifice and Struggle: Ideology and Identity Among Black High School Students" Ph.D. dissertation. Johannesburg: University of the Witwatersrand, Department of Sociology, 1989.

Planact. "The Soweto Rent Boycott: A Report by Planact." Commissioned by the Soweto Delegation. Johannesburg, 1990.

Republic of South Africa, Central Statistical Service. *South African Statistics, 1988.* Pretoria: Government Printer, 1989a.

_____ . *South African Labour Statistics, 1988.* Pretoria: Government Printer, 1989b.

Rothschild, Joseph. *Ethnopolitics.* New York: Columbia University Press, 1981.

Schlemmer, Lawrence. "Political Unrest and African Rights: Part One." *Political Monitor* 2 (October 1984): 3.

Slovo, Joe. "A People's War." *Sechaba* 17 (April 1983): 7–13.

Student Committee Against the New Constitution. Photocopy of leaflet. August 4, 1983.

Suttner, Raymond, and Jeremy Cronin. *Thirty Years of the Freedom Charter.* Johannesburg: Ravan Press, 1986.

Tambo, Oliver. "Call to the Nation: The Future Is Within Our Grasp." Pamphlet. April 25, 1985.

Thompson, Leonard. *The Political Mythology of Apartheid.* New Haven: Yale University Press, 1985.

_____ . *A History of South Africa.* New Haven: Yale University Press, 1990.

United Democratic Front. "UDF Launch." Police Transcript from the Karis-Gerhart Collection. Mitchell's Plain, Cape Town, 1983.

_____ . *National Working Committee Conference.* Johannesburg: Khotso House, May 29–30, 1987.

Uys, Stanley. "The Afrikaner Establishment." In Shaun Johnson, ed., *South Africa: No Turning Back.* Bloomington: Indiana University Press, 1989, 206–239.

Weber, Max. *From Max Weber: Essays in Sociology,* H. H. Gerth and C. Wright Mills, eds. New York: Oxford University Press, 1946.

Wolfe, Bertram. *Three Who Made a Revolution.* Boston: Beacon Press, 1948.

6 Everyday Elite Resistance: Redistributive Agrarian Reform in the Philippines

JEFFREY M. RIEDINGER

In the yet-predominantly rural settings of the developing world, agrarian reform remains the most politically charged of the redistributive societal reforms and arguably the most important. Land-tenure structures have long been viewed as fundamental impediments to the enhancement of agricultural productivity and the initiation of a process of sustained economic development based on a vibrant agricultural sector. Moreover, land-tenure–related grievances have been regularly identified as being one, if not the principal, reason for civil conflict and social revolution. At a more general level, agrarian reform has been seen as the principal vehicle for political incorporation and control of the rural poor, a means of promoting peasant political participation tied to a political party or regime (Lipton 1974; Prosterman and Riedinger 1987).

This is not to suggest that there is unanimity of opinion concerning the benefits of agrarian reform. Scholars, landowners, and political elites have challenged the premises of agrarian reform—arguing that many earlier reforms occasioned little improvement in production, that reform beneficiaries escalated their demands on the government, that the threat of rural insurrection proved more apparent than real, and that the political costs in terms of alienated landed support associated with these modest achievements were considerable (Grindle 1986).

Agrarian reform policy—involving both redistribution of landownership and the development of complementary credit, extension, infrastructure, pricing, and research programs—has been central to the recent debate over political and social change in the Philippines. The Philippine People Power revolution of February 22–25, 1986, marked the triumph of a nonviolent populist movement headed by Corazon Aquino, the end of Ferdinand Marcos's authoritarian regime, the restoration of democratic political forms, and—it appeared—a renewed commitment to social and economic reform. These events provide an important new case with which to address questions concerning the links, if any, between the expansion of political rights and the reduction of socioeconomic inequalities. This chapter raises the issue of socioeconomic inequality in developing countries and questions the capacity of democratic regimes to effectuate redistributive reform. Is significant agrarian reform possible under the auspices of a transitional democracy?

Culture and politics converged in the debates over Philippine agrarian reform. Images of landowner and laborer, agricultural productivity, economies of scale, peasant capacities and aspirations, the contractions of paternalism, and connection to land were advanced and debated in political attempts to influence the design of reform policy. This chapter focuses on elite resistance to redistributive agrarian reform and finds that President Aquino and provincial elites shared political and rhetorical strategies to limit the scope and direction of reform. To do so they concentrated on certain critical issues that legitimized the abandonment of important elements of reform, disempowered rural populations on the threshold of democracy, and revealed contradictions in Philippine elite constructions of paternalism and reciprocity. For the present, those resisting reform have largely prevailed in the formulation of government policy, yet the dominant paradigm of agrarian relations is the subject of systematic and increasing challenges by peasants and social activists.

The agrarian reform debate and the various strategies to promote or resist a reformist agenda remind us that political opposition and confrontation entail much more than is ordinarily denoted by the term *violence*. Reductive definitions of violence, concerned only with physical harm and face-to-face confrontation, tend to minimize the power of rhetorical strategies aimed at miscasting the positions or muting the voices of other social actors. To be sure, the acts of physical violence committed by landowners' private armies and local militias (which were often indistinguishable from private armies) and threats of violent resistance were important in shaping the Philippine reform debate (McCoy 1991). This chapter, however, highlights the ways in which depoliticizing and disempowering discourse forms part of the continuum of violence and confrontation practiced by elites in resisting redistributive reform.

CONTESTED STATE-SOCIETY RELATIONS

In pursuing development and reform, the Philippine state has been forced to confront the complex relationship between reform and contested control. In other settings, development and reform initiatives by the state have unleashed unintended tensions and pressures that have threatened state control (Grindle 1986). Social groups have exhibited unexpected powers, pressuring for new state services or challenging the state's capacity to pursue wider reforms. The issue of control is especially problematic in the Philippines where geography, history, the private armies of large landowners, and insurgency all limit centralized control.

The autonomy of the Aquino regime in executing agrarian reform was circumscribed by both the organized political power of the landed elite and the economic significance of the agricultural sector. As in other countries, the Philippine agricultural sector has often been looked to as a source of surplus, providing cheap food for the urban sector and appreciable foreign exchange earnings. In an era of acute foreign indebtedness, there was—in the view of senior government officials—a high priority given to avoiding any disruption in existing sources of foreign exchange earnings. Landowners in the sugarcane sector, for example, played on this concern, repeatedly arguing that land redistribution would sound the death knell for sugarcane production—with sizable concomitant losses in foreign exchange earnings.[1] (At the time, low world prices for sugar appeared more likely than agrarian reform to constrain the Philippine sugar industry.)

Cultural features further defined the Philippine context for democratic rule and state-initiated reform; they include personal and group identifications along regional and ethnolinguistic lines, the principle of *utang na loób* (debt of gratitude) and patron-client relations, and the prominence of peasant grievances in the struggle for independence in the late nineteenth century and in several twentieth-century insurgencies. The changing role of the Catholic church was also pivotal in recent events.[2] Philippine culture has been shaped by the interplay between the local cultures of Philippine villages, which are ethnically and linguistically diverse, and a variety of foreign influences (Islam, Catholicism, and Spanish, U.S., and Japanese rule). Colonial policies and the penetration of the world market economy in the late nineteenth and early twentieth centuries did much to shape present-day state-society relations and the politics of agrarian reform. These policies and influences institutionalized dramatic inequalities in landownership and fragmented social control. Kinship and ethnolinguistic groups and landed regional and local elites contested the central state in governing the details of everyday life. Although the impact of these social groupings is typically limited to specific regions, their aggregate influence on the state and on state policy can be profound (Migdal 1988).

INTERPERSONAL RELATIONSHIPS:
AN ETHOS OF SOCIAL ACCEPTANCE

Although there have been numerous outbreaks of rural unrest in Philippine history, these episodes are treated as historical exceptions. The cultural ethos of rural Filipinos is generally portrayed in terms that suggest it is antithetical to peasant activism or rebellion. This conventional wisdom found scholarly support in several widely cited articles dating from research conducted in the 1960s and early 1970s (Hollnsteiner 1981; Lynch 1981). In the intervening years, scholars have increasingly emphasized the complex dimensions of cultural ethos. We cannot assume that all members of society internalize the cultural "norms"; nor can notions such as those of national personalities or apolitical peasants be accepted uncritically. Questions of current concern include: Where is mass culture created and for whose consumption? Is culture created for certain classes? What legitimizes the cultural ethos? What leads to its resistance and subversion? What segments of society exhibit what level of commitment to what cultural model?

Earlier works have mischaracterized the cultural ethos of Filipinos to the extent that they fail to note that what appear to be the dominant cultural norms are not uniformly subscribed to. Members of Philippine society recognize the dominant ethos, but no one fully internalizes it. Peasants know the dominant ethos and often tailor their behavior to fit it, yet in many instances they do not conform (just as elites do and do not play their assigned role). Peasants have fashioned their survival strategies around everyday forms of resistance; false compliance, feigned ignorance, and the like are their weapons in the everyday class struggle (Scott 1985). Apparent deference toward landlords, patrons, and village elites can mask acute awareness of (and hostility toward) exploitative relations. This chapter provides a dynamic case study of elite constructions of an ethos of paternalistic agrarian relations and peasant challenges to those constructions.

The conventional analysis of Filipino national culture stresses the high value placed on social acceptance (Lynch 1981). This ethos emphasizes smoothness in interpersonal relationships, sensitivity to personal affront, and reciprocity of obligation (Hollnsteiner 1981). Debts of gratitude (*utang na loób*) and the principle of reciprocity traditionally regulated patron-client relations between the village chief (*datu*) and villagers as well as between *hacenderos* (plantation owners) and farm laborers. When patrons made rice advances (*rasyon*) or credit available at times of crisis for clients, recipients were expected to demonstrate gratitude through gift giving and the performance of services for the patron. Festive occasions and elections have long been regarded as important opportunities for exchanges. By contrast, electoral disloyalty (when discovered) has frequently resulted in dismissal of laborers-cum-clients. Partly as a result, Philippine electoral loyalty has generally been viewed in patron-client terms (Landé 1977).

Identities based on interpersonal linkages crosscut and clash with group- or class-based identities around which cohesive ideologically oriented organizations or policy-oriented activities might be organized. Filipino identity and social responsibility are embedded in a web of bilateral-kinship and fictive-kinship relations. Although these relations inculcate a powerful devotion to those within the circle, they tend to distance individuals from the remainder of society (Lynch 1981: 49).

Patron-client ties have typically reinforced and been reinforced by regional and religious identities. As a legacy of Spanish colonialism, *hacenderos* and farm workers generally shared the Catholic faith. However, recently religious identities have become more complicated. With the church's post–Vatican II commitment to social action, elements of the traditional socioeconomic elite have grown disenchanted with the church. There appears to have been a surge in elite membership in evangelical Protestant denominations and the Church of Latter Day Saints (Mormons). If this trend continues, the rural Philippines may witness the emergence of class-based religiosity, heightening elite-poor tensions, to the extent that religious groups address social justice concerns.

The overlap between patron-client ties and linguistic identities is also complex. In the case of landowners and their tenants or farm workers, for example, patrons and clients may both be fluent in the regional language. However, landowners are more likely to also have mastered Filipino, English, or—in an earlier era—Spanish. Access to these other languages has been a significant advantage in economic and legal affairs. It also intensifies the cleavage between landowners-cum-patrons and farm workers–cum–clients.

U.S. COLONIAL RULE

To understand current constructions of democracy and agrarian reform in the Philippines, we need an overview of colonial and postindependence politics. Three hundred years of Spanish colonial rule, marked by indirect rule through local elites, ended with the Philippine war of independence in 1896. Philippine independence was no sooner proclaimed than it was lost to the United States—a casualty of the Spanish-American War. The sugar *hacen-*

deros of Negros Occidental were among the first Filipinos to betray the Philippine independence movement. In part, the *hacenderos* aligned with the United States to secure a stable market for their sugar (Fast and Richardson 1979: 103–112).[3]

As had their Spanish predecessors, the U.S. colonial administrators (1898–1946) relied on Philippine elites for social control. The contest for relative power continued between Manila and the localities. U.S. introduction of political parties and periodic elections actually strengthened local elites. The clientelist networks of these elites became the foundation for national political alliances. The sugar bloc was particularly effective in utilizing its considerable economic resources to build patron-client networks and exercise regional and national political power (Lopez-Gonzaga 1989: 78–87).

The colonial era thus set the stage for a postindependence Philippine democracy on which the vast majority of the population exerted little influence and from which it derived little benefit. Many of the same social conditions that limited the development of effective parties—powerful regional elites, dependency relations embodied in patron-client networks, private landlord armies, and crosscutting social cleavages that constrained solidarity along class lines—similarly hindered the emergence of mass-based social organizations. However, some cultural traditions and norms have potentially revolutionary implications. For instance, folk Catholicism, although traditionally a conservative force, has nurtured a millennial undercurrent that has repeatedly facilitated the organization of peasant protest movements and rebellions in times of economic and political crisis in the Philippines (Ileto 1979).

MARTIAL LAW

President Ferdinand Marcos halted the evolution of Philippine democracy with his declaration of martial law on September 21, 1972. Martial law was justified by Marcos as a response to several factors, including widespread lawlessness, much of it the work of local armies and "goons" employed by politicians and landowners; the incompetence and corruption of Philippine democracy; and the threats posed by two incipient rebellions—those of the communist New People's Army (NPA) and of the Muslim separationist Moro National Liberation Front.

Marcos also justified martial law as a means of breaking the landed elite's grip on Philippine politics and effectuating redistributive reform. Agrarian reform was to be the cornerstone of Marcos's "New Society." Coincident with martial law, Marcos declared the entire country subject to agrarian reform.

However, one month later Marcos issued Presidential Decree 27 (PD 27), limiting reform to a mixture of land transfer and tenancy regulation for tenanted rice and corn lands. As in the past, the political influence of large sugar, coconut, and tobacco landowners assured their exemption from the reform process. Marcos soon lost interest in implementing the transfer of rice and corn holdings as well.

For all their harshness in particular instances, Marcos's efforts to supplant the traditional Philippine elite were largely ineffectual. Publicly at least, only as the devastating consequences of Marcos's greed and economic mismanagement hit home in the early 1980s did much of the Philippine elite join the anti-Marcos forces. Prominent sugar *hacenderos* felt particularly betrayed by Marcos. Having contributed to his electoral success, the *hacenderos* became increasingly disenchanted with Marcos's sugar marketing monopoly and resentful of the growing influence and land grabbing of his cronies (Lopez-Gonzaga 1989: 80–87). The assassination of Marcos's principal political rival, Benigno "Ninoy" Aquino, Jr., in August 1983, prompted the voicing of long overdue domestic and foreign concerns about the Marcos government and the Philippine economy. Predicated as it was on the dispensation of enormous patronage resources increasingly borrowed from abroad, the Marcos political machine could ill afford the curtailment of international lending and the flight of domestic capital that followed the Aquino assassination. Two and a half years later, Marcos was ousted by a coalition headed by Ninoy's widow, Corazon Cojuangco Aquino.

As she assumed the presidency, Corazon Aquino had to be concerned with three related agrarian issues: extensive and increasing landlessness, poor agricultural performance, and a history of Philippine land reform initiatives that were limited in scope and impact. Assessments of all three issues varied markedly. Empirical data were scarce, and their interpretations were disputed. Cultural and structural factors established the context for the debate over agrarian reform policy; the competing claims concerning the benefits of reform were the heart of that debate.

A HISTORY OF PHILIPPINE LAND REFORM

Since the turn of the century, there have been repeated—although ineffectual—initiatives to address landlessness, underemployment, and poverty in the Philippines through land reform. These reform programs were limited to tenanted holdings devoted to grain crop production. The political influence of the large sugar, coconut, and tobacco landowners assured the exemption of holdings devoted to export crops. The land reform programs have also pro-vided generous landowner retention rights, reducing the area landowners could retain from 300 hectares in 1955 to 75 hectares in 1963, 24 hectares in 1971, and 7 hectares in 1972.[4]

Prior to the Aquino administration, fewer than 315,000 hectares of private land had been acquired under Philippine land reform, or only 4 percent of the nation's 7.8 million cultivated hectares. Associated with this land were just over 168,000 beneficiary families, a figure equal to roughly 5–6 percent of those presently landless nationwide. This record of accomplishment has neither appreciably furthered the cause of social justice nor been adequate to catalyze significant improvements in national agricultural performance.

NEGROS OCCIDENTAL

Historical Development of Negros Occidental

Regional and ethnic diversity and long-standing conflicts have played a crucial role in the resistance to redistributive reform in the Philippines. The centrality of these factors is well illustrated in the debate over the reform of the sugar plantation economy in the province of Negros Occidental. The out-spoken sugar *hacenderos* of Negros were the most prominent landowner group attempting to influence Senate deliberations.[5]

As part of the regional specialization in agriculture introduced by Anglo-American trading houses in the nineteenth century, the province of Negros Occidental became the focus of Philippine sugarcane production. Located three hundred kilometers south of Manila, Negros is in the center of the Phil-ippine archipelago. Technological innovations—the introduction of foreign sugarcane varieties and *bagasse-* (waste cane) fueled furnaces—and foreign-fi-nanced sugar mill construction led to the rapid expansion of sugarcane pro-duction in Negros Occidental beginning in the mid-nineteenth century (Mc-Coy 1982). In the 1920s the U.S. colonial government facilitated significant further expansion of Negros sugar production by financing the construction of six centrifugal mills (centrals) through the Philippine National Bank. The provinces of Negros Occidental and Oriental have generally accounted for over two-thirds of Philippine sugarcane production. Sugar exports, primarily to the United States, supplied roughly 20 percent of Philippine foreign ex-change earnings in the 1960s and 1970s (Hayami et al. 1990: 108–109).

Expansion of sugarcane production in Negros was marked by extreme concentration of landownership—a pattern exacerbated by land grabbing, which accompanied the introduction of land registration laws in the late nineteenth and early twentieth centuries. Spanish barriers to foreign capital—restrictions on Protestant landownership, inter-island migration, and inter-island travel by foreigners—prompted reliance on Chinese *mestizos* as brokers between European commercial interests and sugar planters. In turn, the Chinese *mestizos* came to dominate the sugar industry in Negros (Wickberg 1964). Sugar production was organized around *haciendas* employing hired labor. *Hacenderos* used three means of land acquisition: cash purchases; *pacto de retroventa* loans to peasant landowners, in which default meant forfeiture of the land; and forcible expropriation of peasant farms.

Agrarian Structure and Poverty

One-third the size of New Hampshire, the province of Negros Occidental was home to just over 2.1 million people, or 351,100 families, in 1985. Forty-nine percent (around 172,000 households) of the province's residents made their living from agriculture. As of 1980, about 249,200 hectares (1 hectare = 2.47 acres) were planted in annual or permanent crops, with sugarcane occupying much of this land. The province's ratio of 1.45 cropped hectares per farm family was appreciably higher than that in countries such as China or South Korea but was lower than that in most Latin American or many African settings.

The increasing population pressure on the province's agricultural land base is exacerbated by severe concentration of landownership (Table 6.1). Farms under 2 hectares account for roughly half (50.2 percent) of all farms in Negros Occidental while encompassing a mere 8.9 percent of the province's farm area. Farms above 10 hectares, by contrast, make up 8.7 percent of all farms yet include 59.8 percent of the provincial farm area.

The continuing skewed distribution of land is evidence of the ineffectiveness and limited scope of previous Philippine land reform initiatives. These reforms were limited to redefining or eliminating tenancy on rice and corn holdings. To avoid the reforms, large landowners often displaced tenant farmers in favor of hired laborers and shifted out of rice or corn production. Other policies such as subsidized credit for imported farm machinery, particularly in the sugar sector (bankrolled in substantial part by the World Bank, especially in the years 1974 to 1979 [McCoy 1984: 60–73]), and the high costs of supervising hired labor exacerbated the substitution of capital for labor. Production was biased toward capital-intensive operations with few hired laborers.

Table 6.1

NEGROS OCCIDENTAL LAND TENURE DATA 1980
Number and Area by Farm Size

Farm Size (Hectares)	Number	Percent	Area	Percent
Under 0.5	4,012	6.7	987	0.3
0.5 – 0.99	9,710	16.2	5,878	2.0
1.00 – 1.99	16,371	27.3	19,587	6.6
2.00 – 2.99	9,461	15.8	20,228	6.8
3.00 – 4.99	8,143	13.6	28,262	9.6
5.00 – 7.00	5,481	9.1	20,813	7.0
7.01 – 9.99	1,604	2.7	13,306	4.5
10.00 – 24.99	3,608	6.0	48,729	16.5
25.00 and over	1,593	2.7	128,129	43.3
Total	59,983	100.0	295,919	100.0

Details may not add to total because of rounding.

Source: National Census and Statistics Office, *1980 Census of Agriculture: Negros Occidental*, vol. 1 Final Report (Manila, September 1985).

Landlessness in Negros Occidental is extensive and is growing. Increasingly, cultivators work agricultural lands as tenants or agricultural laborers (without having ownership or ownership-like rights in land). A conservative estimate for 1985 suggests that of the then-roughly 172,000 agricultural families, around 136,900 made their living entirely or primarily from land they did not own. Of these, about 19,100 families were on holdings entirely or predominantly rented, and an additional 117,800 families were dependent on performing agricultural labor for hire without simultaneously farming land as tenants. By 1985 landless families represented nearly 80 percent of Negros Occidental's agricultural population and almost 40 percent of its total population.

Sugarcane production in the Philippines has experienced dramatic cyclical expansions and contractions. In the early 1970s, skyrocketing world sugar prices combined with crop shifting by landowners wanting to avoid land reform programs that affected rice and corn holdings resulted in a substantial increase in the area devoted to sugar production. This expansion occurred at the expense of tenants, squatters and small owner cultivators, and food crops. With the collapse of sugar prices in 1976, the trend was reversed, and the area harvested declined by almost half. The expansion-contraction cycle was repeated in the early 1980s. Recent price increases have again resulted in appreciable expansion of sugarcane planting. Yet, relative to the boom years of 1974–1975, tens of thousands of hectares of sugar land lie abandoned.

The cyclical contractions of the sugar sector have been accompanied by cutbacks in benefits for the "permanent," or regular, plantation laborers (*duma-ans*), by unemployment, and by labor displacement through mechanization and diversification to alternate, capital-intensive products (McCoy 1984: 61–73). On Negros the retrenchment in sugarcane production also caused a decline in employment opportunities for the traditional harvest labor force composed of migratory laborers (*sacadas*) from other islands. Even in the best of times, sugar workers were among the most impoverished members of the Philippine labor force. As a result of the crisis in the sugar sector in the early 1980s, in the Western Visayas region—which includes Negros Occidental—*nearly three-quarters of the total population was living below the poverty threshold by 1986* (NEDA 1986: 51). In response, militant peasant organizations and the communist New People's Army promoted peasant cultivation of idle or abandoned sugar lands for purposes of food crop production. In other instances, peasant organizations negotiated with banks or the Department of Agrarian Reform for the purchase of farms on which landowners had defaulted on their mortgages or production loans.

NATIONAL FEDERATION OF SUGAR WORKERS

The onerous working and living conditions of the sugar plantation workers and mill workers have spawned several efforts at organization. The most notable organization is the National Federation of Sugar Workers (NFSW). Founded in 1971, this farm-workers' union was the brainchild of Father Luis Jalandoni, scion of a wealthy landowning family and social action director of the Bacolod diocese, and Father Hector Mauri, an Italian Jesuit. Mauri had earlier encountered considerable opposition and frustration in his efforts to establish a chapter of the Federation of Free Farmers (FFF) on Negros in the mid-1950s (McCoy 1984: 115–118).

With Vatican II and the 1966 appointment of Bishop Antonio Fortich to the Bacolod diocese, social reform endeavors received new impetus. In this spirit the National Federation of Sugar Workers was established, led by Ed Tejada—a Catholic student leader—Father Edgar Saguinsin, and Father Mauri. Subsequent leadership changes demonstrated the continuing influence of the church. Robert Ortaliz, a government official active in the church's Sa Maria movement,[6] replaced Tejada as the union's president (and later became an executive in the militant labor federation *Kilusang Mayo Uno*, "the May First Movement"). Serge Cherniguin, vice president of the union, similarly cites the church and the theology of liberation as shaping his decision to resign his position as *encargado* (overseer) on a sugar *hacienda* to work with the union. [7]

Cherniguin also attributes the union's early organizational success to the church. The church's Basic Christian Communities served to organize sugar workers and other peasants. Through these communities, workers were made aware of biblical condemnations of oppression. The Basic Christian Communities redefined community, stressing the importance of united action in confronting social injustices. The groundwork thus laid, union organizers then approached community members and began to focus more specifically on the legal rights of farm and mill workers and the inequities in Philippine landownership.

A bitter contest over a 1974 union certification election at the Binalbagan-Isabela Sugar Company mill revealed sharp divisions among the principal sugar worker organizations, the National Federation of Sugar Workers, and the National Congress of Unions in the Sugar Industry of the Philippines (NACUSIP). Zoilo de la Cruz, NACUSIP president, wrote the secretary of defense charging leaders of the National Federation of Sugar Workers with seditious behavior. De la Cruz claimed that the "foreign priests" aiding the rival union threatened the "peace and order of Negros Occidental" (quoted in Mc-Coy 1984: 144). Landowners and conservative union figures branded church and National Federation of Sugar Workers activists as Communist with little regard for their ideological orientation. Efforts to enforce existing laws were identified as subversive. The Philippine Constabulary responded by harassing, arresting, and torturing National Federation of Sugar Workers organizers and sympathizers (McCoy 1984: 149–158).

Over time, the National Federation of Sugar Workers has shifted to a more militant posture. Initially, the union emphasized the legal rights of the farm workers, challenging instances of labor code violations. Innumerable cases were filed, but virtually all were dismissed.[8] Although legal advice and judicial proceedings remain prominent parts of the union's work,[9] the union's educational work now emphasizes the need to restructure the entire sugar industry and the importance of landownership. By 1989 the National Federation of Sugar Workers reported a membership of around 85,000 workers.[10]

During the height of the sugar crisis in the mid-1980s, the union introduced a "farm lot" program, utilizing idle land—with the landowners' consent—to produce foodstuffs and thereby ameliorate the extensive hunger among the sugar workers, several hundred thousand of whom were unemployed. Around four thousand hectares were made available for food lots, which was barely 1 percent of the farm area in Negros. Large landowners were resistant to land sharing, fearing—despite union assurances to the contrary—that farm workers would lay permanent claim to the land. Viewed by union leaders as a breakthrough in early 1987, the program represented the first instance of land sharing for many landowners. It was the first time farm workers were entitled to their entire production. The program was under attack by mid-1989. Domestic sugar prices rose and many landowners reclaimed the farm lots, often without complying with labor laws or offering their workers a livelihood capable of meeting basic needs.

Labor relations remain a source of constant conflict. Harassment, torture, and assassination of union organizers and sympathizers continue. Many of the abuses are committed by vigilantes and private landowner armies financed by the Negros Democracy and Peace Foundation, a fund established by *hacenderos* and mill owners through an assessment on milled sugarcane. The opening of political space for union activities attendant to the transition from the authoritarian Marcos to the "democratic" Aquino regime—which had seen popular demonstrations involving tens of thousands of peasants in the provincial capital in 1986—has now appreciably narrowed.

AQUINO'S CAMPAIGN PROMISES
OF AGRARIAN REFORM

A variety of political, economic, and social considerations led Corazon
Aquino to make agrarian reform a cornerstone of her rural social and economic program in a campaign that otherwise substituted religious symbolism
for substance. Aquino's resort to the rhetoric of reform was a response to the
history of tenure-related peasant grievances and a stagnant agricultural sector,
the developmental ideologies of Philippine intellectuals, the government's
concern with political legitimacy and the related desire to incorporate the rural poor into political life (motivated both by rural unrest and a commitment
to participatory democracy), and international pressures.

In the first major policy address of her presidential campaign, which was
delivered before the Manila business community, Aquino (1986a: 7) promised to undertake "genuine" land reform. She later tempered her commitment to one of "viable" land reform (Aquino 1986b: 5). The specifics of
agrarian reform received scant consideration in Aquino's inner circle during
the campaign, nor were they debated much in public.[11] Aquino's pledge to
"explore how the twin goals of maximum productivity and dispersal of ownership and benefits can be exemplified for the rest of the nation" on her family's six thousand–hectare sugar estate *Hacienda Luisita* was characteristic of
her public statements (Aquino 1986b: 6).

In agitating for reform, peasant activists regularly stressed Aquino's campaign rhetoric. Her promise of "genuine" agrarian reform echoed the phras-
ing used by more militant peasant organizations and the Communist Party of
the Philippines in their calls for free distribution of land to landless and near-
landless cultivators.[12] Some reform proponents interpreted her pledge concerning her family's *Hacienda Luisita* to be a firm commitment to redistribute
the *hacienda's* lands, to lead by example on the reform issue. (For their part,
landowners cited another Aquino campaign pledge—"I shall ask no greater
sacrifices than I myself am prepared to make" [1986a: 7]—to argue against
any agrarian reform initiatives that might affect their landholdings.)

Landowners distressed by Aquino's reform pledges were further concerned
by her appointment of Heherson Alvarez as minister of agrarian reform.
Alvarez was not outspokenly proreform, but it was feared that in his relative
ignorance of agriculture, he might fashion a reform program that failed to
make adequate allowance for—that is, exempt most of the land of—productive landowners.[13] Shortly after taking office, Alvarez did suggest that agrarian reform be expanded to sugar and coconut sectors, an announcement that

was applauded by peasant organizations (FFF 1986). However, Ramon Mitra, then-minister of agriculture (and owner of sizable cattle and coconut holdings), took immediate and strong public exception to Alvarez's remarks. Mitra argued for a completion of the Marcos-era reform (Presidential Decree 27) and the distribution of idle and public lands before initiating reform in the sugar and coconut sectors. Moreover, Mitra was quoted as claiming that average sugarcane and coconut farm holdings were only three and five hectares, respectively, and thus were inappropriate targets of reform. The president appeared to side with Mitra in this dispute, cautioning against redistribution of productive lands.

LANDOWNER RESPONSE TO AQUINO'S REFORM INITIATIVE

Rhetorical Support for Agrarian Reform

Such was the perceived threat of the Communist insurgency in 1986 and hence the political urgency of reform that few went on record as being against agrarian reform, although some argued there was no need for reform. For the most part, resistance was couched instead in terms of support for the principle of reform but opposition to program specifics.[14] Practicing a landowner version of "everyday forms of resistance" (Scott 1985), Philippine landowners manipulated language to mask their antipathy to reform and their efforts to subvert the reform process. The following remarks are illustrative:

> We are not against reform, just against drastic reform.[15]

> I was not against land reform, I was in favor of it. It can uplift the people and make the land more productive. . . . [But] all the way I was against [the Comprehensive Agrarian Reform Law].[16]

One description of the Philippine agrarian reform debates of 1955 was just as applicable in 1986–1988: "The favored tactics of the reform opponents . . . were to delay and weaken legislation rather than oppose it outright" (Tai 1974: 152).

Landowner Organizations and Resistance

Among the standard-bearers in the fight against agrarian reform were a number of crop-specific planters' organizations and the Movement for an In-

dependent Negros, a sugar planters' organization that threatened armed resistance—even secession—in the event of land reform.[17] Threats of violent resistance and secession continued through the congressional deliberations,
many of them made in open testimony before congressional committees.[18]
For these landowners, agrarian reform was synonymous with communism.
Tadeo Villarosa, a sugar industry consultant, condemned a proposal to redistribute 10 percent of sugar farmlands in exchange for debt relief, branding it a
"ploy of the NPA" that would only serve to "create friction between the
planter and his workers."[19]

Landowners used a variety of strategies to resist reform. Although violence
and electoral machinations figured in this resistance, rhetorical strategies of
resistance dominated the formal deliberations in the Constitutional Commission, the executive branch, and the Philippine legislature. Landowners involved in sugarcane, prawn, and livestock production all argued that the
unique nature of their crop or their relationship with their tenants or farm
workers warranted their exemption from the reform process. A prominent
sugar landowner from Central Luzon contended that agrarian reform should
not include tenanted sugarcane holdings because there was little evidence of
peasant unrest on these farms. By his account, the problem of insurgency was
limited to those areas of sugarcane production typified by hired farm workers.
The relative absence of insurgency in tenanted areas was explained by the relationship between landlord and tenant:

> We do not treat our tenants as workers. We treat them as members of the fam-
> ily. And that's the value which I highly appreciate in Filipino's way of life.
> (Sawit 1987: 40)

Although Luzon sugarcane landowners were seeking exemption from the
reform process because they had tenants, sugarcane landowners from Negros
Occidental sought exemption from the reform precisely because they did not
employ tenants (Acuña 1987: 61). At the same time, Negros sugarcane landowners sought to portray their operations as being so highly mechanized that
their farm workers did not qualify as tillers and thus should not be entitled to
land redistribution (Acuña 1987: 65).

Some landowners denied the need for agrarian reform, arguing that tenants and farm workers were better served either by existing arrangements or
by nonreform alternatives. Congresswoman and sugar *hacendero* Hortensia L.
Starke argued that "land was not necessarily the answer," that farm workers
should be "emancipated from the soil" through the creation of industry.[20] An-

other landowner suggested that equity-based rationales for reform were misplaced:

> In the history of mankind . . . there have always been the rich and the poor, the ruling class and the peasants, the farm workers. It is impossible to eradicate poverty. (Acuña 1987: 62)

Sugarcane landowners blamed the policies of the Marcos-era "crony" monopoly in sugar marketing for the impoverished state of the sugar sector: "There was no hunger, no insurgency [in Negros Occidental] before Marcos."[21] The planters argued, in effect, that all would be right with the rural economy and that the well-being of the rural poor would be assured once this monopoly was eliminated (coupled with an increase in the U.S. import quota—something the United States was "duty bound" to provide the Philippines, in the view of many planters).[22]

Many sugarcane landowners emphasized the benefits farm workers supposedly enjoyed under current agricultural arrangements. As these landowners would have it, farm workers had little cause to complain or to agitate for reform; nor by their account did farm workers aspire to landownership, preferring instead the security of employment as farm laborers (Acuña 1987: 76). Sugarcane landowners characterized the benefits they gave farm workers as "cradle to old-age care"—including medical, housing, educational, and recreational services (NFSP and PSA 1960). The landowner-as-benevolent-patron line of argument is well represented, as is the standard rationale for landowners' failure to pay minimum wages, in the remarks of the then-president of the largest sugar landowners' association:

> The farmers in the sugar farms in Negros are provided with free housing, free electricity, free water, free medicines, free hospitalization. Well, it is true perhaps that in some instances there are landowners, sugar landowners who have been remiss in their duty and obligation to pay their laborers the minimum wage. But, Mr. Chairman, that is more of an exception than the rule. And in fairness to those planters who are unable during certain crop years to meet their obligation to their farm laborers . . . it was because they themselves had great difficulty making both ends meet. . . . During the time of President Marcos, the industry was plundered. Besides that, Mr. Chairman, we had this [sic] depressed world market prices. Now, on top of that, the high interest rates in the banks. (Acuña 1987: 58–59)[23]

What landowner remarks of this sort evaded was the considerable evidence that a substantial minority, if not the overwhelming majority, of landowners did not pay the minimum wage. Few *haciendas* provided hospitals or medical clinics, schools, garden plots of any consequence, or the other services cited by landowners as typical benefits. The conditions under which most permanent *hacienda* laborers (*duma-ans*) lived and worked little resembled those portrayed by landowners; the living conditions of the migratory laborers (*sacadas*) were often abominable (Jesena 1969). Yet in the contest over the symbols and language of agrarian relations, the exceptional *hacienda* became the norm cited in landowner discourse. Ironically, in so doing landowners indirectly lent legitimacy to peasant grievances: The owners established a rarely met standard by which peasants could measure and critique landowner behavior.

AN ETHOS OF PATERNALISM

If Philippine cultural values have constrained class-based action among the peasantry by directing feelings of affinity along other axes, such norms are also part of a broader ideology used by elites to justify their status and behavior. Elite paternalism appears central to dominant elite ethos. Peasants are regularly described as "children" who are incapable of independent action. Political and economic elites constantly evoke this disempowering imagery to their own political and strategic advantage. To be certain, significant costs are associated with conformance to the paternal role, costs many self-styled patrons are unwilling to bear even as they evoke the language of responsibility for laborers' welfare.

The paternal ethos also entails appreciable costs for peasants. Internalization of this ethos involves working within relationships of hierarchical interdependence predicated on peasant deference and passivity. The dominant discourse casts peasants as mirroring the discipline required of their masters. Among other consequences, peasant recourse to violence is thus viewed as irrational, as a temporary fury. Despite recurrent episodes of peasant unrest, elites express considerable surprise when peasant grievances give rise to violence and expect that token concessions coupled with forceful reprisals will alleviate the momentary crisis. The structural and behavioral features that are obscured by the paternalistic discourse remain, however, as does the enmity that fueled the violence.

Illustrative of elite attitudes regarding the rural poor are remarks made by Corazon Aquino in a 1983 interview. Asserting that rural Filipinos were less likely to demonstrate against Marcos, Aquino noted:

My husband always explained to me that these [rural] people's No. 1 concern is to get three meals a day. They don't really care about the freedoms as long as they get the three meals. (*Christian Science Monitor* 1983)

The record of the agrarian reform debate is similarly replete with remarks bespeaking elite disdain toward farm workers and tenants. The use of paternalistic narratives as a means of diffusing the agrarian reform initiative is particularly notable. In the words of politicians and landowners, we find expressions of elite resistance to changes in the cultural and political terms of the paternal relationship—in other words, to changes in the paternal "contract." For example, a representative of the sugarcane sector claimed that farm workers were profligate spenders and, by implication, were incapable of the saving behavior demanded by amortization obligations in the event of reform:

The moment they have extra money, what do they do? They spend it on their daughter so that their daughter will become queen in the barrio. That is their priority. They will buy luxury things like stereo or TV, that is why our people in the farm, they have the transistor. They buy all those luxury goods also . . . and if there is anything left, on Sundays, they will go to the cockpit. (Acuña 1987: 79)

In similarly disputing the need for land reform and farm worker preparedness for the responsibilities of landownership, Joaquin Villarosa, a sugar landowner, asserted:

Our workers do not love farming. They are paid for their work—by the day or by piecework. But there are people who really love farming—they are us landowners. If you give the workers the farm immediately, it's like giving a baby that has been used to spoonfeeding the real food. He will get indigestion; he will not know what to do with it. (Collins 1989: 46–47)

Most landowners as well as some Department of Agrarian Reform (DAR) and union officials claim that farm workers prefer the security of *hacienda* employment to the vagaries of landownership. [24] Yet landowners and government officials rarely pose the question of landownership to the farm workers. Rarer still are instances in which farm workers view offers of landownership as credible or as offers to which they can respond without being branded as subversives.

In arguing that farm workers would derive little or no benefit from landownership, two planters' organizations listed disabilities that render farm workers incapable of coping with farm production:

These are his low educational attainment, deficiency in technological know-how, inferior management ability, no capitalization, coupled with the necessity to provide for daily sustenance, and, *above all, his mentality and attitudinal behaviors which need much room for improvement.* (PLADAR and DATU-Panay n.d.: 2 [emphasis added])

In fact, most farm workers and tenants—long disadvantaged in their access to credit, improved inputs, and managerial training—are less able to bear the risks attendant to agricultural landownership. However, crop insurance, farm credit, and technical and managerial training could do much to address these handicaps. For those activities requiring greater education or experience, the farm workers can contract for management services, just as most large and corporate landowners employ managerial personnel. Moreover, the risks associated with agriculture are not unique to landownership. Past episodes of massive unemployment provide ample evidence that the risks of farming extend to those engaged as tenants or farm workers as well.

More insidious in the comments of the various landowners and DAR officials is the implication that farm workers and tenants are somehow inherently inferior to landowners and bureaucrats. Underlying many of these remarks is a class variant of social ideologies of genetic inferiority-superiority.

CONTESTED TERMINOLOGY

The paternal construct of Philippine landowners notwithstanding, agrarian relations are not characterized by a hegemonic ideology, if by that we mean the existence of a universally embraced construct of agrarian relations. Debates over the proper interpretation of theoretical and empirical materials relating to agrarian reform in the Philippines begin with contested terminology and meanings—that is, with differences over the very terms with which to describe Philippine "reality." The debates over land reform in the Philippines involve debates about historical and current events and their meanings. In an important sense there is no objective "reality" waiting to be discovered; instead, there are conflicting versions of past and present realities. In turn, the reform debate became a contest over which of these competing paradigms would dominate Philippine policymaking.

Both laborers and landowners use language to describe their centrality to agriculture rather than the particulars of their role in usual forms of production. Tenants, landless laborers, and other nonlandowning cultivators term themselves "farmers" to emphasize their central role in agricultural production. For their part, landowners typically term themselves "planters" as a means of similarly signaling an essential role in the production process, although they are frequently absentee landowners or otherwise manage their holdings indirectly.

The concept of agrarian reform has been the subject of contested meanings, ranging from the introduction of Green Revolution technological innovations to tenancy regulation, from land resettlement to land redistribution. Those wishing to minimize the redistributive core of agrarian reform, however, have frequently promoted technological interventions under the guise of agrarian reform and as a substitute for land redistribution (cf. Ledesma 1980).

In a similar fashion, the terminology used to denote larger Philippine landholdings is the subject of orchestration. Landowners often explicitly reject terms such as *hacienda* that suggest the existence of large farms. "Only 12 percent of the planters own more than 10 hectares. Even the large holdings are getting smaller because of inheritance," asserted a group of Negros elites.[25] These claims are flatly contradicted by census and survey data that in 1988 showed operational farm holdings in excess of one hundred, two hundred, even five hundred hectares.[26] When pressed, large landowners will acknowledge the existence of sizable farm holdings. However, the landowners emphasize how few large holdings there are in number, ignoring the significant portion of farm area encompassed by such farms.[27] For the landless, by contrast, it is the issue of land concentration in the hands of the few that elicits such determined proreform sentiments.

The debates over meanings and terminology were not simple semantic exercises; they have been central to Philippine policymaking. Conflicting constructions of past and present agrarian relations occupied a significant part of the agrarian reform deliberations. Although the Aquino government's reform legislation suggests the continuing dominance of a particular paradigm—one that is purveyed by large commercial landowners—challenges to that paradigm are considerable and are mounting. In the case of landowner retention limits (that is, the amount of land existing landowners could retain), three issues have been contested: the appropriate definition of "small landowner"; the economies of scale, if any, associated with the production of various agricultural commodities; and the bases of present land rights.

Without defining small landowners, the 1987 Constitution obliged the government to respect the rights of such landowners in determining retention limits. Senator John Osmeña has termed owners of fifty-hectare farms "small farmers," although their holdings were among the top 4 percent of all

Philippine farms by size.[28] A Department of Labor study defined "small farms" to be all those with fewer than forty hectares (Inocentes et al. n.d.). By contrast, Renato Tilanas, a tenant on one-half hectare of rice land and coordinator of the Small Farmers Association of Negros, described any farmer with more than two hectares as a "rich farmer" (Collins 1989: 107).

FARM SIZE, LAND TENURE, AND AGRICULTURAL PRODUCTIVITY

A central element of political and scholarly debates over agrarian reform has been the relation, if any, between farm size and productivity and between tenure forms and productivity. In this area, the reform debate in the Philippines was no exception. Somewhat curiously, the issue of farm size and agricultural productivity, although relatively settled internationally, was the aspect of the tenure-productivity relationship most disputed in the Philippines. Meanwhile, the more complicated and unsettled empirical link between tenure type and productivity elicited relatively little debate. This focus reflects the relative influence of large plantation owners.

The issue of economies of scale in Philippine agriculture—although largely settled among economists, who have found no persuasive evidence of such economies—has remained a matter of considerable contention in the political arena. It has been an article of faith among large landowners that agrarian reform means subdivision of their holdings, with a concomitant decrease in agricultural output.[29] Sugarcane landowners in particular have argued repeatedly for higher retention limits, if not outright exemption from reform legislation, on the basis of supposed economies of scale inherent to that crop. Indeed, by the account of one sugar-sector representative, even the New People's Army objected to land redistribution in Negros Occidental because of the belief that fragmentation of the holdings would mean the collapse of the sugar industry, causing massive unemployment (Acuña 1987: 62).

In the view of large sugar landowners, fragmentation of their holdings would not only result in reduced sugar yields but would occasion a diversification of production away from sugar to the detriment of foreign exchange earnings, sugar mill operations, and mill-related employment (Sabino 1987: 17–19; Sawit 1987: 40). These concerns were echoed by the National Congress of Unions in the Sugar Industry of the Philippines, one of the leading unions in the sugar sector. Reflecting its considerable and relatively wealthy dues-paying mill worker membership, the union has urged potential land reform beneficiaries to continue planting sugarcane, lest production declines lead to mill worker unemployment.[30] The National Federation of Sugar Workers, by contrast, emphasizes the importance of land redistribution and generally urges beneficiaries to attend first to food crops.[31]

In 1986, at the height of the sugar crisis, many landowners acknowledged a need to permanently reduce the area planted in sugar by as much as 50 percent.[32] As domestic sugar prices began to rise in 1987 and 1988, however, lands that had been shifted to rice and corn production as well as idle and abandoned lands were brought back into sugar production, and earlier plans to diversify were forgotten. By the time of the legislative debates over agrarian reform, sugar landowners were expressing great concern that reform would mean curtailment, if not cessation, of sugar production, with a variety of attendant negative consequences (Nasol 1987: 21).[33]

So persistent were the arguments suggesting the existence of economies of scale in Philippine crop production that some representatives of landless cultivators accepted the notion. Jeremias U. Montemayor, longtime president of the Federation of Free Farmers, has argued that in contrast to large plantations, "the moment you go on a six or five hectare [coconut] plantation, that plantation will become inefficient. That is also true with sugar, banana, and other plantations" (remarks reported in *Solidarity* 1986: 23).

Some Philippine scholars of agrarian relations have similarly posited the existence of economies of scale in counseling against subdivision of existing estates.[34] Those evaluating agrarian relations from a Marxist paradigm have also accepted the premise of scale economies; their prescription is typically for agrarian reform along collectivist lines. Other proreform activists have sought to dispel the idea that economies of scale existed in Philippine agriculture or elsewhere, viewing scale economies as an argument by which redistributive agrarian reform might be defeated (ICSI 1987: 2–3).

Internationally, small farms have generally demonstrated an ability to make more efficient use of scarce land and capital resources than do large farms, primarily through more intensive use of relatively abundant labor resources and of the land resources that were available.[35] Most international data thus belie notions of economies of scale in agricultural production.

Economies of scale do exist in the purchase of agricultural inputs and the marketing of production. Agricultural credit and individualized agricultural extension similarly exhibit certain economies of scale. Finally, the farm mechanization often—although inappropriately—associated with the Green Revolution entails large, indivisible ("lumpy") investments such as tractor combines. As a consequence, some analysts argue there are reasons to expect that individual small farms are likely to be disadvantaged relative to large farms in the present era of technological change.

Yet in principle, input, credit, and marketing cooperatives will enable small farmers to enjoy the same scale and cost advantages available to large farmers. Cooperatives can be a vehicle for extension outreach, reducing extension costs per farmer served while circumventing the social barriers that have often confounded efforts to diffuse innovations through "progressive" farmers. Further, cooperatives facilitate group bargaining, empowering small farmers in the competition for scarce government and institutional resources.

This latter point is particularly important because large farmers have historically enjoyed preferential access to government-provided resources and services. The exercise of political and institutional influence by large farmers and their consequently enhanced access to credit resources and extension information should not be mistaken for evidence that technical change is no longer scale-neutral or that the comparative productivity advantage of small farms no longer exists. Rather, these farm size-related inequities in access to scarce productive resources and the evidence of greater social factor productivity on small farms argue all the more forcefully for redistributive agrarian reform.

SCALE ECONOMIES AND PHILIPPINE SUGARCANE PRODUCTION

At the national level, the 1980 agricultural census showed sugarcane yields generally increasing with farm size, with significantly higher yields on the largest farms (NCSO 1985a). However, the data for Negros Occidental, where sugarcane yields are above the national average for all farm sizes, are far less suggestive of economies of scale. As of 1980, farms of 25 hectares or more had average yields of 75.23 metric tons per hectare. Farms in the 1.00- to 1.99-hectare range followed with average yields of 72.26 metric tons per hectare. The lowest yields were found on farms in the 5.00- to 7.00-hectare range (63.44 metric tons per hectare).

Data from the Philippine Sugar Commission indicate that small sugarcane farms are more efficient in terms of total factor productivity. As of 1985, farms under 10 hectares produced a picul, or 140 pounds, of sugar at an average cost of 107 pesos. On farms of over 50 hectares, production costs averaged 120 pesos per picul (Guevarra 1987: 8). Moreover, data from my fieldwork in Taiwan and India reveal that Philippine sugarcane yields are on average little more than one-half those of the small (1- to 2-hectare) owner-operated farms of Taiwan and only one-quarter the yields obtained on small owner-operated farms in Maharashtra state in western India.

An Institute of Agrarian Studies (IAS) review of recent Philippine sugar-sector research found contradictory results in terms of the link between productivity and farm size. The review concluded:

> It is now a common observation that economies of scale [are] more critical in sugar processing than in farm production. . . . Where economies of scale in production [are] indeed critical, a reform program that democratizes control of the land without disrupting operational units can be evolved. (IAS 1987: 2)

Planters claim that scale economies do exist in the sugar sector—at least on farms of up to fifty hectares (Nasol 1987: 19; Sabino 1987: 18), which is the farm area planters deem necessary to support efficient use of the large tractor (seventy-five–eighty horsepower) needed for the more productive deep plowing (forty-five–sixty millimeters rather than the twenty-five-millimeter maximum attainable using a water buffalo for traction) and related soil preparation operations (McCoy 1984: 60–63). Where tractor rental or custom plowing markets are found, as in the Batangas and Bukidnon provinces, this basis of scale economies ceases to exist. Such markets do not presently exist in Negros Occidental because most sugar plantations are large enough to justify ownership of a tractor. This situation should pose no barrier to agrarian reform, however. Even in the event that agrarian reform beneficiaries opt to subdivide affected sugarcane plantations, the advantages of deep plowing can be realized through cooperative ownership and use of the plantations' tractors or through the development of a market in custom plowing services.

This assumes that reform beneficiaries would continue to plant sugarcane, an assumption that is at odds with the preferences of some potential beneficiaries who face capital constraints and recall the significant downturns in the sugar market in recent decades.[36] In the event the farm workers elect to grow sugarcane, they must make a contribution of five pesos per picul toward the sugar planter's fund—the Negros Democracy and Peace Foundation—which is presently used to finance vigilantes and private armies. Farm worker members of the militant National Federation of Sugar Workers are in effect helping to underwrite the costs of union harassment, an irony not lost on the union.[37]

Another supposed scale economy attendant to sugar relates to milling. Large plantations are argued to be better suited to coordinated delivery of cane to sugar mills, maximizing efficiency of mill use and minimizing the loss in sugar content of the harvested cane.[38] Observations of mill operations by the author confirm, however, the almost complete absence of effective scheduling of cane deliveries. The one notable exception is the *Central Azucarera de Don Pedro* (CADP) in Batangas. The third-largest mill in the country, CADP coordinates deliveries from around four thousand planters. Because the actual sugarcane cultivation is done by about twenty thousand share tenants, this experience suggests that coordination of harvesting by small holders is possible on a massive scale.[39]

In the context of Philippine deliberations over agrarian reform policy, what was most important about the ongoing theoretical and empirical debate over the relative efficiencies of various farm-tenure arrangements and scales of operation was the very existence of that debate. The contradictory empirical results and increasingly complex analysis in the literature on economic theory made economic-based decisionmaking problematic for the executive and legislative branches of the Philippine government. With both pro- and antireform political forces able to cite scholarly support for their positions, political considerations—rather than Pareto efficiency—drove the decisionmaking process.

LAND DEVELOPMENT: WHOSE SWEAT AND BLOOD?

As with the argument about economies of scale, it is an article of faith among landowners that the land is theirs—not simply in legal terms but in a more metaphysical sense. Indeed, judging from the arguments proffered by landowners and landless laborers (or tenants) alike, the justness of their respective claims to a given parcel of land turned on their respective contributions to making that land productive. These contributions are contested in the terminology used by landowners and laborers to describe themselves as "planters" and "farmers," respectively. At issue, however, was not merely who paid for or provided particular services or inputs in recent crop years. The debate frequently dated from the original clearing of the land and encompassed the relative contributions of each party (and his or her ancestors) from that date to the present. Being contested were differing constructions as to who had shed more "blood, sweat, and tears" in the nurturing of the land. One planter's organization argued:

> Most sugarcane landowners acquired their lands, not through inheritance, but by the sweat of their brow through the years. (NOPA and AABT 1987: 4)

In urging that the landless be resettled on public lands rather than becoming the recipients of redistributed private lands, Congresswoman Starke sounded this same theme:

> And they will not just be getting somebody else's land because that is developed already. They should start from zero, like the rest of us did. I started from zero; why should they not start from zero.[40]

By contrast, peasants and their representatives emphasized both their contribution to the productive value of the land and the unjust means by which their forebears were dispossessed of land. Jaime Tadeo, president of *Kilusang Magbubukid ng Pilipinas* (Philippine Peasant Movement), claimed:

> Those pieces of land were handed down to us by our forefathers, and for centuries have been tilled by the peasants. If the landlords have been able to buy those lands, we have more than paid for them—five times, ten times, twenty times we have paid for them. (Tadeo 1986: 14)

Similarly, in attacking free market value as a basis for determining landowner compensation, Federation of Free Farmers president Jeremias U. Montemayor wrote:

> The free market does not consider the special relationship of the tenant or tiller to the land which he has conserved and made productive for the benefit both of himself and of the owner for many years.[41]

In his presentation to the Philippine Congress, Germelino M. Bautista (n.d.: 5) argued that tenants shouldered a disproportionate share of current operating costs, suggesting that at present it was the tenants' sweat and capital that was making the land productive. The issue of "sweat equity" in the land was also reflected in calls by peasant organizations for a zero retention limit for noncultivator landowners.[42]

LANDOWNER RETENTION RIGHTS UNDER THE NEW REFORM LAW

After the reform policy was successively deliberated in the Constitutional Commission, the cabinet, and the Philippine Congress, a Comprehensive Agrarian Reform Law was adopted in June 1988. This law provides for retention areas that will "vary according to factors governing a viable family-sized farm ... but in no case shall retention by the landowner exceed five (5) hectares" (Republic Act 6657, Section 6). An additional three hectares could be awarded to each child of the landowner provided the child was at least fifteen years old (as of what date is not stated) and was actually tilling the land or directly managing it. Landowners whose lands had been previously taken under Presidential Decree 27 were allowed to keep their original retention area (seven hectares). Homestead grantees or their direct compulsory heirs were permitted to retain their homestead areas (twenty-four hectares).

Inclusive of the retained areas of landowners with farms in excess of the retention limit, a universal five-hectare retention limit would exempt over 75 percent of total farm area in the Philippines from the reform. If on average one to two heirs per landowning family also receive the maximum retention rights, the effective retention limit will be eight to eleven hectares. Under this scenario, farm holdings with two-thirds to three-quarters of all land in farms will be completely exempt from the reform. Of those farms that remain subject to the reform, only the excess above eight to eleven hectares would be available to the reform. When such retention areas are netted out, even without evasive landowner behavior only 13 to 16 percent of the land in farms nationwide will be available for redistribution under the combination of pre-existing and new legislation, and much of this may not be subject to reform for a decade or more.[43]

The potential redistributive impact of the reform was further narrowed by a series of provisions concerning the implementation schedule and commercial and corporate farms. The law envisioned a decade-long process of implementation; commercial farms were exempted from the reform process for ten years or more; and corporate farms were effectively insulated against land redistribution because they were permitted to distribute corporate stock in lieu of land.

Landowner Reactions

For all the provisions that limit the scope of the reform, landowners and their representatives in Congress view the new law as anathema. Congresswoman Hortensia L. Starke, despite voting for the reform law, denounced it as "extremely faulty ... the most radical and encompassing agrarian reform law in the history of the world."[44] Meanwhile, Congressman Jose "Peping" Cojuangco, Jr.—President Aquino's brother—offered an amendment to decentralize implementation of the reform program to the regional and provincial levels, on the premise that the people are familiar with their own economic and social conditions, and they are in a better position to decide what is best for them. (*Business World* 1990a)

By its reference to "the people," this argument deliberately obscures the dynamics of local politics in settings such as the Philippines. Without forceful administrative arrangements to the contrary, provincial and local economic and political elites can be expected to dominate the decentralized deliberative process at the expense of the landless and other marginal elements of local society (Prosterman and Riedinger 1987: 137–139, 165). Thus, Cojuangco's proposal was widely viewed as an attempt to emasculate the reform (*Business World* 1990b).

Landowners were also looking to the 1992 elections. "There will be another election ... we will be careful not to re-elect these [proreform] people."[45] Noting that 1992 was also the year in which landholdings of fifty hectares and less were targeted for redistribution, Senator Osmeña urged affected landowners to organize in support of appropriate candidates: "There is an indirect referendum built in this CARP law" (Cruz 1988).

Peasant Reactions

Militant and nonmilitant peasant organizations have denounced the new law for its provision on retention limits as well as for deferring reform of commercial farms, permitting stock distribution in lieu of land transfer on corporate farms, and establishing beneficiary repayment obligations they deem unaffordable. Several peasant organizations have responded by initiating land invasions.

Meanwhile, the Congress for a People's Agrarian Reform—pursuant to provisions in the Constitution (which were to be but have not yet been formalized in legislation)—has begun a nationwide signature campaign for a national referendum on its alternative, the People's Agrarian Reform Code. This reform proposal sets a single five-hectare retention limit, eliminates the deferment for commercial estates, establishes a program of selected and progressive compensation, and improves the beneficiary repayment provisions. Over half a million of the estimated two and a half to three million signatures needed have been gathered.

The campaign's greatest achievement may lie in its role as a vehicle for education and democratic mobilization of the peasantry. Democratic grass-roots organizational activities are still in their infancy, a legacy of the years of martial law. At the same time, a substantial violent Left—the New People's

Army—has opted out of the ongoing political process. In consequence the leaders of the Congress for a People's Agrarian Reform acknowledge their continuing political weakness, holding little hope that in the near to medium term they will be able to successfully pressure the Philippine Congress into adopting progressive amendments to the reform.

CONCLUSIONS

The People Power revolution of February 1986 was accompanied by heightened rural expectations concerning comprehensive agrarian reform. More than two years passed before a new reform law was enacted—a law that reflected the successive deliberations of the Constitutional Commission, the cabinet, and the Congress. Although the Aquino government initially touted agrarian reform as the "centerpiece" of its development program, the new reform law is very circumscribed in its potential redistributive impact. Indeed, most of the reform could have been accomplished under a combination of previous legislation, bank foreclosures, and voluntary land transfers.

In the end, the transition from authoritarian rule in the Philippines ushered in a political restoration rather than a revolution.[46] There has been a return to a brand of democratic governance characterized by weak parties, factionalism based primarily on personalities rather than ideology, and the dominance of traditional provincial elites. Important elements of the military have resisted a return to a less political role, and a nationwide insurgent movement continues to threaten the foundations of the Philippine state.

Reflecting the resurgence of the traditional elite, all of the congressional members from Negros Occidental were sugar *hacenderos.* These legislators led the recent largely successful fight to curtail the proposed comprehensive agrarian reform program. Sugar *hacenderos,* their representatives in Congress, and President Aquino shared political and rhetorical strategies to limit the scope and direction of the reform. They concentrated on certain critical and contested issues as they worked to legitimize the abandonment of important elements of reform and the disempowerment of landless peasants on the threshold of democracy. In the effort to shape reform policy, both elites and peasants advanced and debated images of landowners and laborers, connections to land, economies of scale in agricultural productivity, peasant capacities and aspirations, and the contractions of paternalism.

At the same time, large landowners have expanded their private armies while anti-Communist vigilante organizations have proliferated through the assistance of landowners and the Philippine armed forces. After a brief hiatus in the early months of the Aquino government, human rights abuses have increased; the targeted "subversives" include members of the church community and union activists. In some instances militarization of the countryside has increased under the "democratic" Aquino regime as military units previously posted in the greater Manila area to protect the Marcos regime have been reassigned to the countryside.

By their rhetoric and actions, the Philippine elites have revealed striking contradictions in their constructions of paternalism and reciprocity, establishing rarely met standards by which Philippine peasants can measure and critique elite behavior. Although the new reform law suggests the continuing dominance of the paradigm of agrarian relations purveyed by the commercial landowners, challenges to that paradigm are considerable and are mounting. Assisted by progressive elements of the Catholic church, Philippine peasants have adopted a more militant stance in pressing for social reform since the early 1980s. Yet the peasant organizations—many of them still in their infancy—remain politically weak, with little hope in the near to medium term of successfully influencing the Philippine government to adopt reforms with a more redistributive thrust.

The experience in Negros Occidental and the Philippines generally suggests that nonrevolutionary processes of regime transition and political liberalization are unlikely in and of themselves to foster significant redistributive economic reform. When regime transitions do not materially alter the political influence of national or regional economic elites, democratizing the electoral process holds little promise of concurrent democratization of wealth within the society. (Some analysts have gone further, raising the possibility that democratic political transitions may be inherently incompatible with income redistribution [Przeworski 1986: 63]. Others challenge the transition imagery, emphasizing the persistence of authoritarian features in nominally democratic polities.)[47] The obstacles confronting agrarian reform proponents are particularly acute in settings such as the Philippines, where democratic institutions are superimposed on historic and continuing patterns of fragmented social control and acute disparities in landownership and wealth.

NOTES

This chapter was written before the 1992 elections. The issues continue to be salient under the new Fidel V. Ramos government.

I owe *utang na loób*—"a debt of gratitude"—to Henry Bienen, Jonathan Fox, Joel Migdal, James Scott, John Sidel, and Kay Warren for their comments on earlier drafts of this chapter. Much of the field research on which this chapter is based was funded by the John D. and Catherine T. MacArthur Foundation.

1. See Sabino (1987: 21).

2. Most notable has been the influence of Liberation Theology. See O'Brien (1987) and Giordano (1988).

3. The *hacenderos'* actions further fueled the *Babaylan* Movement (1896–1907), a peasant rebellion with religious overtones originally launched against the abuses of Spanish colonial rule. See Cullamar (1986).

4. The successful postwar land reforms of Japan (1947–1949), South Korea (1949–1952) and Taiwan (1953–1955) all featured much lower retention limits. See Dore (1959), Harrison (1968), and Cheng (1961). These land reforms and others were well known in the Philippines. See Ledesma (1980).

5. Interview with Senator Heherson Alvarez, February 24, 1989. Alvarez's counterpart in the House of Representatives, Bonifacio H. Gillego, identified mid-range landowners as the most vocal opponents of reform (interview with Congressman Bonifacio H. Gillego, February 22, 1989). With their leading members elected to the lower house, sugar planters may have felt less need for overt politicking there.

6. Sa Maria seminars involved four days of intensive Christian training and dialogue. Originated by a sugarcane landowner as a means of promoting passivity among farm workers, the movement set the stage for the establishment of Basic Christian Communities and the attendant process of social analysis and criticism. See O'Brien (1987) and McCoy (1984: 112–114).

7. Interviews with Serge Cherniguin, National Federation of Sugar Workers, March 3, 1989, and July 5, 1989; Collins (1989: 69–79).

8. Cherniguin interview, July 5, 1989.

9. The costs to the farm worker–complainants—in time away from work, travel costs, and the like—are not inconsiderable. Yet failure to appear at any one hearing may result in the rendering of a default judgment against the complainant. Judicial proceedings are often a war of attrition, with *hacenderos* much better equipped to go the distance.

10. Cherniguin interview, March 3, 1989.

11. Interview with Joaquin G. Bernas, S.J., president, Ateneo de Manila University, July 10, 1989.

12. For example, the *Kilusang Magbubukid ng Pilipinas* (KMP, Peasant Movement of the Philippines) defined genuine agrarian reform as (1) confiscation and free distribution of lands owned by Marcos and his cronies to the actual tillers, (2) expansion of free distribution to all croplands, and (3) nationalization of transnational agribusiness plantations (KMP 1986).

13. Interview with Emilio M. Benedicto, Jr., sugarcane landowner, June 18, 1986.

14. See the position of the Council of Agricultural Producers of the Philippines as described in Guevarra (1987: 6). For a general discussion of the "I am for land reform, but" phenomenon, see Ledesma (1980: 36–37).

15. Interview with Congresswoman Hortensia L. Starke, June 23, 1989. In other settings, Congresswoman Starke showed much greater antipathy to agrarian reform. See Simons (1987: 166).

16. Interview with Congressman Romeo G. Guanzon, president, National Federation of Sugarcane Planters, July 1, 1989.

17. Matt Miller, "Land Reform Polarizes the Philippines," *Asian Wall Street Journal,* March 24, 1988, 1.

18. See Acuña (1987: 69).

19. Interview with Tadeo Villarosa, consultant to NFSP and First Farmers (Milling) Association, June 19, 1986.

20. Interview with Congresswoman Hortensia L. Starke; Eduardo M. Alunan, vice president, Rafael Alunan Agro-Development, Inc.; and Teresita Montilla Araneta, June 16, 1986.

21. Interview with Eduardo M. Alunan, vice president, Rafael Alunan Agro-Development, Inc., June 16, 1986.

22. Guanzon interview; interview with Enrique D. Rojas, executive vice president, National Federation of Sugarcane Planters, and guests—Joey de la Paz, Antonio de Leon, José Mari Miranda, Willy Cimafranca, Carmelo Locsin, Emilio H. Hernay, Modesto P. Sa-onoy, and Mr. and Mrs. Sevarino—June 17, 1986; Starke et al. interview.

23. Acuña went on to assert that "the landowner never allows [the farm workers] to go hungry."

24. See Del Rosario (1989) and NFSP (n.d.: 7).

25. Rojas and guests interview.

26. A comprehensive survey of landholding patterns in Negros Occidental revealed that less than 2 percent of all landowners in the province had holdings of over 100 hectares. However, these holdings averaged nearly 278 hectares each and together accounted for over 35 percent of the province's total farm area (Lopez-Gonzaga 1988: table 5, p. 27).

27. Alunan interview.

28. Cited in M. Ronquillo, "Exemption of 50-ha. Estates Proposed," *Philippine Daily Inquirer,* June 14, 1988.

29. See Acuña (1987: 62), Sabino (1987: 17), and NFSP (n.d.: 1–8).

30. Interview with Pedro Jimenea and Edgardo Gison, officials, National Congress of Unions in the Sugar Industry of the Philippines, March 1, 1989.

31. In addition to the divergent interests of their principal members (which in turn differed from those of tenants and *sacadas*), the continuing animus between NFSW and NACUSIP and the difficulties of organizing the transient *sacadas* (and the off-island origin of many *sacadas*) as well as dependency relations and cultural norms stood as obstacles to effective mobilization of the rural poor of Negros in favor of a common program of agrarian reform.

32. Interview with Jose Marie Locsin and Margarita Locsin, sugarcane landowners; Roger Z. Reyes, Ernesto Treyes, and Eutiquio Fudolin, attorneys, Sugar Industry Advisory Council, June 14, 1986; Rojas and guests interview.

33. However, Dr. Nasol also noted that fragmentation would result in small farms that would be "more efficient," maximizing their use of abundant resources and minimizing their use of scarce resources.

34. Interview with Violeta Lopez-Gonzaga, Social Research Center, University of St. La Salle, June 17, 1986.

35. See World Bank (1987: 79–83) and Prosterman and Riedinger (1987: 58–65).

36. It was the consensus of thirty-two union officials from eleven Negros Occidental sugar haciendas that the laborers they represented would grow food crops if given individual parcels under the reform program (interview with NACUSIP officials).

37. Interview with Gerundio Dago-ob, deputy secretary general, National Federation of Sugar Workers, October 25, 1988.

38. See Bautista et al. (1983: 76); cf. World Bank (1987: 83).

39. See Hayami et al. (1987: 15–16).

40. Quoted in Baliao (1987). Starke's claim that she "started from zero" is pure mythology, as she has indicated elsewhere (Simons 1987: 163). By birth, Starke (née Lopez) is a member of one of the richest families in the Philippines.

41. Jeremias U. Montemayor, "Moral Issues on Compensation for Land," *Business World* April 13, 1988, 5.

42. See Bascog (1987: 48–49).

43. The extreme concentration of landownership in Negros Occidental means that proportionately more land will be available for reform there than is suggested by national figures. A five-hectare retention limit would exempt around 46 percent of total farm area in the province from the reform. A retention limit of eight to eleven hectares would exempt 50–56 percent of farm area.

44. Cited in Fely C. Gob, "Laurel Backs Landowners Opposing CARP," *Philippine Daily Globe,* September 25, 1988.

45. Interview with Congresswoman Hortensia L. Starke, president, New Alliance of Sugar Producers, June 23, 1989.

46. Interview with Congressman Bonifacio H. Gillego, June 17, 1989; Wurfel (1988: 323–324).

47. In neither Peru nor Guatemala, for example, has political liberalization meant an end to political violence and repression. See Bourque and Warren (1989) and Carmack (1988).

BIBLIOGRAPHY

Acuña, Arsenio R. Testimony of Arsenio R. Acuña. *Transcript of Hearing of the Senate Committee on Agrarian Reform.* Manila, August 14, 1987.

Aquino, Corazon C. "Building from the Ruins." *Veritas* 3 (January 12, 1986a): 6–8.

———. "Broken Promises in the Land of Promise." Speech delivered at Ateneo de Davao University, Davao City, January 16, 1986b.

Baliao, Ricarte M. "A Starke Reality in Agrarian Reform." *Manila Bulletin* (1987): 2.

Bascog, Laurentino. Testimony of Laurentino Bascog, Chairman, Congress for a People's Agrarian Reform; president, Lakas ng Magsasaka, Manggagawa at Mangingisda ng Pilipinas; and member of Agrarian Reform Alliance for Democratic Organizations. *Transcript of Hearing of the Senate Committee on Agrarian Reform.* Manila, August 14, 1987.

Bautista, Germelino M. "Agrarian Reform in Sugarlandia: Some Considerations for Constructing Alternative Models of Land Redistribution." Mimeograph. Quezon City: Department of Economics, Ateneo de Manila University, n.d.

Bautista, Germelino M., William C. Thiesenhusen, and David J. King. "Farm Households on Rice and Sugarlands: Margen's Village Economy in Transition." In Antonio J. Ledesma, Perla Q. Makil, and Virginia A. Miralao, eds., *Second View from the Paddy: More Empirical Studies on Philippine Rice Farming and Tenancy.* Quezon City: Institute of Philippine Culture, Ateneo de Manila University, 1983, 73–92.

Bourque, Susan C., and Kay B. Warren. "Democracy Without Peace: The Cultural Politics of Terror in Peru." *Latin American Research Review* 24, no. 1 (1989): 7–34.

Business World. "LDP Seeks Decentralized Implementation of CARP." April 3, 1990a.

———. "Senate Likely to Reject Cojuangco Proposal to Decentralize CARP." April 4, 1990b: 12.

Carmack, Robert M., ed. *Harvest of Violence: The Maya Indians and the Guatemala Crisis.* Norman: University of Oklahoma Press, 1988.

Cheng, Chen. *Land Reform in Taiwan.* Taipei: China Publishing Company, 1961.

Christian Science Monitor. "Mrs. Aquino Picks up from Her Husband in Philippines: Interview." November 25, 1983, 1.

Collins, Joseph. *The Philippines: Fire on the Rim.* San Francisco: Institute for Food and Development Policy, 1989.

Cruz, Benjamin B. "CARP Law Has Loopholes Favoring All Landowners." *Business World,* June 21, 1988.

Cullamar, Evelyn Tan. *Babaylanism in Negros: 1896–1907.* Quezon City: New Day Publishers, 1986.

Del Rosario, Corazon Paredes. Letter from undersecretary of agrarian reform to the author. December 27, 1989.

Dore, R. P. *Land Reform in Japan.* London: Oxford University Press, 1959.

Fast, Jonathan, and Jim Richardson. *Roots of Dependency: Political and Economic Revolution in 19th Century Philippines.* Quezon City: Foundation for Nationalist Studies, 1979.

Federation of Free Farmers (FFF). "FFF Hails Expansion of Agrarian Reform." Press release. Quezon City, May 2, 1986.

Giordano, Pasquale T. *Awakening to Mission: The Philippine Catholic Church 1965–1981*. Quezon City: New Day Publishers, 1988.

Grindle, Merilee S. *State and Countryside: Development Policy and Politics in Latin America*. Baltimore: Johns Hopkins University Press, 1986.

Guevarra, Carolina I. "Agrarian Reform a Daunting Challenge." *Business Star*, October 20, 1987, 6.

Harrison, Gregory. *Korea: Politics of the Vortex*. Cambridge: Harvard University Press, 1968.

Hayami, Yujiro, Agnes R. Quisumbing, and Lourdes S. Adriano. *In Search of a Land Reform Design for the Philippines*. University of the Philippines at Los Baños–Agricultural Policy Research Program Monograph Series no. 1. Los Baños: University of the Philippines, Los Baños, June 1987.

_____ . *Toward an Alternative Land Reform Paradigm: A Philippine Perspective*. Quezon City: Ateneo de Manila University Press, 1990.

Hollnsteiner, Mary. "Reciprocity in the Lowland Philippines." In Frank Lynch and Alfonso de Guzman II, eds., *Four Readings on Philippine Values*. IPC Papers no. 2. 4th ed. Quezon City: Institute of Philippine Culture, Ateneo de Manila University, 1981, 69–91.

Ileto, Reynaldo. *Pasyon and Revolution: Popular Movements in the Philippines 1840–1910*. Quezon City: Ateneo de Manila University Press, 1979.

Inocentes, Antonio A., Amelita M. King, and Ruben Torres. "The Living and Working Conditions of Sugar Plantation Workers: Negros and Iloilo." In *The Sugar Workers: Two Studies*. Institute of Labor and Manpower Studies. Manila: Ministry of Labor and Employment, n.d.

Institute of Agrarian Studies (IAS). *The Sugar Industry: Issues and Directions on Agrarian Reform*. Los Baños: University of the Philippines at Los Baños, February 1987.

Institute on Church and Social Issues (ICSI). "Major Issues Concerning the Agrarian Reform." Mimeograph. Quezon City: ICSI, September 17, 1987.

Jesena, Arsenio C. "The Sacadas of Sugarland." *Action Now* 1, no. 44 (1969): 4–11.

Kilusang Magbubukid ng Pilipinas (KMP). *Program for Genuine Land Reform*. Quezon City: KMP, June 1–4, 1986.

Landé, Carl H. "Networks and Groups in Southeast Asia: Some Observations on the Group Theory of Politics." In Steffen W. Schmidt, James C. Scott, Carl Landé, and Laura Guasti, eds., *Friends, Followers, and Factions: A Reader in Political Clientelism*. Berkeley: University of California Press, 1977, 75–99.

Ledesma, Antonio J. "Land Reform Programs in East and Southeast Asia: A Comparative Approach." *Philippine Studies* 28, nos. 3 and 4 (1980): 305–343 (no. 3), 451–481 (no. 4).

Lipton, Michael. "Towards a Theory of Land Reform." In David Lehmann, ed., *Peasants, Landlords, and Governments: Agrarian Reform in the Third World*. New York: Holmes and Meier Publishers, 1974, 269–315.

Lopez-Gonzaga, Violeta. "The Context and the Resource Base for Agrarian Reform and Development in Negros Occidental." In Antonio J. Ledesma, S.J., and Lourdes T. Montinola, eds., *The Implementation of Agrarian Reform in Negros: Issues, Problems, and Experiences.* Bacolod: Social Research Center, University of St. La Salle, September 1988, 5–25.

_____ . *The Socio-Politics of Sugar: Wealth, Power Formation, and Change in Negros (1899–1985).* Bacolod: Social Research Center, University of St. La Salle, 1989.

Lynch, Frank. "Social Acceptance Reconsidered." In Frank Lynch and Alfonso de Guzman II, eds., *Four Readings on Philippine Values.* IPC Papers no. 2. 4th ed. Quezon City: Institute of Philippine Culture, Ateneo de Manila University, 1981, 1–68.

McCoy, Alfred W. "A Queen Dies Slowly: The Rise and Decline of Iloilo City." In Alfred W. McCoy and Ed. C. de Jesus, eds., *Philippine Social History: Global Trade and Local Transformations.* Quezon City: Ateneo de Manila University Press, 1982, 297–358.

_____ . *Priests on Trial.* Victoria: Penguin Books Australia, 1984.

_____ . "The Restoration of Planter Power in La Carlota City." In Benedict J. Kerkvliet and Resil B. Mojares, eds., *From Marcos to Aquino: Local Perspectives on Political Transition in the Philippines.* Quezon City: Ateneo de Manila University Press, 1991, 105–142.

Migdal, Joel S. *Strong Societies and Weak States: State-Society Relations and State Capabilities in the Third World.* Princeton: Princeton University Press, 1988.

Nasol, Ramon. Testimony of Ramon Nasol. *Transcript of Hearing of the Senate Committee on Agrarian Reform.* Manila, August 14, 1987.

National Census and Statistics Office (NCSO). *1980 Census of Agriculture: National Summary* 1, Final Report. Manila: NCSO, 1985a.

_____ . *1980 Census of Agriculture: Negros Occidental* 1, Final Report. Manila: NCSO, 1985b.

National Economic and Development Authority (NEDA). *Medium Term Development Plan 1987–1992.* Manila: NEDA, 1986.

National Federation of Sugarcane Planters (NFSP). *Land Reform in the Philippine Sugar Industry.* Bacolod: NFSP, n.d.

National Federation of Sugarcane Planters (NFSP) and Philippine Sugar Association (PSA). *The Story of Sugar in the Philippines, 1521–1960.* Manila: NFSP and PSA, 1960.

Negros Oriental Planters' Association, Inc. (NOPA) and Asociacion Agricola de Bais y Tanjay, Inc. (AABT). "Land Reform—A View from the Standpoint of the Sugarcane Planters of Northern Negros Oriental with 23,000 Hectares of Private Land Planted to Sugarcane in Bais, Tanjay, Manjuyod, and Mabinay." Mimeograph. Bais City, August 24, 1987.

O'Brien, Niall. *Revolution from the Heart.* New York: Oxford University Press, 1987.

Panay Landowners Alliance for Democratic Agrarian Reform (PLADAR) and the Democratic Alliance for a Truly Unified Panay (DATU-Panay). "Position Paper on the Comprehensive Agrarian Reform Program." Mimeograph. Iliolo City, n.d.

Prosterman, Roy L., and Jeffrey M. Riedinger. *Land Reform and Democratic Development.* Baltimore: Johns Hopkins University Press, 1987.

Przeworski, Adam. "Some Problems in the Study of the Transition to Democracy." In Guillermo O'Donnell, Philippe C. Schmitter, and Laurence Whitehead, eds., *Transitions from Authoritarian Rule: Prospects for Democracy.* Baltimore: Johns Hopkins University Press, 1986, 47–63.

Sabino, Mr. Testimony of Mr. Sabino, sugarcane landowner. *Transcript of Hearing of the Senate Committee on Agrarian Reform.* Manila, August 14, 1987.

Sawit, Mr. Testimony of Mr. Sawit, president, Central Azucarera de Tarlac Planters Association, and managing director, Paniki Sugarmills Cooperative Marketing Association. *Transcript of Hearing of the Senate Committee on Agrarian Reform.* Manila, August 14, 1987.

Scott, James C. *Weapons of the Weak: Everyday Forms of Peasant Resistance.* New Haven: Yale University Press, 1985.

Simons, Lewis W. *Worth Dying For.* New York: William Morrow and Company, 1987.

Solidarity. "Agrarian Reform Now!" 106 and 107 (1986): 3–48.

Tadeo, Jaime. "Reflections on Genuine Land Reform." In Romulo A. Sandoval, ed., *Prospects of Agrarian Reform Under the New Order.* Quezon City: Urban Rural Mission—National Council of Churches in the Philippines, 1986, 11–22.

Tai, Hung-Chao. *Land Reform and Politics: A Comparative Analysis.* Berkeley: University of California Press, 1974.

Wickberg, Eric. "The Chinese Mestizo in Philippine History." *Journal of Southeast Asian History* 5 (March 1964): 62–100.

World Bank. *Agrarian Reform Issues in the Philippines: An Assessment of the Proposal for an Accelerated Land Reform Program.* Washington, D.C.: World Bank, May 12, 1987.

Wurfel, David. *Filipino Politics: Development and Decay.* Ithaca: Cornell University Press, and Quezon City: Ateneo de Manila University Press, 1988.

7   Striking with Hunger: Cultural Meanings of Political Violence in Northern Ireland

BEGOÑA ARETXAGA

This entire book is a novel in the form of variations. The individual parts follow each other like individual stretches of a journey leading towards a theme, a thought, a single situation, the sense of which fades into the distance.

—Milan Kundera, *The Book of Laughter and Forgetting*

In 1981 ten Republican men fasted to their deaths in the Long Kesh prison of Belfast while attempting to achieve Special Category (political) status denied them by the British government. For the prisoners, political status amounted to five concrete demands: use of their own clothes instead of prison uniforms; no prison work; free association inside the jail; a parcel, a letter, and a visit per week; and restoration of lost remission of sentence. The strike was the culmination of a long fight in which dirt and nakedness were the prisoners' weapons. During this fight the refusal of the prison uniform became an encompassing and emotionally loaded symbol of a transforming political culture. At first, the fact that four hundred men would be willing to live for years naked, surrounded by their own excreta, and to face death by starvation before putting on a prison uniform may seem perhaps a bizarre show of stubbornness. After all, the Nationalist community (the main IRA audience) did not accept British standards on Irish affairs and did not consider IRA prisoners to be regular criminals.[1] The British administration on the other hand implicitly acknowledged the prisoners' special character by de facto applying special legislation to them. Why, then, engage in a long and torturous battle to settle an identity—political versus criminal—that seemed obvious from the start? The struggle over political identity was a struggle over the power to define the terms of the conflict in Northern Ireland. But this is clearly insufficient to understand the powerful motivations and symbolic constructions that enabled the prisoners to create and endure horrific living conditions and to orchestrate their own deaths. It also does not explain why the British adminis-

tration did not accede to the prisoners' demands when their refusal was stran-
gling political relations with Ireland and increasing the already high level of
political tension in Northern Ireland.

This chapter is an exploration into the cultural construction of political violence, both as a form of colonial domination and of resistance to that domination, through an interpretation of the 1981 Irish hunger strike. I consider
this hunger strike a complex political event and a rich multilayered cultural
text in which different political, historical, and personal strands converge—
overdetermining and deconstructing each other—to create a situation gener-
ative of cultural meaning and social change. I do not present here, however, a
full history of the multiple political and social relations that resulted in the
hunger strike. Nor do I assess its political implications for the different parties
involved (Nationalists, Loyalists, the British administration, the Irish administration). My attempt, rather, is to apprehend the "bizarre" reality of a group
of men who forced their way out of prison in a line of coffins.

I suggest that the hunger strike is best understood when placed into the
larger context of the Anglo-Irish colonial relationship and the set of meanings
and cultural identities that relationship created. In this light I interpret Nationalist narratives of history and personal memories of dispossession. I also
examine key categories used by colonial England in defining its political and
economic relations with Ireland and their bearing on the British view of the
current Northern Ireland conflict.

The meaning of the prisoners' identity is a central question in understanding the experience of political relations in the Northern Ireland Nationalist
communities. This experience is condensed in the 1981 hunger strike, a historical event that renewed old scars and added new ones to the heavily bur-
dened political consciousness of Northern Ireland.

THE "TROUBLES": HISTORICAL NOTES AND
THEORETICAL CONSIDERATIONS

The current conflict in Northern Ireland—or, as the locals call it, the
"troubles"—began in 1968 with the campaign for Catholic civil rights. Its
roots, however, are grounded in the formation of the Northern Ireland
statelet[2] and extend back to the seventeenth century when the native Ulster
population was dispossessed and displaced by Protestant Scottish and English
settlers.[3] In the eighteenth century, the ill-fated rebellion of the Jacobin
United Irishmen against the British colonial government gave rise to the Republican tradition in Ireland. The nineteenth century saw the growth of the

Industrial Revolution in what is now called Northern Ireland, the beginning of communal riots between Protestants and Catholics, and the organization of Protestant Ulster in favor of the union with England and against self-government for Ireland.

The identification of the Conservative party in England with Ulster Unionists fostered the growth of the latter and set the political conditions leading to the partition of Ireland in 1921. The partition was a product of British imperialist contradictions, which—having fed Ulster unionism with its opposition to Irish autonomy—devised no better form of reconciling the conflicting interests of Ireland's Nationalist majority and Ulster's Unionist minority than to create a new statelet in which Protestant Unionists would constitute a permanent majority over Catholic Nationalists. To this end, the boundaries of Northern Ireland were explicitly drawn to include six of the traditional nine counties of Ulster, ensuring a religious cleavage of 820,000 Protestants (most of whom supported the British connection) and 430,000 Catholics (most of whom were against it) (Darby 1983). The result was an inherently unstable state, riddled with discrimination and political violence.

Northern Ireland was born amid bloodshed and social disturbance. The formal opening of its parliament in June 1921 was preceded and followed by riots and attacks on Catholic districts. Between July 1920 and July 1922, 453 people were killed in Belfast: 37 members of the Crown forces, 257 Catholics, 157 Protestants, and 2 of unknown religion. Of the 93,000 Catholics in Belfast, 11,000 were fired or intimidated into leaving their jobs, and 23,000 were driven out of their homes by police forces and Protestant mobs (Farrell 1976).

Soon after the formation of Northern Ireland, the Unionist government established the bases for the political and economic discrimination of the Catholic minority. In 1922 the existing electoral system of proportional representation, which hitherto had given Nationalists certain control in local government, was abolished. Simultaneously, electoral boundaries were redrawn to ensure a Unionist majority, even in the councils of Nationalist enclaves such as the city of Derry. The government of Northern Ireland also restricted franchise by excluding nonratepayers from voting.[4] Because the Unionist councils actively discriminated against Catholics in housing allocations and public employment, also encouraging discrimination in the private sector, Catholics were twice as likely to be poor as were Protestants and therefore much more likely to be left out of electoral politics. As a result, a quarter of the adult population was disenfranchised, the majority of whom were Catholics (Cameron Report 1969).

The structure of Northern Ireland was underpinned by a heavy security apparatus (Flackes and Elliott 1989). The regular police force, the Royal Ulster Constabulary (RUC), was overwhelmingly Protestant; and the parttime voluntary police known as B-specials were exclusively Protestant and were known for their anti-Catholic practices (Farrell 1976). Repressive legislation gave the police wide-ranging powers. The Civil Authorities (Special Powers) Act of 1922, used most often against the Catholic population, provided extensively for actions that represented a practical abrogation of civil and legal rights in the rest of Britain (Hillyard 1983). Such actions included arrests and internment without trial, house searches without a warrant, and censorship. This piece of legislation also introduced the death penalty for possession of explosives and gave the minister of home affairs power to examine the bank accounts of citizens and to seize money if he suspected terrorism (Rowthorn and Wayne 1988).

The judiciary also gave Catholics little confidence. The majority of judges who have been appointed since 1922 in Northern Ireland have been associated with the Unionist party and therefore have been openly anti-Nationalist. The formation of Northern Ireland exacerbated tensions between Catholics and Protestants, deepening existing resentments and creating new fears and suspicions. Rioting and violence occurred during the economic depression of the 1930s and again during the 1950s.[5]

In 1967 the Northern Ireland Civil Rights Association (NICRA) was formed to campaign for housing, an end to job discrimination, and universal franchise. The government failed to make the minimal reforms necessary to appease Catholic discontent, and the campaign intensified. Political tension reached a breaking point in August 1969 when Protestant mobs and local police attacked and burned houses in the Catholic Bogside district of Derry and the Catholic Lower Falls area of Belfast. On August 14, the day after the attack on Lower Falls and two days after that on Derry, the British government sent its army into Northern Ireland. The scene was set for the rebirth of the IRA and the longest violent conflict in Irish history.

Since 1969 a range of social scientists has contributed to the rapidly growing literature about the conflict in Northern Ireland.[6] Most researchers have used the categories from political economy to explain the crisis. They locate the knot of the problem in clashing economic interests and market relations, thus seeing political violence as the result of British or Unionist capitalism in its different shapes and contradictions (Collins 1984; Farrell 1976; O'Dowd et al. 1980). The assumption here is that colonialism is first and foremost an economic phenomenon masked as religious sectarianism in Northern Ireland. There is no question about the economic motivations of colonialism; yet as interpretative sociology has suggested since Weber, economics is not devoid of cultural meaning. Colonialism not only exploits and despoils, it also creates meanings and shapes feelings. As with other political categories (e.g., class) that appear to be "natural," colonialism is also a historically made cultural phenomenon.[7] The political conflict in Northern Ireland, I argue, is shaped by and interpreted through cultural models and symbols deeply rooted in the history of the Anglo-Irish colonial relationship. Anthropologists (Burton 1978; Feldman 1991; Sluka 1989) working in Belfast have been more concerned than other social scientists about the cultural conceptions permeating the structures of inequality in Northern Ireland.

The importance of cultural narratives has been also addressed by historians (Foster 1988; Lyons 1979; Steward 1986) and cultural critics (Deane 1983, 1984; Kearney 1988). Yet these cultural critiques have frequently ignored the webs of power through which cultural narratives are spun. There is still a need to develop a view of political behavior that is capable of apprehending historical actors as they move through cultural space interpreting, manipulating, and changing power relationships. The notion of culture as multidimensional space through which people move in purposive action has been elaborated by James W. Fernandez (1986). In this chapter I attempt to endow this space with those relations of power and dominance that so strongly delineate the contours of people's experience in Northern Ireland. This chapter has a twofold aim: first, to show the weaknesses of simplistic political causalism by showing political relations as culturally constructed through time and second, to critique a view of culture as decontextualized structural systems.

The 1981 Irish hunger strike provides a frame in which it is possible to meaningfully explore the interweaving of historical, political, and cultural processes. When Bobby Sands decided to fast to death against Britain, he was following an international political legacy that had gained moral legitimacy since the time of Gandhi. At the same time, he was reinterpreting and enacting the cultural model of the Christian sacrifice. Furthermore, he was introducing a cultural change because in the process of reinterpretation and enactment, he gave this model new meanings by infusing it with mythological images of Gaelic warriors and modern ideas of national liberation.[8]

But Sands was also simultaneously fighting a concrete political battle in a way that influenced, at least temporarily, the balance of power between Britain and the Republican movement in Northern Ireland. For the people in Northern Ireland, history took a new, unexpected turn. By history I do not mean simply a chronology of events or a determining cultural narrative or the interplay of both, as Marshall Sahlins (1981, 1985) has suggested. The Irish writer Colm Toibin (1987) has compared narratives of Irish history to poetry in the sense that both enable similar emotional moves. I take this emotional quality seriously because I think it is what empowers people in political action. In Northern Ireland, history is understood primarily in existential terms—as a predicament that gives meaning to people's lives, legitimizing their politics and charging their actions with emotional power. This history is condensed in key events that, taken from Irish historical chronology, have become part of the cultural consciousness of people. To miss the existential quality in the "making" of history, both as event and narrative, is to disown history of agency and leave the creative force of human emotion unaccounted for or reduced to structural determinism. In this chapter I see history as a continuous attempt to resolve existential paradoxes, on both the individual and collective levels, in a cultural field inscribed with the changing meanings of the colonial relationship. Bobby Sands and nine other men died, and the horror of these deaths created a new space of meaning.[9] It is to the exploration of that space that I now turn.

FASTING AGAINST BRITAIN

The 1981 Irish hunger strike became an international event, so much so that representatives of different foreign countries attended the funeral of or sent their official respects to Bobby Sands, the first hunger striker to die.[10] The British political establishment termed the hunger strike suicide and reasserted its resolve not to give in to criminals. Although eager to negotiate a way out, the Catholic church also condemned the strike as suicide and warned the prisoners that they were committing a mortal sin. The prisoners and their supporters—that diverse community of relatives, friends, neighbors, acquaintances, and fellow Republicans of the Catholic ghettos—believed the prisoners, far from being suicidal, were fighting for their dignity with the last weapon left to them: their bodies—their lives.

When conversing about the social impact of these deaths with Republican people, I was surprised to hear a local cultural argument. Hunger striking has become part of modern political culture since the time of Gandhi and has been widely used by political movements in different parts of the world. Yet the lack of allusion to this internationally shared political weapon is striking. Instead, the prisoners and their supporters drew on a past native tradition for the meaning of the fast. The hunger strike, I was told, had a deep cultural resonance because it was an ancient Gaelic practice that if one were unjustly wronged and the wrong was not recognized and remedied, one was entitled to fast at the door of the wrongdoer until justice was done. If one died, moral and social responsibility for that death fell onto the person against whom the fast had been carried out.[11]

There is evidence of fasting as a juridical mechanism for arbitration of certain disputes in Gaelic Brehon law (Foster 1988; Kelly 1988). Yet there is probably little resemblance between the cultural milieus of Gaelic Ireland and industrial Belfast. The link between ancient Gaelic practices and contemporary political ones is an imagined (in the sense of culturally constructed), although a powerful, one. For the Republican people I talked to, however, the linkage was not a cultural construction but an "objective fact"; it made up a clear historical continuity. It is interesting that the existence of this Gaelic practice was being used in the 1980s to confer meaning and legitimacy to a controversial political action and to fashion it—not in terms of an international political culture but in terms of Irish history. In Northern Ireland, where national identity is perennially questioned, Republicans were reconstructing their Irish identity by establishing a lineal historical continuity between them and their preconquest ancestors.

The reinterpretation of Irish mythology and folklore for political purposes was not novel. It had its precedent in the literary renaissance that characterized the cultural and political turmoil in turn-of-the-century Ireland. W. B. Yeats elaborated on the theme of the hunger strike in his play *The King's Threshold,* in which a poet fasts against the king who abolished the customary right of the poets to sit at the king's council.[12]

By the 1970s, hunger strikes in Ireland were if not a survival of ancient custom at least a well-known practice in political culture. Ironically, political fasting owes its popularity in Ireland not to Republican men but to suffragist women, who were the first to resort to hunger striking as a means of political pressure in 1911–1913.[13] The tactic proved quite successful and was soon adopted by Republican Nationalists. In 1917 Tomas Ashe, president of the Irish Republican Brotherhood (a forerunner of the IRA), died on a hunger strike for refusing to wear the prison uniform and do prison work. Terence MacSwiney, Lord Mayor of Cork and officer commanding the local IRA, died similarly in 1920.[14] There were hunger strikes in 1923, 1940, and 1946. But by the 1960s, all this history was fairly distant for Nationalists in the north.

It would appear that the young Republicans of the late 1970s, many of whom grew up in the urban ghettos of the northern working class during the relative calm of the 1950s, shared little with the Irish heroes of the first part of the century, many of whom belonged to a cultural or social elite and who for the most part had not directly experienced sectarian or class oppression. Furthermore, that Republicans have resorted to hunger strikes in different historical moments does not necessarily imply they endowed it with the same meanings. We must ask, therefore: What was the meaning of the fasting that resulted in ten dead men in 1981? A Republican woman recalled that time in these terms:

> It was so bad during the hunger strike that people actually turned to praying; 'cause if they [the British army] killed children [in the streets], what wouldn't they do? We thought we all were going to die.[15]

Republicans talk about the hunger strike with a deferential respect, almost awe. Voices are lowered, and their gaze gets lost in distant space. In many houses, portraits of the hunger strikers or memorials of Bobby Sands can be seen hanging on the wall under the rubric "our martyrs" beside a picture of the Sacred Heart or the Virgin Mary, and the Victorian landscape of Catholic West Belfast still shows the vestiges of that time. For Republicans it was a point of no return. As with Easter 1916,[16] for them May 1981 was "the beginning of the end." The end of what beginning?

OUT OF THE ASHES AROSE THE IRA[17]

In 1934 Lord Craigavon, the first minister of Northern Ireland, declared in a memorable discourse, "All I boast is that we have a Protestant parliament and a Protestant state."[18] In 1968, when the Northern Ireland Civil Rights Association increased the pressure to change the sectarian character of Northern Ireland and win civil rights for Catholics, the inner contradictions of the state had become so entrenched that it proved irreformable. Repression was unleashed, riots broke out, and the conflict came to a head with the burning of Catholic houses in Belfast and Derry by Loyalist mobs and B-specials in August 1969. It was after what one participant called "this nightmare" that the Provisional IRA was formed in January 1970.

In 1969 the IRA had practically disappeared, leaving the Catholic districts without the community defense force the IRA had become during the riots of the 1920s and 1930s. People expressed their mounting helplessness and frustration on the walls, where graffiti bitterly screamed: "IRA = *I Run Away*." The IRA, which had remained practically inactive after the violence of the 1920s, launched a campaign in the late 1950s. Operation Harvest, as it was called, consisted of a series of attacks on police stations along the border with the Irish Republic. This was conceived to stir up nationalist feeling and create an insurrectionary mood. The Catholic population, however, was unreceptive to an armed campaign. The result was a political failure reflected in the 1959 Westminster elections, with the vote for Sinn Fein (the political wing of the IRA) declining drastically (Farrell 1976: 216). Following this, the IRA leadership—embittered by the lack of popular support and divided over future tactics—called off the campaign.

The 1962 IRA convention marked the beginning of a turn toward a more socialist republicanism that was increasingly concerned with socioeconomic issues. The shift from military struggle to agitational politics left the IRA ill prepared for the upsurge of sectarian violence in 1969. The Catholic Lower Falls area, which suffered the brunt of intimidation and house burning, had only a handful of IRA volunteers and a few rusty weapons. The lack of infrastructure made the IRA deeply reluctant to intervene because it feared the use of arms would justify harsh repression from local police (RUC) and B-specials, to which the IRA would be unable to respond logistically. In addition, the leadership—which at the time was located in Dublin, fairly far from the unfolding reality of the north—feared armed intervention would further polarize the Protestant and Catholic working class and preclude their alliance along common class interests.

From the vantage point of the community, however, the situation was quite different because people were being intimidated, threatened, and burned out of their homes by voluntary police and hostile Protestant mobs. In their view, if the IRA had a role it was as a defense force—as in the 1920s and 1930s—and in August 1969 they expected the IRA to take on that role. One citizen told me a story that illustrates the mood of the community in those early days:

> I think everybody was involved then, everybody. But there were no arms. I was driving with Tony one night and we had a flat tire, and Tony suddenly pulls out a gun and gets out of the car and says to me to change the tire, and we went around the corner because the Loyalist mobs were getting closer and closer. I had not a clue he had a gun, but thank God he had it. And he fired a few shots to scare them [the Loyalists], and then our people [were] shouting for him to fire more and becoming angry [that] he was not shooting enough. And I remember a man shouting at him, "Give it [the gun] to me if you are not going to shoot." But he couldn't because he didn't have enough bullets, and the Loyalists had [ammunition] and they were many.

There was increased community pressure for the IRA to use whatever weapons it had. Its reluctance and inadequate preparation resulted in resentment and discomfort on the part of many people in the Catholic ghettos. Some IRA volunteers disagreed with the organization's leadership and its policy of subordinating armed struggle to other political tactics. Under these circumstances the IRA was split at its annual convention in January 1970, and a new organization—the Provisional Irish Republican Army (PIRA)[19]—was established. PIRA immediately attracted hundreds of young men, especially in Belfast and Derry where the violence of 1969 and the ensuing presence of the British army had left them eager to take some "real" action.

In April 1971 PIRA launched a major bombing campaign against commercial targets. Four months later internment without trial was introduced by the government of Northern Ireland upon consent of the British government, and thousands of people in the Catholic ghettos were arrested (Farrell 1976: 281). After increasing pressure from the internees, Secretary of State for Northern Ireland William Whitelaw conceded political status to Republican prisoners in June 1972. In March 1976, however, under the so-called Policy of Normalization, the British government put an end to internment and abolished Special Category status for political prisoners. From then on, Republican prisoners were to be considered and treated as ordinary criminals and be forced to wear prison uniforms and do prison work.

Republican prisoners rejected the criminal label. Ciaran Nuget—the first political prisoner to experience the new policy—could wear only a blanket when he spurned the prison uniform, thus inaugurating what became known as "the blanket protest," which lasted four and a half years. Protesting Republican prisoners were confined to isolation without reading materials or other sorts of stimulation, locked up in their cells twenty-four hours a day—naked except for a blanket—and routinely sentenced to the punishment cells. The only time the prisoners—three-quarters of whom were between seventeen and twenty-one years of age—left their cells was for their monthly visit, weekly shower, and daily slop out.

In March 1977 the prison authorities decided that the prisoners would not be allowed to wear a blanket while outside the cells. This meant they had to leave their cells naked, exposing themselves to the warders' jeering at their bodies—especially their genitals—as well as to frequent beatings.[20] After eighteen months of this treatment, the prisoners responded with the "no-wash protest." They refused to leave their cells either to wash or to slop out. At first, chamber pots were emptied through the spy holes in the cell doors and the windows. When these were blocked by the warders, the prisoners began to smear their excreta on the walls of their cells (Fairweather et al. 1984). The indefinite continuation of this stalemate led in 1980 to the first hunger strike[21] and in March 1981 to the second hunger strike and ten men dead.

For Margaret Thatcher, the prisoners' suffering was self-inflicted because it would end at once if they conformed with the law and put on the prison uniform. For the Republican prisoners, however, to do so was to renounce their very identity. The meaning of this identity, as soldiers of an army of liberation fighting a war with Britain, transcends the individual self to constitute the defining terms of a power struggle. The philosopher Albert Memmi (1965: 128) noted the political significance of the military identity in the colonial context when he talked about the use of khaki uniforms by Tunisian rebels: "Obviously they hoped to be considered soldiers and [be] treated in accordance with the rules of war. There is profound meaning in this emphatic desire as it was by this tactic that they laid claim to and wore the dress of history."

For the IRA prisoners, to wear a prison uniform meant to assume Britain's definition of reality and accept the judgment that Ireland's history was no more than a concatenation of criminal acts. That attitude contradicted not only their symbolic construction of nationality but, as we see later, their very existential experience. Furthermore, the prison uniform meant downgrading to the level of criminals not only themselves but also their families and the community to which they belonged. Ultimately, wearing the uniform was to admit that moral and ethical distinctions lay only in the weight of the dominant force.

Only an arbitrary date marked the distinction between a political prisoner and a criminal. Those Republicans sentenced before March 1976 were considered prisoners of war and enjoyed the privileges accorded this status. Those sentenced after that date were regarded as criminals. For members of the same organization—sharing principles, goals, and gaol—nothing but a "decree" differentiated them, a decree that, cast as "the Law,"[22] exempted the British establishment from political responsibility for the prison crisis while forcing Republicans to the last line of subversion. For Republicans, to reject the moral value of the law that classified them into opposed categories was to defy the arbitrariness of a superior power, to reassert their dignity and humanity. Paradoxically, to achieve that aim, Republicans sentenced after March 1976 lived in the most degrading and inhuman conditions and ultimately died.

The criminal–political dichotomy that converted the prison uniform into such a charged symbol is ultimately about ethical distinctions and political legitimation. Most people I talked to emphasized the low level of criminality in Northern Ireland. With internment, the jails—filled with Catholics—and prisons took a central place in people's lives. This was a difficult adjustment that was made only because of the shared knowledge of the political reasons for imprisonment. The pretense of criminality was not only unbelievable for people but was unpalatable, especially for Republicans for whom the new policy represented a criminalization of Irish history. A popular song of the time expressed this sentiment clearly:

> But I wear no convict's uniform
> Nor meekly serve my time
> That Britain's might call Ireland's fight
> Eight hundred years of crime.

The importance of the word *dignity* was soon evident in my fieldwork. It epitomized the accumulated feelings of the experience of being a Catholic in Northern Ireland: "Some outsiders think they understand what is going on here, but they don't. They don't know what it means to be observed, humiliated, made to feel inferior, day by day in your own country." That the Republican prisoners saw the prison uniform as a denial of their identity and therefore of their human dignity was clearly expressed by Bobby Sands (1982: 93):

> That's a word: "Dignity." They can't take that from me either. Naked as I am, treated worse than an animal, I am what I am. They can't and won't change that. . . . Of course I can be murdered, but while I remain alive, I remain what I am, a political prisoner of war, and no one can change that.

Bobby Sands legitimized his politics on a plane surpassing contingent law. The premises guiding his actions rest on an ethically superior order. It is this transcendental conviction, along with a deep emotional bond among them, that allowed the prisoners to create moral value out of the most degrading conditions. The first day of his hunger strike, Bobby Sands (1982: 153) wrote, no doubt as testament for the future:

> I am a political prisoner because I am a casualty of a perennial war that is being fought between the oppressed Irish people and an alien, oppressive, unwanted regime that refuses to withdraw from our land. I believe and stand by the God-given right of the Irish nation to sovereign independence, and the right of any Irishman or woman to assert this right in armed revolution. That is why I am incarcerated, naked and tortured.

I agree with Michael Taussig (1987) when he says that it is not in conscious ideology, as customarily defined, but in a dialectics of images and story-like creations that people delineate their world, including their politics. How did those young men and women prisoners of the late 1970s arrive there? What supported them during those years in which they survived practically naked and surrounded by their own excreta? What was the meaning of such apparently stubborn and irrational conduct? As an anthropologist I am interested in the cultural formations of meaning and their articulation through personal experience because it is at the intersection at which cultural constructions blend together with unique personal (or collective) experience that modes of feeling are shaped and new meanings created.

The protesting prisoners in the late 1970s were the children caught in the riots of a decade before. Mairead, twenty-nine years old when I met her, was sentenced to twenty years imprisonment in March 1981. She was nine years old when the "troubles" started and twelve when she and her family moved—as a consequence of intimidation—from their predominantly Protestant district to Twinbrook, a new Catholic housing estate at the outskirts of West Belfast. Mairead's grandparents lived in Falls Road—the heart of Catholic West Belfast—at the center of the intimidation, burnings, and killings in the early stage of the present conflict. When the "troubles" began, Mairead and her sister stayed with their grandparents on the weekends and witnessed some of what was going on:

> At eleven years of age we had to be actually escorted to and from the school buses by our teachers because the local Protestant youths living near our school would gather and throw bottles and stones at us. One day I can remember witnessing them trailing three young Catholic boys from the bus—a crowd of about twenty of them did it—and they gave them really bad beatings with sticks, and the rest of us were terrified and turned to get help from the other people standing by, but whether because of fear or whatever, none of them would interfere. The young boys in question had to be taken to hospital, they were that badly beaten.

As with many other refugees fleeing from other parts of Belfast, Mairead's family went back to the ghetto they had left in 1966 and began to live in unfinished houses without doors, windows, electricity, water, or anything else:

> I'm not kidding you; in fact the BBC made a Panorama film about the slum conditions the people in Twinbrook had to live in, and in the film they interviewed my mother and filmed us sitting eating on the floor by candlelight. I can remember hearing of a young boy of seventeen from the Twinbrook state being shot dead by Loyalist gunmen at the garage where he was apprenticed at the Lisburn Road—that happened the night we moved to the [housing] estate.

Mairead later came to know the sisters of this boy, and they told her the details of his killing. Mairead's world was changing dramatically; and this change was becoming meaningful through whispers, memories, and stories:

> My granny would take us around the Falls and explain who had been killed. They'd recall the Belfast riots of the 1920s and 1930s, the execution of Tom Williams and other such things.

When she tells me about why she became involved in the armed struggle, it is not a conventional ideology or a set of doctrinal ideas about socialism or national liberation that is described. That came later during the obligatory reflection imprisonment imposes on so many people. When she recalls her early motivations, what comes to her is experience encapsulated and conveyed—as it always is—in images and stories: "Witnessing RUC/British army brutality left a profound image on most of the young teenagers then." Witnessing violence is mentioned again and again in the reminiscences of the people I talk to. "I learned my politics in the street, by witnessing what was going on," said Anne, another protesting prisoner.

A friend, Pauline, evoked the smell of the houses burning in the Lower Falls where she was living and the terror of abandoning the house with only a trash bag full of clothes, not knowing where to go or what was happening. The world shaped by those early impressions created a mode of feeling that led those young teenagers to get involved in a war they came to interpret as theirs. That world was also rendered meaningful by earlier memories, those of parents and grandparents who were marked by the riots of the 1920s and 1930s. Individual experience was embedded in collective memory as a frame of interpretation.

Bobby Sands was no exception in the formation of those early modes of feeling. He was fifteen when the "troubles" began. He was living in Rathcoole, a predominantly Protestant area. There were only six Catholic families on his street. One day the Ulster Defense Association (UDA), a paramilitary group that became notorious for assassinating Catholics, staged a march down his street. The Sands family kept the lights out while Bobby waited on the stairs clutching a carving knife. On another occasion he was coming home when two men stopped him. One produced a knife and cut him. Groups of youths began to gather outside the house shouting "taigs out!"[23] The intimidation increased until the Sands fled Rathcoole for Twinbrook in 1972. Shortly afterwards Bobby Sands joined the IRA (Beresford 1987: 58–59).

THE CREATION OF THE WILD IRISH

The Irish intellectual Seamus Deane (1983: 11) has said that

the language of politics in Ireland and England, especially when the subject is Northern Ireland, is still dominated by the putative division between barbarism and civilization. Civilization still defines itself as a system of law; and it defines barbarism (which by the nature of the distinction cannot be capable of defining itself) as a chaos of arbitrary wills, an Hobbesian state of nature.

The use of the barbarism-civilization dichotomy to convey colonial relationships between Ireland and Britain has a long history that goes back to the sixteenth century. In 1600 Elizabethan England undertook a massive colonizing effort in Ireland, which until then had been very much under the control of Gaelic chiefs and their native Brehon laws with the exception of "the Pale," as the area around Dublin was known. Prior to 1600, during the years 1565–1576, there were a number of privately sponsored colonizing efforts in Ireland. These campaigns were accompanied by an outpouring of rhetorical justifications underlying the uncivil and savage nature of the Irish (Canny 1973). Queen Elizabeth I, who wanted her Irish subjects to be "well used" during the colonizing campaign, was later willing to condone the massacres of colonizers such as Essex in Ulster and Gilbert in Munster on the grounds that the Irish were a "rude and barbarious nation . . . whom reason and duty cannot bridle" (Canny 1973: 581). This posture was not unusual; it had previously been adopted by the Spaniards to justify the massacres of Indians in the New World.

In the sixteenth century, the newly "discovered" people were still very much perceived through a medieval prism deformed with the fantasies of the marvelous and the monstrous. Despite evidence to the contrary, voyagers and explorers presented the natives of Africa and America to the European public as "half-human, hairy wild men, degraded by daily tumults, fears, doubts, and barbarous cruelties" (Hodgen 1964: 362). The Renaissance "savage" (with its profound pejorative connotations) replaced the medieval human monster, becoming a central category in European thought. Not only was savagery projected onto people of distant lands, but the Irish neighbors fell into this category as well. Edmund Spenser's *A View of the Present State of Ireland,* written in 1596, summarized the then-current arguments for the wildness and barbarity of the Irish and advocated harsh military policy as the only path by which to civilize them.

The Elizabethan colonizers not only were familiar with travel writings and Spanish literature on the conquest of the New World and their images of barbarism; they were also well versed on available "knowledge" of the Irish. Two popular sources dealing with the Irish were Sebastian Muenster's *Cosmographiae Universalis* written in 1544 and *Theatrum Orbis Terrarum* written by the geographer Abraham Ortelius in 1570. Both describe the Irish as wild, uncivil, and cruel. Sixteenth-century colonizers in Ireland were also strict Protestants to whom the Catholicism of Gaelic Ireland (which did not fully conform with Roman liturgy) was simply paganism. The Irish, said historian William Camden in 1610, were "in some places wilde and very uncivill," among whom there was "neither divine service; nor any form of chapella . . . no Altars at all . . . the Missal or Masse booke all torne" (quoted in Hodgen 1964: 365).

The social structure was similarly interpreted according to medieval models of barbarism. Although Gaelic society was structured in a complex and hierarchical form, the positions of political authority as well as land tenure were not fixed by right of inheritance but had a contractual character and could be redefined in every generation. This coupled with the Gaelic practice of transhumance accounted for a great deal of fluidity in Gaelic society, which the English interpreted as barbaric chaos (Foster 1988). Once the barbarous and pagan character of the native Irish was established, Elizabethan England concluded that "it was England's duty to educate the Irish brutes" (Smyth as quoted in Canny 1973: 588). Many English colonizers cited Spanish sources to justify their harsh measures in dealing with barbarous people.[24] By the beginning of the seventeenth century, 85 percent of the land in Ireland had been expropriated and given to Protestant planters and Cromwellian soldiers.

The sixteenth-century English held a dualistic conception of barbarian societies. Against all evidence, there were—for Smyth as well as for Spenser— two kinds of people in Ireland: the tyrannical and cruel lords governing the docile and simple tenants. It was part of the civilizing mission to liberate the latter from the tyranny of the former (Canny 1973). The official English view in the 1600s argued that it was not a war of conquest that was being waged in Ireland but the "rooting out" of a few "unnatural and barbarous rebels" (Foster 1988: 35). In a similar vein, it has been characteristic of British officials since the early 1970s to portray the Catholic community in Northern Ireland as composed of ordinary peace-loving people who are sick of the wicked terrorists who dominate them. The British army has been portrayed as a neutral third party whose duty it is to defend the common people from the tyranny of terrorists cast as brutal gangsters.

As with the English of four centuries ago, during the last twenty years in Northern Ireland the British government has combined the imagery of a murderous and hated group of terrorists with generalized intimidation against the Catholic minority. The incongruity of this policy has not deterred British governments, who seem systematically reluctant to learn from their own history.[25] When the military occupation and the policy of criminalization failed to "normalize" the political climate in Northern Ireland, the British establishment—instead of reassessing its policies—went back to its deep-rooted anti-Irish prejudices and concluded that the Irish were irrational and untractable. From the standpoint of British dominant ideology, the 1981 hunger strike was the ultimate proof of Irish irrationality because it was perceived as a totally arbitrary and self-inflicted action (O'Malley 1990). The situation was blamed on prisoners' depravity in the same way seventeenth-century colonizers such as Moryson blamed Irish ills on Gaelic perversity (Foster 1988). That they still think of the Irish—at least those in Northern Ireland—as basically barbarian is expressed by many comments: Two suffice as examples.

The BBC broadcast a series of interviews on the "Tonight" program in the spring of 1977, with Bernard O'Connor—a school teacher—and Michael Lavelle—a production controller at a factory—in which the two made allegations about the use of torture by the interrogators at Castlereagh interrogation center. After the program, conservatives in England and Northern Ireland protested strongly, accusing the BBC of aiding terrorism and demanding tougher security measures. The respected *Sunday Times* added to the controversy by stating that "the notorious problem is how a civilized country can overpower uncivilized people without becoming less civilized in the process" (quoted in Curtis 1984: 55). If the Tories saw the allegations of torture as a sign of the strength of terrorist propaganda in the media, the liberal English were concerned about degeneration. The dilemma is an old one. The problem is not the legitimacy of overpowering others—that is granted by the others' inferiority—but how to avoid degradation while in contact with them. Far from being "naturally" superior, civilized morality seems easily corruptible.

A more recent instance of the resilience of British anti-Irish prejudice is the reply of the former lord chancellor Lord Hailsham to the suggestion made by the Irish government in September 1989 that the Diplock courts—trials without jury presided over by only one judge—in Northern Ireland should be replaced by a more suitable alternative such as a three-judge court. Lord Hailsham dismissed the suggestion as silly and ignorant. When a journalist challenged him, saying the Diplock courts were a cause of deep grievance for the Nationalist community, Lord Hailsham answered, "That is because they don't think. It's as simple as that, they just don't think and on certain subjects they are incapable of thought."[26] Nationalists responded to this statement with sarcasm. For them it was nothing new; they had heard it many times and felt it many more.

Perhaps nothing embodies the image of the wild Irish people more clearly than the image of the terrorist. They are the "other" par excellence, criminals depicted with apelike features maintaining an armed tyranny over the Nationalist community.[27] This image legitimizes the permanent deployment of the British army and local police, who—according to the British master narrative—are in Northern Ireland to defend "ordinary people" from the tyranny of the terrorists. That this idea is challenged by the everyday contempt of these "ordinary people" for the security forces in the Catholic districts has not changed British officials' perceptions of the problem.

In a 1989 TV program about British troops in Northern Ireland, soldiers openly expressed their anxiety at moving in a terrain that was perceived as impenetrable, unknown, and filled with danger.[28] It is interesting that British soldiers perceived Belfast ghettos as exotic and untamed much as the sixteenth-century Elizabethan soldiers perceived the Irish landscape—whose dense woods, bogs, lakes, and mountains concealed and sustained resistance (Foster 1988). Yet little in West Belfast distinguishes it from the working-class neighborhoods of Liverpool, Newcastle, or Glasgow—the hometowns of the British soldiers. Little differentiates their styles of life, customs, or language—except, of course, the multiple army posts and police barracks dotting the area as landmarks competing with the chimneys of the now-abandoned linen mills for historical hegemony and the murals and political graffiti endlessly painted over by the army and repainted by the natives.

The impoverished landscape of West Belfast is familiar; yet, like the remote Irish woods, it still conceals resistance. For the British soldiers it remains impenetrable, even when every household is surveilled; by virtue of this perceived impenetrability, the landscape becomes defamiliarized and the people who inhabit it become strangers. The soldiers' perception, however, is far from innocent or spontaneous estrangement. They are trained in special sessions to see the population and the environment as things to be wary of and to tame. When they get to Belfast, they see what they are conditioned to see: potential criminals on every corner rather than people too similar to themselves to be aliens. Some soldiers admitted seeing every person as a potential terrorist who could slay them at any moment. Others spoke of being seduced in the vertigo of the game, of having fun by beating someone now and then. The cultural dynamic reinforces itself. Their patrolling, arbitrary searches, and continual harassment anger the population, which views them with obvious disdain; this in turn reinforces the soldiers' perception of the Irish as hostile strangers. The contradiction is clear: Although the problem of Northern Ireland is defined by the British government as one provoked by an organized bunch of criminals, the British policy criminalizes—de facto—the entire Catholic population.

In 1976 the British government defined IRA members as criminals, yet the treatment of these criminals was insidiously different from standard procedure. Torture was used to extract confessions, and special courts without juries were created to try IRA members. Yet for Britain, the prisoners' refusal to accept this disparity was a new example of their barbarism. The horrific imagery of degradation the "no-wash" protest provided could not to the British mind be anything but proof of a bizarre nature.[29]

When Bobby Sands began to fast, all attempts at mediation by Irish politicians, human rights organizations, and the Catholic church were in vain. When, in the middle of his fast, Bobby Sands was elected to Westminster Parliament by 30,492 votes, people in the Catholic ghettos thought the British government would be obliged to recognize the political character of the prisoners. Their hopes were frustrated. Margaret Thatcher's response was her now-famous phrase: "A crime is a crime is a crime. It is not political, it is a crime" (Beresford 1987: 115). This answer further alienated the Nationalist community and convinced many people that the only language Britain would understand was the language of force.[30] If Thatcher's intransigence was aimed at breaking the Republican movement and undermining its popular support, it achieved the opposite: The IRA and Sinn Fein rose in popularity. After the success of Sands's electoral campaign, Sinn Fein initiated a process of reorganization to lead a more comprehensive political strategy known as "the armalite and the ballot box" (a combination of political organizing, electoral campaigning, and armed struggle), which has consistently secured it representatives in the local and Westminster elections. Most important, perhaps, the British strategy during the hunger strike left a deep scar in the consciousness of many Nationalists:

Nobody who went through that experience can say that it didn't profoundly affect their lives. No matter what happens we cannot give up the struggle now.

THE SYMBOLISM OF THE HUNGER STRIKE

You gather strength when you think of the people in the outside and your comrades, from their deaths, because you know they have died for you.

—Republican prisoner

Some commentators on Irish Republicanism have emphasized the ideology of martyrdom that impinges on this movement. It has frequently been claimed that the mythology of sacrifice determines IRA violence and the support the IRA receives in the Catholic ghettos (Kearney 1988). This explanation assumes that myths have a force of their own and are capable by themselves of inducing people's behavior. It implies a vision of human conduct devoid of consciousness and choice. This view also presupposes both a powerful IRA leadership skillfully using its militants' suffering to draw people's support and a blind following of the rank and file. These interpretations fail to explain why people have responded to that symbolism at certain moments but not at others. It is important to remember that Nationalists have not always supported the IRA to the degree that they do now. As mentioned previously, the IRA campaign of the late 1950s had to be abandoned for lack of popular support, and the IRA was bitter about this. Little attention was paid to the IRA prior to 1969. People from the Catholic ghettos of Belfast voted mainly for the conservative and parliamentarist Nationalist party and the moderate Labor party.

The mythology of sacrifice as the alleged cause of the current political violence in Northern Ireland seems to me to be a new origin myth that conveniently allows one to ignore the field of power relations at play in the use of political violence, both by the state and by the IRA, and its ramifications. Further, this mythology reinforces the too common view of Irish people as irrational myth followers. This is not to deny the existence of a mythology of sacrifice in the Nationalist community, especially in the Republican section; rather, it is to deny that the sacrificial narrative constitutes the etiology of the IRA violence. Such violence belongs more to the history of British colonization in Ireland and, in its contemporary fashion, to the peculiarly sectarian form that colonization took in the North. I thus wish to explore how the symbolism of sacrifice embedded in Catholic mythology becomes at certain political conjunctures, such as that of the 1981 hunger strike, a meaningful frame for political action.

The heroic symbolism of Republican culture has its origins in the Irish cultural revival of the turn of the century. W. B. Yeats perhaps did the most to create the image of the sacrificial hero that became so important to the imagi-nation of the 1916 uprising.[31] And if Yeats reinvented a glorious mythological past populated with Gaelic warriors, Patrick Pearse infused it with Christian imagery and revolutionary action. One of the artificers of the 1916 uprising, Pearse conceived heroic sacrifice as an act of renewal, firmly believing that the sacrifice of a selected few would stir the dormant spirit of the nation and lead it to statehood. Not coincidentally, the day chosen for the revolt was Easter Monday.[32] The rebellion, which lacked popular support and was badly orga-nized, was crushed rapidly; the participants were arrested and their leaders ex-ecuted. Yet Pearse was right in a sense because the intended exemplary execu-tions provoked generalized social disturbances in Ireland, leading ultimately to the war of independence and the Anglo-Irish treaty of 1922 that severed the northeastern corner of Ireland from the rest of the country. Easter 1916 became a glorified, crucial event—not only in Republican mythology but also in the official historical narrative of the new Irish state.

Myths as meaningful frames of interpretation require a social context in order to become more than interesting stories. By the 1950s, the political sig-nificance of the symbolism of sacrifice was eclipsed for Nationalists in North-ern Ireland. It was after the violence of 1969 that this symbolism was en-dowed with a new life and meaning in terms of political behavior. The imagery of sacrificial heroism then took on a new "force," in Renato Rosaldo's sense of the term—that is, it became not only a cognitive structure but also an emotional experience defined by the subjects' position within the field of social relations (Rosaldo 1989). During the "blanket protest," a profusion of religious imagery emphasized the Christ-like sacrifice of the Republican pris-oners. Yet it was not the leadership of the IRA or of Sinn Fein who created this imagery. In fact, Sinn Fein paid little attention to the prisoners in the early stages of the protest, and the IRA was opposed to the hunger strike.[33] It was the prisoners themselves and their relatives who increasingly saw in their existential predicament a parallel with the Christian narrative.

When I asked Pauline, a Republican supporter who had been in jail her-self, what the era of the hunger strike was like, she said: "It was a dramatic time for all of us but specially for the families. They say about Jesus, well, Bobby Sands died for us all." There is virtually no house in Catholic West Belfast that does not have an image of the Sacred Heart and one of the Virgin Mary, just as there is no house that has not experienced military searches, po-lice harassment, or the loss of a loved one. Religion is as deeply anchored in the Catholic experience of the world in Northern Ireland as is dispossession. Starting with the Penal Laws introduced by Britain in 1695, to be a Catholic

became progressively synonymous with being Irish.[34] After Ireland was parti-
tioned in 1922, religion in Northern Ireland became—more clearly than ever
before—a parameter of one's position in the web of social relations. Being
Catholic in the new statelet signified being disadvantaged and discriminated
against. Religion continued to be another word for national identity. Eamonn
McCann (1980: 9) begins his story of growing up in a Catholic ghetto by saying, "One learned quite literally at one's mother's knee that Christ died for
the human race and Patrick Pearse for the Irish section of it."

The Catholic church was not eager to propagate revolutionary values,
however. The church was careful to keep on good terms with the political establishment, systematically condemning the IRA and any serious attempt to
challenge the status quo by political or military means. The emergence of the
IRA in 1970 seriously threatened the tight control priests had maintained
over the Catholic community. This is how Siobhan (a Nationalist woman) recalls it:

> They [the priests] had complete control of people then; if there was trouble in
> a family or in the street, the priest would come with a stick and beat up the
> troublemakers or sort out the family problem. Because, even in those days [be-
> fore the "troubles"] Catholics did not call the police. There were the priests
> who had the social control and knew everything about everybody.

The generalized violence that accompanied the beginning of the "troubles"
upset these traditional relations of authority just as it upset social relations in
general.

People did not mechanically apply religious models to the political arena;
these were re-created and infused with new meanings. Thus, if the Christian
ideal of sacrifice and endurance had served the church in preaching resigna-
tion to the suffering of this world, Republicans transformed it into a model of
resistance. Suffering and endurance were now understood as active ways of
changing this world. The statement of Terence MacSwiney (the Republican
mayor of Cork who died in a hunger strike in 1920) was revived: "It is not he
who inflicts the most but he who suffers the most that will conquer." The
church condemnation of IRA violence and the prisoners' protest alienated
many people who found too great a disjuncture among religious convictions,
priests' political opinions, and their own experience:

> My cutting point was when "so and so" was killed and the priest would not al-
> low his coffin into the church for his funeral. I thought that was terrible, be-
> cause let's put things straight, if somebody steals you something, that's stealing

isn't it? Well, that's what England has done: steal a part of this country. And I thought, this priest has been in the war and what is the difference? People go to war and kill hundreds of other people for no other reason than to steal somebody else's land, and they get a proper funeral. And what is the IRA doing? Fighting a war against Britain who stole this land! And they are Catholic men, and they cannot get a proper Catholic funeral? I told this to the priest and he had no answers, so I said this is it, and I didn't go back to church.

Forced out of the institutional frame, people discovered new meanings for their religiosity and new expression in the readily available political field. A Republican prisoner put it this way: "I am not an atheist, I don't think I could ever be, but I don't believe in the church. It is difficult to be critical of the church because it is so much a part of your upbringing, and we had never heard before of a feminist Christian or a socialist Christian. But people [are] looking now for other models, like the theology of liberation for instance."

During the years of the "blanket protest" and the hunger strike, a proliferation of leaflets and murals in support of the prisoners portrayed them as Christ-like figures. The physical appearance of the prisoners (with long hair and beards, their bodies covered only with blankets) strengthened this identification. As conditions worsened in the jail and solutions to the stalemate seemed far away, the parallel with the religious model of Christ became even stronger. For the relatives and prisoners, this model contained the moral legitimation for their struggle in the face of widespread condemnation from the church, the media, and the political establishment. The Yugoslavian philosopher Elias Canetti observed that praying is a rehearsal of wishes. During the "blanket protest," the prisoners went to mass and prayed the rosary daily. When the hunger strike began, they started praying the rosary twice a day while relatives and supporters prayed it on the street at the same time. "Praying was a form of drawing strength," said the former prisoner Eileen. "Even I who am not very much of a believer prayed when I was arrested." Many of the prisoners were believers, and so were their supporters on the outside. Bobby Sands was a strong believer, and he defended his political position in religious terms when the chaplain of the jail, Father Faul, tried to dissuade him from his strike on moral grounds: "What greater love hath a man than to lay down his life for the life of his friends?" And that is how much of the Nationalist community felt as well.[35]

Sands's writings are filled with religious imagery. Metaphors of sacrifice and also of hell transpire from his imagination. Sacrifice and hell are intimately woven together to capture an experience bordering on the surreal. "The Crime of Castlereagh" is a poem of 145 stanzas in which Sands talks

about interrogation and jail.[36] Sands (1982: 44) imagines the space of
Castlereagh interrogation center—with its cells and its corridors—as hell
with its devils torturing him, trying to eat his mind and rip his soul apart,
tricking him into evil deals, and offering comforts in exchange for his secrets:

> This Citadel, this house of hell
> Is worshipped by the law.
>
> Some bear the stain of cruel Cain,
> These are the men of doom.
> The torture-men who go no end
> To fix you in that room.
> To brutalize they utilize
> Contrivances of hell,
> For great duress can mean success
> When tortured start to tell.

In a space that is neither life nor death, Bobby Sands (1982: 50) perceives
other prisoners as nightmare phantoms carrying the burden of a fate heavier
than themselves: "Each looked like a loss, each bore a cross / Upon his
bended back."[37]

In the interrogation center the parameters of reality blur. Space is distorted; unmastered; changing; pregnant with fear, threats, and promised
comfort. Nor is there control of time; permanent lights make day and night
indistinguishable. Creating uncertainty and confusion in the detainee is a big
part of the interrogation game. There one is left to one's most inner solitude
to confront the ultimate dilemma of confession, that crucial operation of
power producing truth through "the body of the condemned" (Foucault
1979). The production of truth was, in Northern Ireland as in any society
founded on the degradation of a human group, vital to its justification and
survival. In extracting confessions, the point is not the congruity of fact and
evidence but the fabrication of social truths. "The truth-power relation remains at the heart of all mechanisms of punishment," Michel Foucault
(1979: 55) has said. An important component of this relation is, of course,
the humiliation of the confessant. Obliged sometimes to confess nonexistent
realities incriminating oneself and others, the confessant is deprived of indi-
viduality and of the last ground from which to resist normalization. Yet confession also represents a tempting relief from the agony of interrogation.
Hence the dilemma, the distorted reality, the displacement of meanings that
frequently produce a hallucinatory quality. Sands's devils turn into serpents,
and he sees himself surrounded by the inferno's beasts (1982: 56):

A demon came his eyes aflame
And round him was the law.
They danced like in Hades and rats in plagues
And Christ I froze in awe.
They spun a cord this gruesome horde
On loom of doom and sin,
To make a noose that would induce
A tortured soul within.

His is a journey between life and death. Despite its nightmarish quality, there is a literalness in this space of death because Sands does not know if he is going to come out of it alive or (like detainee Brian Maguire) die on the path. This literalness becomes chillingly real during the hunger strike. As Michael Taussig (1987) has shown, the meaning of this experience cannot be conveyed in rational discourse because reality loses its cleavages and appears as a bad dream, leaving an indelible print. Sean, a blanket prisoner, expressed it one night: "For some people prison time is like a nightmare from where they never come out again even if the sentence is served and they can go home." As one woman said, "How do you explain a nightmare?" Only deep-rooted metaphors and images can convey the inexpressible. For Sands, religious imagery and poetic language provided the semantic and emotional space to interpret and transmit his experience.[38]

In the horror of incarceration, amid deprivation and dirt, there is always the temptation of giving in, of ending the torture by conforming with prison rules. But salvation—that is, victory over the evil wrongs of Britain—demands endurance. Sands (1982: 64) saw in his predicament a Christ-like Calvary:

The time had come to be,
To walk the lonely road
Like that of Calvary.
And take up the cross of Irishmen
Who've carried liberty.

If Bobby Sands saw himself walking to Calvary, the last step would be the ultimate sacrifice. Sands's decision to go on a hunger strike against Britain was a coldly weighted one. It was made, contrary to the media interpretations of the time, against the wishes of the IRA leadership.[39] Sands and the other prisoners saw it as a political last resort; but once the crisis escalated and the decision to fast to death was taken, it was the Christian myth of sacrifice—deeply rooted in his upbringing—that he seized.

If the Christian myth provided Bobby Sands with a "model for action" (Geertz 1973), it also constituted an interpretative frame for Nationalist supporters. The "force" of the sacrifice metaphor can thus be seen not only in the graffiti and murals of the urban landscape but also in how it moved people in the political arena. I agree with James Fernandez (1986: 6) that metaphoric assertions people make about themselves or about others "provide images in relation to which the organization of behavior can take place." In the Catholic ghettos, demonstrations and riots escalated. If the Nationalist community moved in the direction of revolt, the Loyalist community was affected in the opposite direction. Among Protestants, the hunger strike stirred deep fears and anxieties about the Catholics. As Padraig O'Malley (1990) has pointed out, the "no-wash" protest reaffirmed their belief in the inherent dirtiness and inadequacy of Catholics: "If cleanliness is next to godliness," asked Peter Robinson, MP, leader of the Democratic Unionist party, "then to whom are these men close?" (quoted in O'Malley 1990: 163). The prisoners' deprivation was, from the viewpoint of Protestants, as self-imposed as their second-class status and only deserved disdain. If Catholic walls cried, "Don't let Sands die," Protestant wards demanded, "The time is now for Sands to die" (Rolston 1987). Tension rose as the countdown went on. Assassinations of Catholics by paramilitary Loyalists increased,[40] as did the number of people killed by British troops in nonriot situations. Among the latter were seven children.

Sean MacBride (1983: 5), winner of the Nobel Peace Prize in 1974 and the Lenin Prize for Peace in 1977 and founding member of Amnesty International, concluded: "The hunger strike must be understood in terms of the historical memory of British colonial misrule."[41] This historical memory is a contested subject in Ireland. But whatever the different constructions, historical memory plays a deep role in political legitimacy. Historic actors do not play in an atemporal space or in a symbolic vacuum. The prisoners protesting in Long Kesh, especially the hunger strikers, saw themselves as the perpetuators of a long tradition of resistance that went back eight centuries. The force and immediacy of this history transpire in Bobby Sands's writings when he juxtaposes men from different generations and sociopolitical contexts to create a single, identical tradition: "I remember, and I shall never forget, how this monster took the lives of Tom Ashe, Terence MacSwiney, Michael Gaughan, Frank Stagg, and Hugh Coney" (1982: 91).

History for Republicans is not merely an intellectual legacy. If religious symbolism gives meaning to the incomprehensible—people willing to die of starvation—history makes meaningful the present as it unfolds in existential experience, directing action in the world. As Siobhan commented, "Some people say we have to forget history, but we have to remember it because history repeats itself, and we have to be prepared." And Mary: "The troubles in 1969 caught us completely unprepared, but that shouldn't have happened. We should have known better with the history we got."

History for the Republican prisoners was not a detached knowledge learned at school but was the crystallization of a mode of feeling: "History was forced on me," said Anne. It conveyed for Republicans the kind of inevitability contained in tragedy because tragedy is ultimately about facing paradoxical dilemmas. For the hunger strikers the choice was to accept the criminal definition, in which case they were psychologically if not politically defeated, or to die, in which case they were also damned. Feeling deprived of everything else—their country, their history, and their self-definitions—death became the only act to preserve their humanity. Yet the nature of the tragedy appears strongest in the experience of the women, mainly mothers, who had to decide between saving the lives of their sons by betraying them or being loyal to them by losing them:

> It was traumatic for the mothers because it's a reversal of all [that] it means to be a mother, a reversal of all [that] you have done for your son. You've struggled all your life to put food in their bellies, sometimes at the expense of yourself, and to watch them die of starvation.

*   *   *

The scars of the past are slow to disappear
the cries of the dead are always in our ears
Only the very safe
Can talk about right and wrong . . .

—Paul Doran

The hunger strike was a watershed in Irish history, the social and political consequences of which are still being assessed. My concern here has been to reflect on a kind of experience that appeared to me as inexpressible. I have tried to show meaning in what seemed bizarre, meaningless, and futile. In the process, what seemed rational and civilized has became irrational and strange. Is it not the task of the anthropologist to show how porous, vulnerable, and context-bound our categorizations of reality are? The leading question of this chapter was how the ten Irish men—terrorists, criminals, martyrs: that for us matters little—who died voluntarily in 1981 came to make that decision. In answering this question, I have tried to decipher the interlocking contexts encompassing their actions with meaning and the new cultural meanings created through their own interpretation and the interpretation of others. It is not for me to decide whether the hunger strikers were right or wrong or if what they achieved was worse than what they were trying to overcome. In her superb novel *Beloved*, Toni Morrison tackles this dilemma. When it is suggested to Sethe that killing her baby to save her from slavery might be worse than slavery itself, she answers, "It ain't my job to know what's worse. It is my job to know what is and to keep them away from what I know is terrible. I did that" (Morrison 1987: 165). And that, too, is what the hunger strikers did. Just as Sethe's killing her baby cannot be understood without the unforgettable scar of slavery, so the starved bodies of the Irish hunger strikers are meaningless outside the ongoing imprint of British colonization.

NOTES

Many people contributed to the final version of this chapter. I am especially grateful to Kay Warren who first encouraged me to write it and who tirelessly commented on the subsequent drafts. I must also thank the participants in the Culture and Conflict seminar at Princeton University, particularly Davida Wood and Michael Hanchard with whom I have had many challenging discussions. I have benefited greatly from the critiques and suggestions of James Boon, Barbara Corbett, James Fernandez, Ernestine Friedl, John Kelly, Michael Jimenez, Michael Merrill, Gananath Obeyesekere, and Darini Rajasingham. The responsibility for possible mistakes and misinterpretations is, of course, only mine. Thanks also to Pauline Caulk who typed an early draft and helped with numerous queries about word processing. This chapter is based on fieldwork research conducted in Belfast from October 1988 to December 1989 and September to October 1990. My major debt is to the people in Belfast who shared their lives and concerns with me and made my work possible. I respect their wishes to remain anonymous. The research was funded by a Social Science Research Council Doctoral Dissertation fellowship and a MacArthur Foundation grant, administered through the Center of International Studies of Princeton, directed by Henry Bienen.

1. People in Northern Ireland use the terms Catholic or Nationalist community to signal an ethnic-political identity vis-à-vis Protestant-Loyalist or British. Thus, "the Nationalist community" is in this sense a homogeneous "imagined community"— to use Benedict Anderson's celebrated notion—of shared history, cultural forms, and ethos. Far from being homogeneous, however, the Nationalist community is characterized by dissenting social and political positions that at times have accounted for acute intracommunal conflict. With this in mind, it is possible, however, to talk about a Nationalist community to refer to that shared culture and ethnic identity in which

Nationalists of different persuasions partake. It is in this sense that the notion of Nationalist community is used in this chapter.

2. Although not completely independent, from the start Northern Ireland enjoyed a high degree of autonomy with its own parliament, government, judiciary, and police bodies. The term statelet is generally used to refer to the small size as well as the quasi-independent character of Northern Ireland.

3. In regard to the Ulster Plantation, see Canny (1987) and Foster (1988).

4. Ratepayers refers to people who own houses or who rent them from the local council. An adult person without a tenancy did not pay rates (nonratepayer) and according to the Northern Ireland legislation, was not entitled to vote in local elections.

5. The 1930s also witnessed a short-lived alliance between the Catholic and Protestant working class in response to the terrible economic conditions of life. The brief coalescence, however, was dismantled by selective repression against Catholics and the stirring up of the Protestant supremacist ideology by the Unionist leaders and members of the government, who constituted the landowners and financial class of Northern Ireland. For more information, see Farrell (1976).

6. For a guide to and a recent appraisal of this literature, see Darby (1983) and Whyte (1990).

7. For an excellent and now-classic account of the cultural construction of a political phenomenon, see Thompson (1963).

8. The polyvalent significations of the sacrifice model can be seen in the Republican funerary memorials as well as in murals seen throughout the Catholic districts. The use of these mythical models, such as the Gaelic warrior Cuchulain and Jesus Christ, in the political arena has its main antecedent in Patrick Pearse, leader of the 1916 uprising.

9. Michael Taussig (1987) has insisted on the need to examine the cultural meanings created in contexts in which political terror and violence are endemic. In these contexts torture and death become a privileged space in the creation of meaning.

10. The U.S. government expressed deep regret. The president of the Italian senate sent his condolences to the Sands family. Thousands marched in Paris. The town of Le Mans named a street after him. In India the *Hindustan Times* accused Britain of allowing a member of the Parliament to die of starvation, and the opposition of the Upper House stood for a minute of silence. Iran sent an ambassador to the funeral. The Soviet Union condemned Britain for its policies in Northern Ireland. Poland paid tribute to Sands. Bombs exploded near British premises in France, Milan, and Lisbon; and there were demonstrations in several countries (Beresford 1987: 132).

11. The interpretation of Irish political hunger strikes in the light of the ancient Gaelic practice of fasting is not idiosyncratic of Republican nationalists. Researchers have often referred to it in their analysis; see, for example, Beresford (1987), Fallon (1987), and O'Malley (1990).

12. W. B. Yeats wrote *The King's Threshold* in 1904. The first version of the play ended with the poet still alive. In 1924, after the death of Terence McSwiney, he rewrote the play. In his second version, the poet dies and so do his followers.

13. These women must have been influenced by the history of political fasting in other parts of the British empire, especially in India and overseas (Morris 1978). For discussion of the Irish suffragists, see Fallon (1987) and Owens (1984).

14. MacSwiney was a poet, playwright, and philosopher. The symbolism of the single, ultimate sacrifice is transparent in his writings. Like Pearse, he believed a symbolic act would awaken the consciousness of Ireland.

15. Unless otherwise indicated, unidentified quotes come from discussions I had with Republican people during fieldwork in Belfast. To preserve anonymity, I have left the quotes unidentified in some cases and used pseudonyms for the sake of the narrative in others.

16. The Easter 1916 rebellion, with its subsequent executions, was the prelude to the war of independence and the Anglo-Irish treaty that gave rise to the Irish Free State and Northern Ireland.

17. Graffiti in Catholic West Belfast.

18. Northern Ireland Parliamentary Debates, House of Commons, vol. 16, cols. 1,091–1,095, cited in Farrell (1976). Lord Craigavon was a company director and a landowner; he also held various positions at Westminster Parliament.

19. The other part of the split, the Official IRA, laid down its arms in 1972. I use the general IRA or the Provisionals to refer to the PIRA. For a comprehensive history of the IRA, see Bell (1980) and Coogan (1980).

20. The Long Kesh medical officer recorded 114 cases of injury to H Block prisoners in 1978. Minister of State Don Concannon denied the abuse of prisoners, stating that no punishment had ever been imposed on warders for that reason.

21. The first hunger strike, led by Brendan Hughes, began in 1980. It was called off after fifty-three days when the British administration produced a document that seemed to concede implicitly to the prisoners' five demands. Once the hunger strike was abandoned, the British government claimed the demands were not contained in the document, a position that prompted the second hunger strike.

22. Corrigan and Sayer (1985) have shown the centrality of the ideology of "the Law" in the development of the British state and the role it played in different historical moments in advancing upper-class and imperialist interests.

23. "Taig" is a derogatory word for Catholic, something like "nigger" in the United States.

24. The most extended Spanish influence was Peter Martyr Anglerius's *De Orbe Novo* (1555). According to Margaret T. Hodgen (1964), Peter Martyr was an "inveterate gossip" whose account of the discovery of America departed greatly from Columbus's descriptions, employing the fabulous invention of the medieval travel genre more than any kind of realist description.

25. The British introduced internment despite its having been proven disastrous in the past. The same applies to the criminalization policy.

26. "Hailsham in Bitter Attack on Irish," *Irish News,* September 19, 1989, 1.

27. This is not only reserved for Nationalists. When it comes to British mainstream perceptions of Ireland, Catholic and Protestants alike are frequently portrayed as brutish and irrational.

28. In her chapter in this volume, Kay B. Warren calls attention to the cultural construction of space as a symbolic map of interethnic power relationships. In Guatemala, the army manipulates Mayan cultural meanings to infuse the local geography with new symbolic marks of violence and institutionalized terror. See also Warren (1989: 40–44).

29. I refer here to that dominant ideology that creates and shapes public opinion. This dominant ideology was contested in Britain, if only by small groups who campaigned in favor of the Irish prisoners.

30. Despite the general perception that Thatcher was the main obstacle to a political resolution, the leaders of the main political parties, including the Liberal party and the Labor party, shared her position on the issue.

31. For the imagery of the 1916 uprising, see Thompson (1982). For an account of the 1916 rebellion in Ireland in the broader context of the British empire, see Morris (1978).

32. For an excellent biography of Patrick Pearse, see Edwards (1977).

33. The Relatives Action Committee was formed in 1976 by relatives of Republican prisoners (mainly women) to campaign in support of the prisoners' demands. The organization was a response to the apparent indifference of political parties, including Sinn Fein, to the prisoners' predicament.

34. The Penal Laws disenfranchised Catholic and Presbyterian religious practice. They denied Catholics and dissenting Protestants access to education, the right to vote, and access to government jobs. In the case of Catholics, they drastically curtailed land rights so that in 1775, Catholics held only 5 percent of the land. The Penal Laws must be understood in relation to the role of Protestantism in the formation of the English state. To Corrigan and Sayer (1985), it was the establishment of a state church in the 1530s that laid the ground for a potent fusion of Protestantism and English nationalism. Catholics in England and Ireland became the immediate "Papist" enemy that reinforced English national unity.

35. There were other feelings as well—a sense of powerlessness produced as much by the British attitude as by the inability to disengage from the hunger strikes. The situation was so polarized that not to support the hunger strikers was to support the British. There was also anger at the IRA, even among supporters of the hunger strikers, because many people believed the IRA had the power to order an end to the fast.

36. It falls outside the margins of this chapter to explore the larger cultural tradition of the Irish ballad wherein much of Sands's poetry is embedded. Suffice it to mention the interesting resemblance between "The Crime of Castlereagh" and "The Ballad of Reading Gaol"—the celebrated work of that other great Irish poet, Oscar Wilde, who was also condemned to jail for being an outcast (if of a different type) by a British court.

37. For an account of the uncertainty and surrealism of the experience of interrogation, see Timerman (1981). For an excellent interpretation of this experience, see

Taussig (1987). The experience of living in a space between life and death, where the line between the real and the imagined blurs, has been exceptionally captured by Mexican writer Juan Rulfo in his novel *Pedro Paramo* (1987).

38. As Lila Abu-Lughod (1986) has suggested, poetry can provide an alternative cultural discourse that allows people not only to express deep experiential feelings but also to persuade others to action, especially in situations of intense personal suffering. By using a stylized cultural form, poetry can resort to images and metaphors that may differ greatly from everyday discourse. Thus, the religious imagery and emotional vulnerability contained in Bobby Sands's poetry contrast strongly with the hardened, uncompromising attitude of Sands, the military strategist and officer commander of the IRA, in Long Kesh prison. Both the poetic and politico-military discourses were inextricably linked cultural devices through which collective and personal meanings were constructed, articulated, and enacted by Bobby Sands during the prison protest.

39. For the IRA leadership, priority had to be given to the military effort. A hunger strike was seen as divesting its resources because of the need to give attention to campaigns and propaganda and due to the political risk of the unsure outcome.

40. Bernardette Devlin, elected member of Parliament in 1971 and forefront campaigner for the prisoners, was badly wounded; and several outspoken supporters were killed by Loyalist paramilitary organizations.

41. A key event in this sense is the Irish Famine of 1854 when English economic policies in Ireland allowed one million people to die of hunger. No doubt the 1981 fast had deep historical resonances; many people in Ireland, although disagreeing with the hunger strikers, thought the English were again starving Irish people.

BIBLIOGRAPHY

Abu-Lughod, Lila. *Veiled Sentiments: Honor and Poetry in a Bedouin Society.* Berkeley: University of California Press, 1986.

Anderson, Benedict. *Imagined Communities: Reflections on the Origin and Spread of Nationalism.* London: Verso, 1983.

Anglerius, Peter Martyr. *De Orbe Novo.* (The Decades of the Newe Worlde or West India), translated by Richard Eden. 1555.

Bell, J. Bowyer. *The Secret Army: The IRA 1916–1979.* Cambridge, Mass.: MIT Press, 1980.

Beresford, David. *Ten Men Dead: The Story of the 1981 Irish Hunger Strike.* London: Grafton Books, 1987.

Burton, Frank. *The Politics of Legitimacy: Struggles in a Belfast Community.* London: Routledge and Kegan Paul, 1978.

Cameron Report. *Disturbances in Northern Ireland: Report of the Cameron Commission.* London: Her Majesty's Stationary Office, Command 532, 1969.

Canetti, Elias. *The Human Province: Notes 1942–1972.* New York: Seabury Press, 1978.

Canny, Nicholas P. "The Ideology of English Colonization: From Ireland to America." *William and Mary Quarterly* 30 (1973): 575–598.

_____ . *From Reformation to Restoration: Ireland 1534–1660.* Dublin: Helicon, 1987.

Collins, T. *The Centre Cannot Hold.* Dublin: Bookworks, 1984.

Coogan, Tim Pat. *The IRA.* London: Fontana Books, 1980.

Corrigan, Phillip, and Derek Sayer. *The Great Arch: English State Formation as Cultural Revolution.* New York: Basil Blackwell, 1985.

Curtis, Liz. *Ireland: The Propaganda War: The British Media and the "Battle for Hearts and Minds."* London: Pluto Press, 1984.

Darby, John, ed. *Northern Ireland: The Background to the Conflict.* Belfast: Appletree Press, 1983.

Deane, Seamus. *Civilians and Barbarians.* Derry: Field Day Theatre Company, 1983.

_____ . *Heroic Styles: The Tradition of an Idea.* Derry: Field Day Theatre Company, 1984.

Edwards, Ruth Dudley. *Patrick Pearse: The Triumph of Failure.* London: Gollancz, 1977.

Fairweather, Eileen, Roisin McDonough, and Melanie McFadyean. *Only the Rivers Run Free: Northern Ireland: The Women's War.* London: Pluto Press, 1984.

Fallon, Charlotte. "Civil War Hungerstrikes: Women and Men." *Eire-Ireland* 22 (1987): 3.

Farrell, Michael. *Northern Ireland: The Orange State.* London: Pluto Press, 1976.

Feldman, Allen. *Formations of Violence: The Narrative of the Body and Political Terror in Northern Ireland.* Chicago: University of Chicago Press, 1991.

Fernandez, James W. *Persuasions and Performances: The Play of Tropes in Culture.* Bloomington: Indiana University Press, 1986.

Flackes, W. D., and S. Elliott. *Northern Ireland: A Political Directory, 1968–1988.* Dublin: Gill and Macmillan, 1989.

Foster, R. F. *Modern Ireland 1600–1972.* London: Penguin, 1988.

Foucault, Michel. *Discipline and Punish: The Birth of the Prison,* translated by Alan Sheridan. New York: Vintage Books, 1979.

Geertz, Clifford. "Religion as a Cultural System." In Clifford Geertz, ed., *The Interpretation of Cultures.* New York: Basic Books, 1973, 87–126.

Hillyard, Paddy. "Law and Order." In John Darby, ed., *Northern Ireland: The Background to the Conflict.* Belfast: Appletree Press, 1983, 32–61.

Hodgen, Margaret T. *Early Anthropology in the Sixteenth and Seventeenth Centuries.* Philadelphia: University of Pennsylvania Press, 1964.

Kearney, Richard. *Transitions: Narratives in Modern Irish Culture.* Manchester: Manchester University Press, 1988.

Kelly, Fergus. *A Guide to Early Irish Law.* Dublin: Dublin Institute for Advanced Studies, 1988.

Kundera, Milan. *The Book of Laughter and Forgetting.* New York: Alfred A. Knopf, 1980.

Lyons, F.S.L. *Culture and Anarchy in Ireland 1890–1939.* Oxford and New York: Oxford University Press, 1979.

MacBride, Sean. "Introduction." In Bobby Sands, *One Day in My Life.* London: Pluto Press, 1983.

McCann, Eamonn. *War and an Irish Town.* London: Pluto Press, 1980.

Memmi, Albert. *The Colonizer and the Colonized.* Boston: Beacon Press, 1965.

Morris, James. *Farewell the Trumpets: An Imperial Retreat.* New York: Harvest/HBJ, 1978.

Morrison, Toni. *Beloved: A Novel.* New York: Alfred A. Knopf, 1987.

Muenster, Sebastian. *Cosmographiae Universalis.* Basilea: Henrichum Petri, 1554.

O'Dowd, Liam, Bill Rolston, and Mike Tomlinson. *Northern Ireland: Between Civil Rights and Civil War.* London: CSE Books, 1980.

O'Malley, Padraig. *Biting at the Grave: The Irish Hunger Strikes and the Politics of Despair.* Boston: Beacon Press, 1990.

Ortelius, Abraham. *Theatrum Orbis Terrarum.* Antuerdiae: A. R. Sandensen, 1570.

Owens, Rosemary Cullen. *Smashing Times: A History of the Irish Women's Suffrage Movement 1889–1922.* Dublin: Attic Press, 1984.

Rolston, Bill. "Politics, Painting and Popular Culture: The Political Wall Murals of Northern Ireland." *Media, Culture and Society* 9 (1987): 5–28.

Rosaldo, Renato. *Culture and Truth: The Remaking of Social Analysis.* Boston: Beacon Press, 1989.

Rowthorn, Bob, and Naomi Wayne. *Northern Ireland: The Political Economy of the Conflict.* Cambridge: Polity Press, 1988.

Rulfo, Juan. "Pedro Paramo." In *Obras.* Mexico: Fondo de Cultura Economica, 1987.

Sahlins, Marshall. *Historical Metaphors and Mythical Realities: Structure in the Early History of the Sandwich Islands Kingdom.* Ann Arbor: University of Michigan Press, 1981.

———. *Islands of History.* Chicago: University of Chicago Press, 1985.

Sands, Bobby. *Skylark Sing Your Lonely Song: An Anthology of the Writings of Bobby Sands.* Cork and Dublin: Mercier Press, 1982.

———. *One Day in My Life.* London: Pluto Press, 1983.

Sluka, Jeffrey A. *Hearts and Minds, Water and Fish: Support for the IRA and INLA in a Northern Ireland Ghetto.* Greenwich, Conn.: JAI Press, 1989.

Spenser, Edmund. *A View of the Present State of Ireland.* 1st ed. Dublin: Sir James Ware, 1633. Oxford: Clarendon Press, 1970.

Steward, A.T.Q. *The Narrow Ground: Patterns of Ulster History.* Belfast: Pretani Press, 1986.

Taussig, Michael. *Shamanism, Colonialism, and the Wild Man: A Study in Terror and Healing*. Chicago: University of Chicago Press, 1987.

Thompson, E. P. *The Making of the English Working Class*. London: Penguin, 1963.

Thompson, William Irwin. *The Imagination of an Insurrection, Dublin, Easter 1916: A Study of an Ideological Movement*. West Stockbridge, Mass.: Lindisfarne Press, 1982.

Timerman, Jacobo. *Prisoner Without a Name, Cell Without a Number*. New York: Alfred A. Knopf, 1981.

Toibin, Colm. *Martyrs and Metaphors*. Letters from the New Island Series. Dublin: Raven Art Press, 1987.

Warren, Kay B. *The Symbolism of Subordination: Indian Identity in a Guatemalan Town*. 2d ed. Austin: University of Texas Press, 1989.

Whyte, John. *Interpreting Northern Ireland*. Oxford: Clarendon Press, 1990.

Yeats, W. B. *The King's Threshold*. 1st ed. London: A. H. Bullen, 1904. London: Macmillan, 1937.

About the Book and Editor

This book explores a range of contemporary conflicts in which culture has become an explicit issue: ethnic nationalism, religious fundamentalism, the militarization of civilian life, opposition movements in authoritarian states, political resistance to redistributive agrarian reforms, and racism in racial democracies. The authors show that one cannot understand current conflicts or crises without studying long-term patterns of social, political, and cultural change. At issue throughout the book is how anthropologists and comparative political scientists conceptualize the interplay of culture and politics. The result is a volume that offers readers a sophisticated introduction to new currents in cultural analysis, demonstrates realms of convergence and continuing debate between the two disciplines, and offers focused analyses of contemporary conflicts from the perspective of those caught up in them. The case studies for this volume focus on movements and communities in Guatemala, Brazil, Israel/Palestine, Iran, Egypt, South Africa, the Philippines, and Northern Ireland.

Kay B. Warren is professor of anthropology at Princeton where she earned her Ph.D. Her research on racism and religion in Guatemala during the early 1970s was published in *The Symbolism of Subordination: Indian Identity in a Guatemalan Town* (Texas 1978/89). Her collaborative project with Susan C. Bourque on gender, class, and community in Peru appeared as *Women of the Andes: Patriarchy and Social Change in Rural Peru* (Michigan 1981). Currently she is finishing *Meanings of Ethnic Resurgence: Race and Representation in the Americas,* based on her return to Guatemala after two decades to examine culture, conflict, and ethnic renewal, and *Making and Remaking 'Americas': A U.S.-British Experiment in Social Documentary for TV.*

About the Contributors

Begoña Aretxaga recently completed her doctoral dissertation, "A Topography of Dignity: Gendered Politics and Transformative Symbols in Northern Ireland," in anthropology at Princeton University, where she is currently a lecturer. She was born in the Basque Country and received her *licenciatura* from the Universidad del País Vasco. Her earlier research, focusing on gender and Basque political culture, appeared in *Mujer vasca: Imagen y realidad* (Barcelona: Anthropos 1985), *Los Funerales en el Nacionalismo Radical Vasco* (San Sebastian: Baroja 1988), and *Critical Matrix* (1988). Aretxaga's chapter for this volume draws on sixteen months of fieldwork in Belfast, Northern Ireland, during 1988–1990. Her research interests include gender, political violence, and ethnic nationalism.

Guilain Denoeux is assistant professor of government at Colby College. Born in France, he received degrees in economics, foreign service studies, and political science from the University of Grenoble, Georgetown University, and Princeton University. Since earning his Ph.D. at Princeton University, he has published *Urban Unrest in the Middle East: A Comparative Study of Informal Networks in Egypt, Iran, and Lebanon* (SUNY-Albany 1993). Guilain's analyses of Middle Eastern politics have appeared in *Comparative Politics* and in *Consensus and Conflict in Lebanon* (Tauris 1988). Denoeux has lived, studied, and traveled in Egypt, Jordan, and Syria. He also spent eighteen months on assignment to the Cultural Service of the French Embassy in Baghdad, Iraq.

Michael Hanchard is assistant professor of political science at the University of Texas at Austin. He earned his Ph.D. in politics at Princeton University. His research on race and politics involved twelve months of fieldwork in Brazil and will be published as *Orpheus and Power: Afro-Brazilian Social Movements in Rio de Janeiro and São Paulo, Brazil, 1945–1988* (Princeton 1993). Hanchard has also published on African-American identity in *Social Text* and on social theory in *Socialism and Democracy*. His research interests include social theory, racial politics, and social movements.

Anthony W. Marx is assistant professor of political science at Columbia University. Since earning his Ph.D. in politics at Princeton University, he has published *Lessons of Struggle: South African Internal Opposition, 1960–1990* (Oxford 1991) as well as articles in *Journal of Modern African Studies, Comparative Politics,* and *Political Science Quarterly.* Marx lived in South Africa for extended periods between 1984 and 1989 and participated in the founding of Khanya College, an alternative, black-run educational center. His research interests include nationalism and the ideology of social movements.

Jeffrey M. Riedinger is assistant professor of political science at Michigan State University. He completed his doctoral dissertation, "Redistributive Reform in Transitional Democracies: The Philippine Case," for the Woodrow Wilson School at Princeton University. He also holds a law degree from the University of Washington. Riedinger is coauthor of *Land Reform and Democratic Development* (Johns Hopkins 1987) and a number of monographs and articles on rural development and agrarian reform. Over the last twelve years he has conducted fieldwork on rural development in Central America, the Middle East, and South and Southeast Asia.

Kay B. Warren is professor of anthropology at Princeton where she earned her Ph.D. Her research on racism and religion in Guatemala during the early 1970s was published in *The Symbolism of Subordination: Indian Identity in a Guatemalan Town* (Texas 1978/89). Her collaborative project with Susan C. Bourque on gender, class, and community in Peru appeared as *Women of the Andes: Patriarchy and Social Change in Rural Peru* (Michigan 1981). Currently she is finishing *Meanings of Ethnic Resurgence: Race and Representation in the Americas,* based on her return to Guatemala after two decades to examine culture, conflict, and ethnic renewal, and *Making and Remaking 'Americas': A U.S.-British Experiment in Social Documentary for TV.*

Davida Wood is currently completing her doctoral dissertation, entitled "The Politics of Identity in a Palestinian Village in Israel," in anthropology at Princeton University. Born in Cape Town, South Africa, she immigrated to the United States in 1979. Her field research took her to Israel/Palestine for twenty-six months during 1987–1989. Her research interests include colonialism, nationalisms of resistance, and the politics of gender.

Index